Points of Entry

Points of Entry

How Canada's Immigration Officers Decide Who Gets In

Vic Satzewich

UBCPress · Vancouver · Toronto

23 22 21 20 19 18 17 16 15 5 4 3 2 1

Printed in Canada on FSC-certified ancient-forest-free paper (100% post-consumer recycled) that is processed chlorine- and acid-free.

Library and Archives Canada Cataloguing in Publication

Satzewich, Vic, author
Points of entry : how Canada's immigration officers decide who gets in / Vic Satzewich.

Includes bibliographical references and index.
Issued in print and electronic formats.
ISBN 978-0-7748-3024-9 (bound).–ISBN 978-0-7748-3025-6 (pbk.).–
ISBN 978-0-7748-3026-3 (pdf).– ISBN 978-0-7748-3027-0 (epub)

1. Canada. Citizenship and Immigration Canada. 2. Canada. Citizenship and Immigration Canada–Rules and practice. 3. Canada. Citizenship and Immigration Canada–Decision making. 4. Canada–Emigration and immigration–Government policy. 5. Emigration and immigration law–Canada. 6. Canada–Emigration and immigration. I. Title.

JV7233.S28 2015 353.4'840971 C2015-903815-4
C2015-903816-2

Canadä

UBC Press gratefully acknowledges the financial support for our publishing program of the Government of Canada (through the Canada Book Fund), the Canada Council for the Arts, and the British Columbia Arts Council.

This book has been published with the help of a grant from the Canadian Federation for the Humanities and Social Sciences, through the Awards to Scholarly Publications Program, using funds provided by the Social Sciences and Humanities Research Council of Canada.

UBC Press
The University of British Columbia
2029 West Mall
Vancouver, BC V6T 1Z2
www.ubcpress.ca

For my friend and colleague Billy Shaffir,
who knows a thing or two about ethnography

Contents

Figure and Tables / ix

Acknowledgments / xi

Introduction / 1

1 Stated and Hidden Agendas / 19

2 Delegated Discretion / 37

3 Immigration Policy / 59

4 Visa Offices and Officers / 79

5 Approval and Refusal Rates / 105

6 Spousal and Partner Sponsorships / 139

7 Federal Skilled Workers / 164

8 Visitor Visas / 187

9 The Interview / 215

Conclusion / 239

Appendix / 248

Notes / 250

References / 259

Index / 277

Figure and Tables

Figure

1 Organization of the Kingston mission, 2008 / 89

Tables

1 Selection grid for federal skilled workers / 65
2 Permanent resident visa approval rates, 2012 / 107
3 Permanent resident visa approval rates, by office location, 2012 / 110
4 Approval rates, by overseas region and admission category, 2012 / 113
5 Spousal and partner approval rates, by overseas office, 2012 / 113
6 Approval rates for C-50 federal skilled workers, by overseas office, 2012 / 116
7 Permanent resident operational targets, applications finalized, 2014 / 125
8 Permanent resident overseas operational targets by office, economic applications finalized, 2014 / 126
9 Permanent resident overseas operational targets by office, non-economic applications finalized, 2014 / 129

Acknowledgments

Many institutions and individuals have been directly and indirectly supportive of the work that has gone into this book. This research could not have been undertaken without the generous financial support of the Social Sciences and Humanities Research Council of Canada and the support of Citizenship and Immigration Canada. In particular, I would like to thank the director general of International Region and the individual immigration program managers for allowing me to come and talk to their staff and observe the work in their offices. I also very much appreciate the willingness of the many Canada-based officers and locally engaged staff to take the time to talk to me about how they do what they do. As an outsider, I feel truly privileged to have been given the opportunity to see what the world looks like for Canadian visa officers. Mike Molloy, along with two unnamed individuals, helped open the doors to the immigration department, and without their help, this research may not have been possible. Ben Kelly provided some timely advice about what I should read as I started to write up the results. Danielle Belanger, John Biles, Charlene Miall, and Dorothy Pawluch read and commented on earlier versions of various chapters. Linda Mahood and Dave Goutor, despite being busy with their own work, read and offered useful comments and insights on the complete manuscript. I would also like to thank members of the Friday Night Social Club, including Sue Perry, Kevin Perry, Dorothy Bakker, Pat Devine, Terry Devine, Janet Diebel, Mark Figaro, Joan Fox, Annette Franson, Danny Lui, Cathy Standring, and Sonny

Yuen, for the regular chance to unwind, and to not talk about work. My friend Neil Mcdougald never complained when I asked him to look after my house, cut my grass, and clear my driveway of snow when I was away doing the fieldwork. The staff at UBC Press are truly wonderful to work with. Emily Andrew steered the manuscript through the review process and Lesley Erickson through production. Copy editor Deborah Kerr is a gifted wordsmith who helped make the manuscript much more readable. Some material in Chapters 5 and 6 was previously published in the *Canadian Review of Sociology*, the *Journal of Ethnic and Migration Studies*, and the *Journal of International Migration and Integration*.

Points of Entry

Introduction

Maria enters the interview booth with a broad, confident smile.[1] Brenda, the visa officer responsible for reviewing her application, smiles back and asks her to close the sliding door behind her. There is no chair on Maria's side of the small, six- by eight-foot interview booth, so she takes a few seconds to put her bag on the floor and try to get comfortable for the interview. She ends up leaning against the small ledge in front of the bulletproof glass window that separates visa applicants from visa officers. A few years ago, Canadian embassies installed the special glass in their interview booths because of safety and security concerns. People sometimes get angry when their visa application is refused, and in this day and age, you can never be too careful.

Brenda points to the telephone on the wall and gestures to Maria that she should pick it up. She welcomes Maria and introduces herself as "the visa officer responsible for your case." She asks Maria in English if she can understand what she is saying. Maria nods in agreement, but Brenda asks her to please say "yes" or "no." Maria says "yes." Brenda needs a verbal response because she has to document her decision-making process by keeping notes of the questions asked, Maria's replies, and her own assessment of the answers. Brenda then asks if she is comfortable conducting the interview in English, and since Maria lived in the United States for several years, she says "yes" but asks that Brenda "speak slowly."

Brenda already knows a lot about Maria and her circumstances from the spousal application for immigration that she and her Canadian sponsor submitted eight months ago. Maria's husband wants her to join him in Saskatoon, and as part of the application, couples are asked to tell the story of their relationship. Brenda reviewed the application about a month ago, but something about the couple's story did not add up. Her program assistant contacted Maria to schedule the interview so that Brenda's concerns could be addressed.

Visa officers do not interview every applicant for admission to Canada. In fact, headquarters in Ottawa likes them to keep the number of interviews down and encourages them to make their decisions solely on the basis of the information in the application. Interviews take a lot of time, and time in a visa office is in short supply. Officers are trained to make their decisions to approve or refuse visa applications relatively quickly. Brenda has two or three dozen files stacked on the corner of her desk and on top of two filing cabinets in her office. Her program assistant is working on a couple dozen other files at various stages of processing. Globally, there are thousands of applications in what Citizenship and Immigration euphemistically calls its "inventory," which is its code word for "backlog." The more time Brenda spends on one file, the longer other applicants must wait for a decision.

Officers must also meet their yearly visa issuance targets. It is early December, and Brenda's office has not yet met its target for family class spousal visas. If Brenda fails to meet it, this will reflect badly on her and on her boss, the immigration program manager. Headquarters in Ottawa will also be unhappy because it will have to find another visa office to pick up the slack. All the other offices are also working hard to meet their own targets, so a last-minute request to increase a target because another office has not met its own quota means that something has gone awry. If no other office manages to fill the gap, the overall target for family class admissions will not be met, and the immigration minister will want to know why. The minister announced the targets the year before in Parliament and will be held accountable by the Opposition if the number of visas falls far below, or far above, them. Since politics are politics, Opposition colleagues can be rather unforgiving in their assessment of a cabinet minister's performance and will relish any opportunity to cast the minister as incompetent or as failing to control his or her department.

In a family class spousal sponsorship case, such as that of Maria, Brenda must be "satisfied" that the relationship between Maria and her husband in Canada is "genuine" and that its primary purpose is not for Maria to gain permanent resident status in Canada. Upon reviewing the file a month earlier, Brenda suspected that this might be a marriage of convenience. She uses the interview to figure out whether the relationship is real and whether its primary purpose is immigration.

After asking a few simple, factual questions – Maria's full name, date of birth, and other matters that already appear on the application – Brenda starts to focus more closely: "It says on your application that you lived in the United States for fifteen years and that you returned to Guatemala three years ago. Why did you return to Guatemala after living for so many years in the United States?" Maria explains that she missed her family and returned to Guatemala to be closer to them. This sounds odd to Brenda, who thinks to herself, "Why would someone voluntarily leave the United States to go back and live in Guatemala?" She suspects that Maria is concealing something, so she pointedly asks, "Were you deported from the United States?" After pausing for a moment to reflect on her answer, Maria admits that she was slated for deportation but chose to leave before the American authorities put her on the plane. She does not explain why she was going to be deported, but Brenda puts two and two together and surmises that Maria probably overstayed her original visa and then somehow caught the attention of US immigration authorities. For Brenda, Maria's original evasive answer to the question of why she left the United States confirms her concerns and prompts her to dig deeper.

She moves on. "How did you meet your husband?" Maria explains that they first met at the birthday party of a mutual friend when they were both living in Los Angeles. They dated a few times, but nothing really came of the dates. A few years later, they met again at another birthday party of a mutual friend, this time after she had returned to Guatemala.

Brenda also knows a fair amount about Maria's husband. She has access to the Field Operations Support System database, which contains information about the application history of everyone who has applied for admission to Canada in the past several years. Before the interview, Brenda pulled up the file for Maria's husband, which told her that he, too, is from Guatemala and that seven years ago he submitted a successful refugee claim in Canada. He had lived in the United States for several years but then crossed the border into Canada at Surrey, British Columbia. She suspects that he, too, was scheduled for removal from the United States and that rather than return to Guatemala, he decided to take a chance with the Canadian refugee determination system. When he crossed at Surrey, he must have uttered words to the effect that "I am a refugee." As soon as Canada Border Services

Agency staff heard the word "refugee," a complex refugee determination process came into play. Ultimately, Maria's husband convinced the Refugee Protection Division of the Immigration and Refugee Board that he was genuinely in fear of his life in Guatemala, so he was granted permanent residence status in Canada.

After this, he returned to Guatemala to visit some old friends, where "by chance," he met Maria again. Since he planned to be in Guatemala for a month, they started dating, and this time they fell in love. Within two weeks, they were married at a small civil ceremony. A few close friends attended. Though his mother and two brothers lived in Guatemala, they were not at the wedding. Maria explains that they lived "far away" and could not travel to Guatemala City for the wedding. She adds that her mother and sister stayed away because they thought that her husband was not "good enough" for her.

As Maria explains the circumstances of how she met and married her husband, Brenda looks through a pile of thirty or forty photographs that the couple included in the application to support the story of their relationship. The photos show the marriage ceremony and the small reception that followed it. One shot shows about twelve guests seated at a large restaurant table, all happily toasting the bride and groom.

The other pictures are of the wedding night and the honeymoon. The wedding night photos show the couple in the bedroom. She is wearing lingerie; he is in a bathrobe with his chest exposed. They are lying on a bed, smiling directly into the camera and toasting with champagne. Brenda looks at these pictures and cracks a barely visible smile. She thinks to herself, "Why on earth would they have a photographer in their bedroom on their wedding night?" The honeymoon photos show the couple on a beach in Panama. Maria explains that they chose Panama because they got a good deal on a package offered by a local resort. Shortly after their honeymoon, Maria's husband returned to Canada and began the process of sponsoring her for permanent resident status.

Brenda then turns to the issue of children. "It says on your application that you have a child in the United States." "Yes, she is grown and goes to college." "Were you ever married before?" "No, this is my first marriage."

Finally, Brenda moves on to questions about Maria's relationship with her husband. "It says on your application that you talk to your husband every day for about twenty minutes." Also included in the file are a stack of phone cards that Maria says she uses to call her husband in Saskatoon. The cards provide no information about the numbers that were dialed or the length of the calls. Since, in themselves, they are not evidence of much, Brenda asks, "So what do you talk about with your husband when you call?" Maria says that they talk about how much they love and miss each other, and how they can't wait to be together again. Brenda smiles, but then asks, "Okay, but you can't talk about love all of the time. What else do you talk about?" "We talk about our lives and our future life together, things like that." At this point in the interview, Brenda starts to drill down, to look for specifics. In her view, real couples talk about more than just love: genuine partners have some knowledge of each other's past and everyday lives and circumstances.

"Where does your husband work?" "A trucking company; I think its name is On Time Trucking, or something like that."

"What is the name of your husband's boss?" "I don't know."

"What are the names of some of the people he works with?" "He does not really have any friends at work."

"What are the names of his non-work friends?" "He sometimes talks about a guy named Sam, who lives in the same apartment building."

"What kind of apartment does he live in, and how many bedrooms does it have?" "I don't know."

"What is his favourite meal?" "Hamburgers."

"What does he like to cook for himself?" "Hamburgers."

"What was the last movie he saw?" *"Friday the Thirteenth."* "So, he likes scary movies?" "Uh huh."

This back-and-forth about Maria's knowledge of her husband and his life in Canada lasts about ten minutes, and then Brenda asks, "Are you looking forward to moving to Saskatoon?" "Yes, very much." "What is Saskatoon like?" "I don't really know, but it seems it is a lot like California." Brenda, visibly surprised by this answer, says, "Really? What makes Saskatoon like California?" Maria pauses for a moment and replies, "There is shopping there, it is clean, things like that." "Have you ever seen any pictures of Saskatoon in the winter?" "No."

The interview lasts for about an hour, and after the last question Brenda takes a few minutes to review the overall application and digest Maria's answers. She then tells Maria that she is not satisfied that her relationship with her husband is genuine, and that she believes that the primary reason for her marriage is to gain permanent resident status in Canada. She details the "concerns" that have led to her assessment. Maria listens with apparent surprise that her story is not believed and spends the next few minutes trying to address each of Brenda's concerns by repeating what she has already said. After listening intently, Brenda says, "Thank you, I am ready to make my decision."

In the end, what decision do you think Brenda made? Did she grant Maria her family class spousal visa, or did she refuse the application? Was Maria in a real relationship, or was it a fake? Did she get married primarily because she wanted to become a permanent resident in Canada or because she loved her husband and wanted to start a new life with him?

Canadian visa officers must answer these kinds of questions every day. They make decisions about who should, and should not, be issued a visa to enter Canada, both as permanent and temporary residents. According to the Auditor General of Canada (2011, 1), Canadian overseas visa offices processed 1.36 million permanent and temporary resident visas in 2010 alone. Every application required a visa officer to make a decision. The officers work in a complex bureaucratic environment – the Immigration and Refugee Protection Act spells out the general principles of Canadian immigration policy, the Immigration Regulations specify the criteria to be used in assessing applications, and detailed processing manuals explain how they should conduct and document their investigations. Nonetheless, the decision to issue or refuse a visa is ultimately a matter of discretion. An officer must be "satisfied" that applicants are who they claim to be, that they meet the eligibility criteria for the visa, and that they are not inadmissible to Canada for reasons of public safety, security, or health conditions.

Among other things, a visa officer's job involves fitting immigration rules to individual cases. The world of immigration is a big, messy, and ambiguous place. Many, if not most, visa applicants tell the truth about themselves, their families, and their situations. But some do lie. Others fall in between and embellish or exaggerate certain aspects of their biographies in hopes of looking like a better fit for Canada. Some people fill out an application entirely on their own, but others pay lawyers or immigration consultants to help them. Many of these representatives are legitimate and give good, honest advice. But others are not overburdened with ethics and counsel their clients to answer questions in certain ways because they think they know what Canadian visa officers are looking for. Most applicants are peaceful and law abiding, and are simply seeking better opportunities for themselves and their children, or they want to be closer to their families in Canada. But some are involved in illegal activities at home and may plan to continue them in Canada. Others may have committed atrocities against civilians during their military service in their country of origin. And a very few have been, or are, members of organizations that the Canadian government deems to be terrorist. Most applicants are physically fit and healthy. But some may hope to take advantage of Canada's health care system.

Though visa officers do not make up the rules of the game, separating the "genuine" from the "non-genuine" is part of their everyday routine. They make decisions on a wide variety of applications for permanent and temporary residency: federal skilled workers, spouses and partners, parents and grandparents, dependent and non-dependent children, investors, entrepreneurs, refugees, temporary foreign workers, students, and visitors. As a key part of Canada's border control efforts, they must sort applicants into those who deserve a visa and those who do not. Though they are guided by complex laws, rules, and procedures, these cannot cover every possible scenario and combination of circumstances presented by applicants. As a result, the decision to grant or deny a visa is part of a bureaucratic, yet discretionary, process where the officers are entrusted to use their knowledge, experience, and judgment to apply the law and decide whether particular people ought to be allowed into Canada.

This book is about how Canadian visa officers make decisions about potential immigrants on a day-to-day basis. Canada has one of the most open immigration policies in the world, and immigration is one of the most researched subjects in Canada today, yet what goes on in visa offices is clouded in secrecy.[2] When visa officers do come to public attention, it's usually because of a high-profile case, such as that of Conrad Black. In 2012, after serving time in a US jail for fraud and the obstruction of justice, he was issued a visa that permitted him to return to Canada. Canada's immigration rules are designed to prevent individuals who have records of "serious" criminality from entering the country, so many people rightly wondered how Black could have received a visa, especially as he had so unceremoniously renounced his Canadian citizenship a few years earlier to take up a position in the British House of Lords (Chase 2012). More commonly, though, it is the refusal of a visa that attracts public attention. These cases invariably involve the public condemnation of mostly unnamed, but sometimes named, officers for decisions that, at first blush, seem arbitrary, vindictive, and lacking in compassion, humanity, and even common sense. In addition, Internet-based immigration chat forums contain extensive, and generally uncomplimentary, comments about officers and their decisions, and are full of anecdotes and allegations about unsympathetic, biased officers who are apparently bent on making applicants as miserable as possible.

Since officers are bound by federal privacy rules and thus cannot elaborate on why they made their decisions in specific cases, much of the public's understanding of them is, as a result, one-sided. The mandated silence about controversial cases tends to leave the public with a largely negative impression of officers and how they do their jobs. Though there is little systematic research on how immigrants and the wider public perceive them, there are arguably two diametrically opposed views of officers and how they approach their work. One sees them as detached, dispassionate bureaucrats who mechanically apply immigration rules and procedures. They are utterly lacking in humanity when it comes to the unique and seemingly compelling reasons why an individual desires to move to, or remain in, Canada. At the other extreme, officers are seen as too emotionally invested in their jobs. They are perceived as capricious and vindictive, and as acting on the basis of their personal prejudices. These biases are seen as unfairly informing their decisions and as sidestepping the universally applicable rules and procedures that are designed to make the process of getting into Canada transparent, standardized, and free of bias.

To get at the reality behind the rhetoric, I sought, and gained, access to observe the inner workings of Canada's visa offices.[3] Though I have been a student and keen observer of immigration-related matters since the late 1980s, and have met Citizenship and Immigration officials at various conferences and workshops over the years, when I began writing this book I had only a sketchy understanding of how the decision-making process for visa issuance was organized. Nor did I know the name of a single currently serving officer whom I might interview to get a snowball sample rolling. Although Canada's immigration rules, regulations, and procedures are publicly available, the department's organization of decision making is something of a mystery for those who do not work in the immigration industry. For an outsider such as myself, lacking both a sponsor to help open doors and even a clear sense of who the gatekeepers to individual offices might be, gaining entrée to overseas offices was, to put it mildly, a challenge.

Indeed, Citizenship and Immigration could have written the manual on how to design a truly nameless and faceless bureaucracy. Its International Region branch administers overseas visa offices, but it has little presence on the departmental website. Nor does the website name any official who works for International Region, or for the department as a whole for that matter. In fact, one of the few people whom the website mentions by name is Chris Alexander, currently the Citizenship and Immigration minister. The website lists the location of overseas visa offices and provides links to their websites. In turn, the overseas websites list 1-800 numbers that people can call if they have questions about their applications, and they provide two generic email addresses to applicants: one is for "case specific" inquiries, and one is for general inquiries. All the websites provide copies of application forms, answers to frequently asked questions and the like, and considerable information about how to apply for a visa, but nowhere is it possible to find the name, let alone the email address or telephone number, of an actual person who works for the department, either in Canada or overseas.

Uncertain of how to proceed, I made two rather clumsy, and in hindsight laughable, attempts to penetrate the fortress. My first strategy was to email three overseas visa offices via the general inquiry addresses listed on their websites. In my emails, I briefly explained what my book was about and asked whether I could visit them, interview a few of their officers, and observe interviews with federal skilled worker applicants to better understand how officers exercised discretion. No one replied. In retrospect, this is not surprising. My request would have been highly unusual, given the nature of email correspondence that a visa office normally receives. Moreover, it was probably read first by a locally engaged staff member who would not have known how to categorize it for further action, and it may have gone straight into the trash. If it were passed along to the immigration program manager or her or his executive assistant, it is easy to see why replying would be a rather low priority for them. They work in a high-pressure environment and are extraordinarily busy people, who juggle complex demands, relationships, and expectations, so dealing with everyday management issues monopolizes their time. Moreover, as I later learned, overseas visa offices are highly attuned to criticism and to issues of "risk," and my request had "potential problem" written all over it.

Having garnered a response rate of zero, I knew I needed to change my strategy. Fortuitously, in January 2009, I was invited to be a discussant at a Wilfrid Laurier University conference on Arab immigration to Canada. One of the other invitees was Mike Molloy, a name that I recognized from a 1989 National Film Board documentary called *Who Gets In?* It was about how overseas offices processed immigration applicants, and it featured an officer by the name of Mike Molloy. When I saw his name on the Laurier program, I hoped that he might be the same person and a possible entrée to visa offices.

At the conference, I immediately recognized Molloy from the documentary. As we chatted about his participation in the video, he also talked about his subsequent career in Citizenship and Immigration, and later as a diplomat. He had retired from the public service a few years earlier but was still very interested in immigration matters. Eventually, I explained my interest in the subject, hoping that he might give me some pointers about how to gain access to overseas visa offices. I could see that he was intrigued by my project. He told me that he was involved with an organization called the Canadian Immigration Historical Society and that most of its members were former immigration department employees. It met fairly regularly, and Mike offered to mention my project idea to some of the members to see if they would talk to me about their experiences of working overseas. He then told me that he knew the man who, following the introduction of the Immigration and Refugee Protection Act in 2002, had drafted changes to the Immigration Regulations that changed the way in which the applications of skilled workers were processed. Reluctant to mention his name, Mike called him "Mr. X." He was well placed in the immigration department and might also be able to help me gain access to currently serving officers. Mike agreed to ask Mr. X if he would speak to me.

Needless to say, I was elated. That Mike referred to the contact as "Mr. X" made me feel like a sociological secret agent who was onto something interesting and important. Mike and I corresponded via email for the next several weeks, and eventually he arranged for me to visit Ottawa and meet some of his former colleagues. He kindly opened his home to me and four or five of his colleagues, many of whom had occupied important senior positions in the immigration department during the 1980s and 1990s. True to his promise, he had also approached Mr. X, who had agreed to be contacted, so we began to correspond directly. A former visa officer, Mr. X had worked his way up the ranks and was, at the time we met, a senior department official in Ottawa. We arranged to have breakfast at a downtown coffee shop, and much of our conversation focused on his role in drafting the new Immigration Regulations and on the changes that followed. Toward the end of our breakfast, I explained that I also hoped to visit overseas offices to interview their officers and to observe interviews with applicants to get an understanding of how discretion is applied and understood in the skilled worker system. Like Mike, he seemed genuinely intrigued by my project and thought that having an outsider examine the consequences of the changes to visa processing that he himself had helped to introduce might prove useful to the department.

Although he was not part of International Region, its director general's office was immediately beside his own, and he agreed to mention my research idea to him. Thinking that my project might fall under the purview of the director general of the Research and Evaluation Branch, he also agreed to speak to her. Feeling that I now had two sponsors, Mike Molloy and Mr. X, and having narrowed down the potential gatekeepers, I felt that I was making real progress. To lend more credibility to my request, Mr. X and I agreed that I should email him a copy of my original Social Sciences and Humanities Research Council of Canada grant application and a copy of an article that my colleague Billy Shaffir and I had written, based on our work with Hamilton Police Services. The article, which dealt with racial profiling and policing, had discussed the discretionary power of police officers and had inspired me to discover how overseas visa offices worked (Satzewich and Shaffir 2009). Moreover, given the apparent sensitivity of the topic and the fact that few academics since Freda Hawkins had been admitted to the offices, I wanted to be open and transparent about my intentions. I also thought that the article might help establish my credentials because it showed that I was able to gain the trust and cooperation of senior police officials to conduct research on the sensitive matter of racial profiling.

Mr. X did as promised and contacted the directors general of International Region and the Research and Evaluation Branch on my behalf. He told me that, if they did not reply, I should feel free to contact him again and he would give them a nudge. I emailed them, with a copy of my grant application and profiling article attached, explained my project and what I was asking of them, and offered to answer any questions.

While I waited for a response, an immigration consultant working in southern Ontario got in touch with me. A retired visa officer, he had set himself up as an immigration consultant and had heard from the Immigration Historical Society of my interest in exploring how visa officers used "substituted evaluations." A substituted evaluation is an administrative mechanism that gives visa officers the discretion to approve a skilled worker application from someone who does not meet the entry criteria, and to refuse applicants who do meet the stated criteria. Because I also planned to write about consultants, who charge for giving advice about how immigration officers exercise discretion, I jumped at the chance to meet him.[4] We had lunch a few days later. The lunch was pleasant enough, but I soon discovered that he had his own reasons for meeting with me. He explained that he was having "trouble" with the visa office in Buffalo. He represented a client who was applying as a federal skilled worker but who did not quite satisfy the criteria for gaining permanent resident status in Canada. As a result, he had asked the Buffalo visa officer to exercise his discretion and issue a positive substituted evaluation on the grounds that his client was already working in Canada in a skilled job, was married, and would be "good material" for Canada. Buffalo had refused to comply, so he was contemplating going to the press to publicize the apparent ludicrousness of the decision not to issue his client a visa. He then gave me the name and email address of the immigration program manager in Buffalo and encouraged me "to ask" him about substituted evaluations. I realized at this point that he wanted to use me, and my project, to further his client's case and perhaps embarrass the department.

Nonetheless, our meeting did have a positive side – I now had the name and email address of the Buffalo immigration program manager. So, since my other access strategy had not yet produced a response, I decided to contact him directly. I sent him an email in which I introduced my project, appended copies of my grant proposal and profiling article, and asked if I could meet with him to discuss the work of his office and whether I could interview his staff. He responded the next day. He would be happy to speak with me, he said, but first I needed to get permission from International Region in Ottawa. Somewhat discouraged by his reluctance to speak without authorization, at least I now knew for certain that International Region's director general was the gatekeeper and that I needed to redouble my efforts to contact him.

Eventually, the director general of the Research and Evaluation Branch agreed to meet with me and talk about my research, but I still had not heard from her counterpart at International Region. Nonetheless, I took her response as a good sign. During our half-hour meeting in Ottawa, she expressed interest in my proposal and hoped that it might help the department better understand why some "strange decisions" were being made in skilled worker cases. She described a case where an applicant in his mid-seventies was accepted as a federal skilled worker on the basis of his education, experience, and fluency in English. She said, "This is the kind of case where you shake your head and wonder what they are thinking. The applicant is already in retirement age, and why the officer would not have exercised negative discretion in that case is a mystery to me. The person's working life in Canada is going to be short."[5] Though supportive of my proposal, she explained that permitting access to the overseas visa offices and officers was not her call to make, and she also pointed me in the direction of the International Region director general.

In the end, a chance encounter with another senior immigration official helped me to arrange a meeting with the director general of International Region. I was invited to an Ottawa workshop in March 2010, which was sponsored by the Department of Foreign Affairs and International Trade. At the time, the department was working on what it called its Global Citizens Strategy. One of the people who was involved in shaping the strategy knew my earlier work on diasporas and transnationalism, so he invited me to speak at a panel (Satzewich 2002; Satzewich and Wong 2006; Satzewich 2007–08). Among the federal government employees who attended the workshop was a senior official from the immigration department. I made a point of sitting beside her at lunch to explain my project and seek her advice on getting a response from the director general of International Region. She, too, seemed intrigued by my project and offered to talk to him about it. She also gave me the name and phone number of his executive assistant, and encouraged me to call her in hopes of arranging a meeting.

I immediately called the executive assistant and explained my situation. She said she would get back to me. A day or two later, she called me and said that her boss would meet with me for half an hour in early May. I was delighted. I could finally make the case for my research project to the key gatekeeper.

On the day of the meeting, on Kent Street in Ottawa, I showed up a few minutes early because I knew that my pitch would have to be quick. The executive assistant escorted me up to the director general's office and explained that he was detained at another meeting. After about ten minutes, I was joined by two staff members from adjacent offices who were also slated to attend the meeting. When they decided to start without waiting for the director general, I was deflated. Pinning him down had taken so long, and now, because something had come up, I might not even see him! I spoke for five or ten minutes and could appreciate that the two staff members were interested, but I could also see that they did not have the authority to grant me access to the overseas offices. Thankfully, the director general soon arrived, apologized for being late, and sat down.

I explained my project again, and the staff members spoke positively about my plans. The director general listened intently and asked how many offices I wanted to visit and for how long. I replied that I hoped to visit two or three offices in each of the branch's four regions (the Americas, Europe, Africa and the Middle East, and Asia and the Pacific). Two weeks at each office would probably be sufficient. I had chosen two weeks because, when the immigration department sends teams to audit its overseas offices, their visits seemed to last for about ten working days (see, for example, Citizenship and Immigration Canada 2008, 2009a, 2009b).

After a few more minutes of discussion about how long I could spend at each office, the director general gave me the green light to visit any office I pleased on the condition that its program manager agreed. We eventually concluded that my visits would last between three and five days, in part to avoid disrupting the operation of the office for too long. The director general made no effort to limit or impede my research, but he did ask that I try not to visit the offices during the summer, when their attention is focused on temporary resident processing, which is very time sensitive.

I was thrilled by the outcome of this meeting. What I had not mentioned was whether I could record my interviews. I had simply assumed that this would not be an issue but was quickly disabused of the idea when the security guard at the first visa office I visited made me store my recorder, and my cell phone, in a locker. Though I later tried to convince the director general of International Region to let me record interviews, he did not agree. As a result, I secured oral consent from interviewees, wrote detailed field notes of conversations and observations while at the offices, and typed them up as soon as I could.

My visits were arranged in collaboration with a designated contact in International Region. The program managers probably talked among themselves about me and my project. In fact, at the end of my first visit, the manager explicitly told me that she would be writing a report to International Region in Ottawa, and to her overseas colleagues, about me and my research.[6] I must have made a favourable impression because the branch continued to support and organize my visits. Throughout the next two years, I would email my contact with the places and dates of my proposed visits, and he would confirm them with the program managers. In two cases, they did not agree to my visit. One expected to be elsewhere at the time. In the other case, my visit came too close to the Christmas holidays, and the small office would have had just a skeleton staff. A scheduled visit to the Cairo office had to be cancelled at the last minute because the anti-government protests led to the partial shutdown of the Canadian embassy.

From July 2010 to January 2012, I visited eleven Canadian visa offices abroad, one in each of Europe, the Middle East, the Caribbean, the United States, and South America; two in Africa; and four in Asia. Depending on the size of the office and the schedule of the manager, I spent two to four days in each one. In most cases, I stayed for three full days, but I spent four days in a few larger offices. I devoted two days to one small office. In total, I spent about 220 hours at the various offices, where I interviewed 128 people who were involved with the operation of the immigration program.[7] I also observed forty-two interviews that visa officers conducted with various types of applicants.[8]

Given the importance of immigration to our national identity and economy, a study of how Canada's visa officers make decisions is both timely and important. International migration is arguably growing in consequence globally, and Canada remains a desired destination for people who plan to travel and live abroad. Visa officers are key gatekeepers of its borders, as they sort through who is eligible to enter the country as a visitor or permanent resident. Since few academics have been given permission to talk to visa officers about how they do what they do, and to see how visa offices work, this book helps to shed light on the understudied but complex question of how border control decisions are actually made. To anticipate how this book answers this question, let me outline some of the key points of my argument and findings.

Though the Canadian immigrant and visitor selection system is a highly bureaucratized enterprise that operates on the basis of clearly articulated policies, rules, and procedures, the system is also discretionary. Though bureaucracies function on the basis of written rules and standardized processing procedures, it is difficult, if not impossible, to design an immigrant selection system that is devoid of judgments by immigration officials. The world of immigration is simply too complex and ever changing to have a visa issuance regime that is devoid of a human, discretionary element. Visa officers must assess the credibility of applicants' biographies and the documents that they supply to support the story of who they are and why they want to travel to Canada. In addition, they must try to predict the behaviour of individuals, which as most social scientists know, is incredibly difficult and imprecise. This is why Canadian visa officers, like their counterparts in most other parts of the world, are delegated with discretion in order to carry out their duties. In this sense, discretion and the rule of law are not necessarily incompatible. Rules and laws require interpretation, and in the case of visa officers, those rules and laws need to be applied to real-world visa applicants, in all their diversity.

Since the exercise of discretion almost always sparks the accusation that decision-makers are biased, this book is also important because it unpacks the factors that go into discretionary decisions and discusses the nature of bias in the border-control process. As decisions in visa issuance are based on the notion of "the balance of probabilities," it is not surprising that any two officers who look at the same application might reach different decisions. Individual-level attributes shape the way in which officers assess a file and exercise their discretion. Some apply an enforcement-oriented approach, whereas others are more facilitative, which may lead them to adopt differing interview styles and investigative techniques. Some look to uphold the letter of the law, whereas others look for reasons to approve an application. A seasoned officer who has accumulated a great deal of work experience might detect things in a file that a newly trained officer might not notice or think significant. Though they learn not to get emotionally invested in their work, it is sometimes difficult for officers to completely bracket their own biography as they make decisions, particularly in "hard cases." Immigration is an emotionally charged policy field in which human lives, opportunities, and relationships hinge on whether a visa is issued or denied. Officers understand that refusing a visa to a deserving applicant can have negative consequences for an individual or family, and depending on the nature of the case, they may choose to issue a visa even though they might have certain doubts about the veracity of the person's story or reason for entering Canada. These kinds of individual-level variations in discretion are not necessarily an indication of bad faith or of a faulty decision-making structure; instead, they reflect differences in officer understandings and assessments of credibility and risk.

Canada's immigrant-selection system is often accused of being racially biased. However, this study uncovered little evidence of race-based preference in the visa issuance system. In offices that processed mainly "visible minority" applicants, approval rates were comparable to those of offices that processed mainly white applicants. Moreover, due to certain structural realities in their workplace, racially prejudiced officers would not keep their jobs for long. Visa processing requires that staff produce, and production is measured by the number of decisions made. Refusing a visa generally involves more work than approving one. Thus, officers who regularly and repeatedly denied visas solely on the basis of an applicant's skin colour would work more slowly than their colleagues and would have difficulty surviving in an environment where mass processing is the norm.

Important though it is, individual-level discretion should not be overemphasized. In a sense, this book is about what I call the "social constitution of discretion": in other words, it argues that broader structural and organizational factors are far more significant in influencing officer decision making. The larger context in which officers work and in which individuals apply to come to Canada shapes the exercise of discretion. Officers have a broad understanding of the push-and-pull forces that encourage people to leave their country of origin. They know that, due to global inequalities, individuals from some countries are more desperate than others to get into Canada. They also recognize that such inequalities shape both the opportunities for legal migration and the extent to which people might engage in fraud or misrepresentation to enter Canada. As a result, such inequalities condition their discretionary choices to dig deeper into some files rather than others, and so there seems little doubt that broader social class and socio-economic biases are part of the visa issuance system.

The bureaucratic environment in which officers work also imposes its own set of pressures. All workplaces have expectations regarding staff productivity, and visa offices are no different in this respect. They and their officers must meet certain processing targets and client service expectations, and these too help mould officer decisions to dig more deeply into certain files. In the context of scarce resources, time constraints, and a heavily backlogged system, offices and officers must triage applications, deciding which ones warrant further probing and which ones can simply be approved. They cannot afford to process every file as if it were a blank slate, and so they must use their accumulated training and on-the-job experience to help pigeonhole files. They also rely on locally engaged staff members who are familiar with local conditions, customs, and contexts to help them address issues of credibility and risk.

Moreover, officers are motivated to achieve complex yet sometimes competing goals: they may wish to safeguard the integrity of the immigration system; to protect Canadian society from potential harms; to help Canada achieve its immigration-related economic objectives; to aid the process of nation building by selecting good immigrants; and to issue visas to eligible candidates. They also face numerous client groups that might have competing expectations about their decisions. Clients of the immigration system are not just visa applicants and their family members in Canada, but also employers, business associates, provincial governments, and immigration lawyers and consultants who have interests in specific individuals or groups being admitted to the country. Though the visa issuance system, in theory at least, is designed to insulate officer decision making from client groups, their interests do sometimes enter into the broader policy implementation process.

Sociologists apply the term "front-line bureaucrats" to professionals such as visa officers: vested with discretion in performing their duties, they work on the front lines, conveying certain benefits directly to clients. The sociological literature on front-line bureaucrats emphasizes that discretion is exercised and formed, in part, by face-to-face interaction with clients. Yet, because of resource constraints and a policy environment that demands both transparency and consistency, direct contact between visa officers and applicants is increasingly rare. Officers are explicitly encouraged to ground their decisions solely on the information supplied in an application. Readers may be surprised to learn that relatively few applicants are interviewed and that interviews are now decidedly outside the norm. Though this is understandable from a resource point of view because interviews take time, and time is expensive in a visa office, it is still hard to reconcile oneself to the reality that the vast majority of those who are admitted to Canada as visitors, temporary workers, or permanent residents are never interviewed by an officer. Given that succeeding in an interview is a prerequisite for landing virtually any job in Canada, whether a university faculty position or flipping burgers at a fast-food restaurant, the fact that our visa issuance system is being progressively built around insulating officers from face-to-face interaction with applicants is somewhat disconcerting. Nonetheless, in the absence of direct contact with applicants, discretion is still exercised, as this book reveals.

1

Stated and Hidden Agendas

> *Well, it's part science, and part art. The science part is applying the law. The art part is about understanding the people.* (Field notes, December 13, 2010)

Visa officers make their decisions in the larger context of state efforts to control borders. As key gatekeepers, they mediate between an individual's desire to cross an international boundary and whether the state permits him or her to do so (Simmons 2010). Visa offices and officers occupy the meso level of the migration process: that is, they operate between the broad macro-level factors that prompt people to leave home and the personal decisions that they themselves make regarding whether to migrate (Castles and Miller 2003). In this context, visa issuance functions as a border-control mechanism for states. Though most states justify border control on the grounds that it protects their citizens, academics argue that it is often shaped by hidden agendas, which are themselves structured by class, gender, and race-based prejudices. They point to the discretionary power that states delegate to their border control agents, including visa officers, as facilitating the exercise of such biases.

Understanding Border Control

Stephen Castles and Mark Miller (2003) argue that international migration is best understood through a theoretical model that is based on three levels of analysis: macro, micro, and meso. The macro level consists of the broad socio-economic and political factors that create the conditions for international migration and of the greater socio-economic consequences of large-scale migration. Immigration research at the macro level focuses on issues such as how inequalities within and between states encourage people to move, the relationship between trade and migration, changing global patterns of supply and demand for labour, the role of migrant remittances in national development, and the effects of immigration on local economies and labour markets.[1]

The micro level encompasses the individual and household-level decisions and consequences associated with international migration. Here, research focuses on how and why people decide to leave home and how they restart their lives in their new country. Among the many specific processes and issues studied at the micro level are the transnational ties that immigrants maintain with their homelands, the role that social networks play in migration decisions and settlement outcomes, how immigrants adjust/assimilate/integrate, and how they are treated in the labour market and other institutional spheres of society.[2]

The meso level refers to the individuals and organizations that mediate between the macro and micro levels. According to Stephen Castles and Mark Miller (2003, 28; see also Ford, Lyons, and van Schendel 2012), the meso level includes "the migration industry," which consists of "recruitment organizations, lawyers, agents, smugglers and other intermediaries." It also encompasses state immigration policy and the bureaucratic organizations, structures, and agents that implement it (Simmons 2010).

Castles and Miller (2003) argue that the meso level is the least understood aspect of the migration process. Other theorists tend to agree. For example, Alejandro Portes (1999, 32) writes that "the outside forces and agents that promote continuation of an open door [immigration] policy are easy enough to identify, but the internal dynamics of state agencies, the ways they absorb information and react to conflicting pressures, are not." Douglas Massey (1999, 51) suggests that "hypotheses concerning the interests, role and behavior of the state constitute a missing link in theories of international migration." And Gallya Lahav (2000, 218) notes that "few attempts have been made to disaggregate the state and to identify the agencies and actors involved in regulating immigration."

It is important to study immigration bureaucrats and bureaucracies because they are charged with controlling borders and regulating immigration (Webber 2012; Iacovetta 2007; Bouchard and Carroll 2002; Calavita 1991; Gilboy 1992). Although irregular and undocumented migration is substantial, and may in fact be growing, the vast majority of international migration today occurs through legal, state-sanctioned means (Papademetriou 2005). At some point, legal migrants pass through one or more layers of the bureaucratic border control process of at least one state. Moreover, even in an age of globalization where free trade agreements and other policy mechanisms seek to ensure that capital, commodities, and ideas circulate relatively unencumbered by national boundaries, states rather stubbornly cling to the idea that they can, and should, maintain control over their borders when it comes to the circulation of people (Jordan, Stråth, and Triandafyllidou 2003a and 2003b; Pécoud and de Guchteneire 2007). Indeed, control over physical borders is still seen as an inherent and inviolable element of state sovereignty (Sassen 2006; Zolberg 1999). This is true even in the European Union, which is often cited as a case where states have ceded their border control functions to a larger supranational body. EU states have certainly given up some aspects of control along their shared borders and for EU citizens. However, for those whose origins are outside of "Fortress Europe," EU states still have their own unique immigration policies that define whom they ideally want and how they will acquire permanent resident status and citizenship (Koopmans et al. 2005). Moreover, they vigorously police their borders to exclude those whom they define as unsuitable for social, economic, or ideological reasons.

Though often seen as mechanisms to keep certain individuals or groups out of a country (Fassin 2011, 217), immigration policy and border control, at their most basic level, are simultaneously about inclusion and exclusion (Schrover and Schinkel 2013; Sharma 2006; Abu-Laban 1998; Auditor General of Canada 2003). States control their borders to facilitate the entry of desirable individuals and to bar the undesirable (Schuck 2008). No matter how difficult or narrowly prescribed they make the process, even countries that lack active immigration programs nonetheless have mechanisms and procedures that enable at least some non-nationals to become permanent residents, if not naturalized citizens. Moreover, even the most insular countries in the world have policies that allow visitors, such as tourists and students, to spend short periods (usually highly controlled) in their territory. These "inclusion" policies coexist with other policies and procedures that attempt to keep out certain kinds of visitors and prospective permanent residents. How countries strike a balance between the competing principles of inclusion and exclusion lies at the heart of immigration policy and practice (Hollifield 2008).

Broadly speaking, there are four points at which in-migration states such as Canada exercise border control functions to regulate the inclusion and exclusion of immigrants: before individuals arrive, when they are either issued or refused a visa (Alpes and Spire 2013; Salter 2011); at the physical border or port of entry, when they are screened by customs or immigration officials (Gilboy 1991; Heyman 2001a); after they arrive, when they face deportation or removal if they violate certain laws or immigration procedures (Webber 2012; Golash-Boza 2012; Pratt 2005); and at the point of citizenship acquisition, when they are allowed (or not) to become citizens (Rygiel 2010). Obviously, individual states vary in terms of how they manage the particular mix of border control mechanisms at these four sites of enforcement (Webber 2012; Pécoud and de Guchteneire 2007).

First, at the point of visa issuance, many states create bureaucratic structures and processes to regulate the entry and stay of people who plan either to permanently move to or temporarily visit, work, or study in their territory (Boehmer and Peña 2012). Outside of certain common market zones such as the EU, most states require people to apply for a visa in advance of their arrival if they intend to work or live permanently in the country (Salter 2011). Some allow visitors to apply for work permits or permanent residency after they arrive. In Italy, for example, individuals from outside the EU can apply for "stay permits" after they reach the country, though they must prove that they entered legally (Triandafyllidou 2003). Canada used to require that all permanent resident applications be submitted to, and processed by, an overseas visa office. The idea was that applications for immigrant status should normally come from people who were not living in Canada. However, recent changes to immigration rules allow some categories of temporary residents, such as international students and temporary foreign workers, to apply for permanent residence from within Canada. As a result, more and more permanent resident visa processing now occurs in Canada.

Some states, such as the "Hermit Kingdom" of North Korea, require all short-term visitors to acquire a visa before they arrive, regardless of their nationality, the purpose of their trip, and the length of their stay (Visa Services Canada 2013). More commonly, however, states waive visitor visa requirements for the nationals of certain countries and/or for some types and durations of travel. The variability in visa requirements for short-term stays is based on a combination of geographic, political, and economic considerations (Newman 2003). For instance, neither Canadians nor Americans who wish to temporarily cross their shared border must apply in advance for a visa, because doing so would constitute a major barrier to trade and tourism. Given the volume of travel between the two countries, a visitor visa requirement would necessitate the creation of large bureaucratic infrastructures that would be both expensive and politically unpopular, even in an age of heightened border security.

Visas generally permit individuals to travel to a country and to remain there, either indefinitely or for specified times or purposes. Hoping to push border control beyond their actual physical boundaries, many countries impose fines and other sanctions on carriers that transport passengers without proper documentation, such as a passport or visa, to a port of entry (Comisión de Ayuda al Refugiado en Euskadi 2013). In such cases, the possession of a visa takes on additional significance because it constitutes permission to board an airplane, train, bus, or boat that conveys an individual to a physical border. Between 1997 and 2003, airline officials and Canadian immigration authorities reportedly stopped over forty thousand holders of improper travel documents from catching a flight to Canada (Brouwer 2003).

As a first-line border control measure, the process of issuing a visa essentially involves assessing the identity, eligibility, and intentions of those who wish to enter a country (Salter 2006, 2011). Visa issuance decisions tend to focus on whether individuals are who they claim to be, whether they meet the admission criteria laid out in a country's immigration policy, and whether they will do what they say they will do after they arrive. As Chapter 2 discusses in more detail, such assessments are neither arbitrary nor straightforward. In their official immigration policies and procedures, states usually outline the overall criteria and procedures that their officials will use in granting or denying visas. However, marrying immigration rules and procedures to individual cases is a complex bureaucratic process that is far from mechanical.

Second, at their physical borders, most states engage in another assessment of the identity, eligibility, and intentions of individuals. Even people whose eligibility and intentions have already been evaluated, and who possess a visa, face further scrutiny by an immigration or customs official when they reach the border (Heyman 2001a, 2001b, 2009). At the port of entry, officials attempt to ensure that they do not possess items prohibited by law or in excess of allowable limits. But they also gauge whether passport- and visa-holders are the same people who were issued the passport and visa, and whether they still meet their entrance eligibility requirements. States are under no obligation to admit the possessor of a visa. If, after it was issued, the state acquires adverse information about the individual, he or she may be denied entry upon reaching the border. Alternatively, even if a visa is not required to visit a country, information might be available to a state that will make travellers ineligible for entry. This is true of Canada and the United States. Although American citizens do not need a visa to come to Canada, through information-sharing arrangements with various US police jurisdictions, the Canada Border Services Agency can determine whether they have a US criminal record that will make them ineligible for entry, even as short-term visitors. Americans who have been convicted in the United States of driving under the influence of alcohol are sometimes surprised to find themselves being turned back at the border (except under specific circumstances).

In special cases, most notably that of the EU, there are no inspection services at the borders of member states. However, even EU states do selectively target third-country nationals whom they suspect of entering Fortress Europe without proper documentation. In other cases, the symbolic borders of the state extend beyond their physical border. For example, travellers who are flying from Canada to the United States are legally considered to be in America when they are screened by an American Customs and Border Protection official, even though the screening occurs on Canadian soil.

Depending on one's identity, origins, and destination, physically crossing a border can be more or less problematic (Helleiner 2012; Makaremi 2009). In the aftermath of 9/11, there is little question that Muslims and people with Muslim-sounding names, regardless of their national origins or citizenship, face extra scrutiny when they cross into many Western states. American Muslims who re-enter the United States from Canada report being targets of special and invasive scrutiny by the FBI and by Customs and Border Protection. In response to the seriousness of this, the Michigan chapter of the Council on American-Islamic Relations is suing the two organizations for violating American Muslim First Amendment rights (Macaluso 2012). LGBT travellers also encounter an extra layer of anxiety and uncertainty when they cross a border. The appearance of transgender travellers may not necessarily match their passport photo or the gender assigned to them on their official identity document (Steinecke 2009). In such cases, they are often subjected to additional scrutiny at the border because some officials have difficulty with individuals who do not fit into certain gender boxes.

Third, states control their borders by removing people who enter their territory without permission, who enter lawfully but violate certain laws or conditions of entry, or who misrepresented critical aspects of their identity or biography when they secured their visa (L. Weber 2013; Golash-Boza 2012; Pratt 2005). Many countries also enlist police services and other public-sector employees and agencies in the furtherance of immigration enforcement. Though much of Arizona's controversial 2010 state immigration law (SB1070) was struck down by the US Supreme Court in 2012, it nevertheless upheld the provision that authorized the police to check a person's immigration status while they enforced other laws (National Conference of State Legislatures 2012). Leanne Weber's (2013) account of policing of non-citizens in Australia focuses on the way in which "previously uninvolved actors" such as local police services are increasingly recruited into the regulation and control of national borders. In Ontario during the summer of 2014, Canada Border Services Agency officials accompanied Ontario Provincial Police during vehicle spot checks and ended up arresting twenty-one undocumented workers (CBC News 2014b).

In 2011, the British government removed or deported nearly forty-two thousand people who had violated immigration law (Migration Observatory 2011). In 2012, the United States removed nearly 400,000 individuals, and Canada expelled more than 13,000 people in 2008–09 for violating immigration rules and procedures (*Economist* 2014; Canada Border Services Agency 2010). In Canada, people can be removed if their application for refugee status is denied, if they overstay or violate the terms of entry on their visa, if they commit a major crime in Canada, or if they committed a war crime or major human rights violation elsewhere (Pratt 2005).

Finally, states control their borders by regulating access to citizenship (Koopmans et al. 2005; Rygiel 2010). Citizenship confers certain rights and obligations on individuals within a state. Permanent residence status and citizenship are not necessarily the same thing. In some countries, people may remain more or less permanently without becoming citizens. For some, like many Americans who live in Canada, citizenship in the country of residence is not particularly desired (Matthews and Satzewich 2006). Acquiring Canadian citizenship is relatively easy (although recent changes, such as increasing the pass mark on the test from 60 percent to 75 percent, mean that it is clearly getting more difficult). Nonetheless, many Americans are content to retain their original citizenship and do not feel a compelling need to become Canadians. On the other hand, states such as Germany impose highly restrictive conditions on the acquisition of citizenship and thus reinforce further boundaries between "us" and "them" (Triadafilopoulos 2012). As a number of commentators have argued, restrictive citizenship regimes can create groups of denizens, those who are permanent members of a society but who lack certain fundamental rights such as the franchise or running for public office (Hammar 1990).

States expend considerable resources in their effort to create and enforce these various border control mechanisms. One estimate suggests that the twenty-five richest countries in the world annually spend between US$25 and US$30 billion per year on enforcing their immigration laws (Martin 2003). Despite these vast expenditures, states often fail to completely control their borders. Visa issuance and port of entry screening mechanisms are imperfect, and some individuals are mistakenly given visas or granted entry even though a state might define them as undesirable or ineligible. People who are refused a visa, or who face deportation, sometimes evade authorities and manage to enter, live, and work in a country on an irregular or undocumented basis. Moreover, ever more stringent border control mechanisms usually engender ever more creative, and dangerous, ways to circumvent border controls (Pécoud and de Guchteneire 2007, 5). Some commentators argue that the $2.4 billion 650-mile-long wall built by the United States along sections of its southern border has not appreciably reduced undocumented migration from Mexico (Heyman 2009). In fact, only the ways in which the border is circumvented seem to have changed.

Why Do States Control Borders?

How states control their borders gives rise to the question of why they invest so many resources in doing so. Of course, they provide the official reasons, but other explanations focus on their hidden agendas.

The official justifications are fairly consistent across states. Most cite the interrelated grounds of safety, security, and economic prosperity (Papademetriou and Yale-Loeher 1996; Hollifield 2008). On the exclusion side, they say that border control protects their populations from undesirables. Most feel that drug traffickers, human smugglers, terrorists, and war criminals are threats to their safety and security, so they are deemed unwelcome as either immigrants or visitors. Few would disagree that excluding such individuals is a legitimate objective of border control, although what constitutes a "terrorist" is often debated (Ganor 2002). Countries with relatively high standards of living, and with good social welfare or health care systems, also say that border control protects them from being taken advantage of by people who want access to the benefits without having paid their dues, mainly in the form of taxes. Many states also say that border control protects the livelihoods of their members. In relatively prosperous countries, an uncontrolled border is seen as a recipe for undesirable increases in population and labour supply – uncontrolled migration leads to heightened competition for jobs and eventually to lower wages and standards of living for workers (Harris 2007).

On the inclusion side, most states recognize that admitting tourists boosts their economy. In many countries, tourism generates considerable economic activity and leads to job creation and to improvements in a state's balance of payments. Moreover, some states seek to recruit overseas students to "internationalize" their own student body and to help improve their global reach (Marginson 2014). Many countries also face long-term demographic and economic challenges. Declining birthrates mean that some states worry about the negative consequences of population aging. Immigration is seen as a potential solution to a shrinking tax base and future labour shortages. Finally, some states admit permanent residents and temporary workers in hopes of enhancing short- and/or long-term economic prosperity: they see various forms of controlled in-migration as ways to increase the supply of certain kinds of labour power, to augment capital formation, and to improve the aggregate demand for goods and services (Hollifield 2008).

Authorities in many countries often invoke the safety, security, and prosperity troika when they seek to explain or justify new immigration policies or procedures (Juss 1997, 53). In 2007, President George W. Bush attempted a major overhaul of American immigration policy that involved strengthening border control mechanisms, legalizing an estimated 12 million undocumented migrants, and creating a temporary worker program to give employers access to migrant workers (Smith 2007). In the case of Canada, the broad goals of immigration policy are outlined in the preamble to the Immigration and Refugee Protection Act (2001). However, in Canada, a related explanation cum justification of the need for border control is to maintain public confidence in the immigration system. To put it plainly, aggressive border control leads to public confidence in the immigration system and the maintenance of a robust immigration program. The underlying logic of this view is that weak or poorly designed border enforcement mechanisms simply encourage individuals and/or criminal organizations to circumvent or take advantage of the rules. End runs around border control erode public confidence in, and support for, the immigration program itself. In turn, the diminished support leads to public pressure to rein in, or reduce, overall immigration, which would have negative consequences for a country's economy and long-term demographic prospects. Immigration officials, who are charged with upholding Canada's immigration laws, often invoke this logic; certainly, it was a favourite refrain of former immigration minister Jason Kenney when new enforcement-related policies or practices were introduced.

Though the official reasons for border control are often dismissed by critics as nothing more than political rhetoric, they ought to be taken seriously. Canadian employers are key beneficiaries of Canada's relatively robust immigration program. As the 2013–14 controversy over temporary foreign workers made abundantly clear, Canadian immigration officials, like their counterparts elsewhere, do pay attention to the interests of employers when they draft policy. Anti-immigrant sentiments, and organized political voices, can prompt demands for immigration restrictions and can potentially harm the interests of employers (Stanford 2014). Though government officials sell immigration as being "good for Canada," which at an aggregate level, is true, it is undoubtedly "very good" for Canadian employers who are in search of labour. As a result, employers often strongly pressure government to keep the doors open.

There are other explanations of why states regulate entry to their territory. In some in-migration countries, border control policies and restrictive administrative practices are seen as mechanisms to exclude more than the usual list of "bad guys." Arguably, a hidden agenda underlies the publicly articulated criteria used to define certain individuals or groups as desirable or undesirable, either as visitors or permanent residents. Since legislators and legislatures are sometimes reluctant to reveal the true intentions of certain policies or practices, these hidden agendas are often imputed to political actors such as politicians, lobbyists, and political parties, or are read into certain policy statements or administrative procedures. Moreover, in a geo-political context where universalistic immigration policies are the norm in most Western states, policies that differentiate between applicants on the basis of certain characteristics are generally seen as unacceptable (Joppke 2005), thus creating the need to mask their true purposes.

As a result, some analysts look behind the public pronouncements of immigration officials to see how, either by design or default, apparently neutral and universally applicable policies, rules, and procedures put some groups at a disadvantage in the migration process purely because of their origins. In addition, some suggest that the mechanisms by which immigration policies are implemented are avenues for various types of bias to inform border control. Allegations of hidden agendas in state efforts at border control are often linked to issues of race, ethnicity, and religion. Controls over immigrants and visitors are interpreted as tools that preclude the migration of undesirable individuals on the grounds that they will create frictions with local populations, undermine national unity and identity, and/or challenge the legitimacy of the state (Garner 2010). Many states are often unwilling to acknowledge this, although in the wake of rising Islamophobia, politicians in some countries are becoming less hesitant about doubting the wisdom of admitting certain immigrants, whether they be defined as "Arabs" or "Muslims."

In many Western countries, immigration policy and procedures and immigrant integration policies have become focal points for claims about hidden agendas rooted in racism and Eurocentrism (Mahrouse 2010; Garner 2010). For example, though Australia officially abandoned its explicit "white Australia" policy in the early 1970s, the United Nations Human Rights commissioner asserted in 2011 that the policy was alive and well. As proof, the commissioner cited Australia's English-language test requirements for permanent residency applications and its policy of asking small island states such as Nauru to detain its would-be refugee applicants (*Daily Mail* 2011). In the United States, Tanya Golash-Boza (2012, 85) argues that the Department of Homeland Security's deportation practices are grounded in systemic racism, with the result that "black and Latino noncitizens are more likely to be targets of immigration law enforcement than white or Asian noncitizens." She suggests that the prevailing stereotypes of "black men as criminals" and "Mexicans and Central Americans as undocumented" play a role in how this aspect of border enforcement is carried out.

In Britain, some analysts assert that the British immigration control apparatus is meant to beat back black, Muslim, and Roma migration, and to keep Britain white (Rachel Hall 2002; Marginson 2014; Garner 2010). The state's efforts to control refugee migration, to deport individuals who lack official documentation, and to excessively scrutinize applications for spousal migration are all interpreted as based in racism (Webber 2012). Referring specifically to controls over spousal migration, Jacqueline Bhabha and Sue Shutter (1994) state that the British immigration bureaucracy, as an institution, is racist and sexist in how it conceives of families.

Individual bureaucrats are inevitably tainted by the larger racist organizational culture in which they work, and in Bhabha and Shutter's (ibid.) view, the British state's effort to control family reunification is really designed to curb black immigration (see also Webber 2012). In a biting indictment of the British immigration control apparatus, including both the policies and the officials who implement them, Frances Webber (ibid., 13) argues,

> It is often claimed that immigration law has been decoupled from racism since the bad old days of the 1960s and 1970s, when "immigration" meant settlement of former colonial subjects from Africa, the Caribbean and the Indian sub-continent, and laws emerged from, reflected, legitimated and reproduced colour-coded racism. But the anti-asylum laws and practices of the 1980s and 1990s were informed by a non-colour coded but just as virulent "xeno-racism" directed against poor eastern Europeans, particularly Roma. A ferocious anti-Muslim racism underlay the national security measures of the 2000s and the debate about Britishness instituted by Labour and carried forward in Cameron's critique of multiculturalism which suggests that you can't be properly British and Muslim at the same time ... Institutional racism is alive and well in government, in the United Kingdom Border Agency (UKBA), the modern incarnation of the Home Office Immigration and Nationality Directorate, and in the immigration judiciary. It is of course important to distinguish institutional racism from personal attitudes, although the former informs the latter.

Webber (2012, 14) adds that the systemic suppression of empathy is the main mechanism for the reproduction of racism among British immigration officials. Recognizing that officials are not "evil monsters," she suggests that the system in which they work dehumanizes immigrants and refugees, creating an indifference to the plight of people who are desperate to get into, and stay in, Britain. Drawing on Zygmunt Bauman's (1989) analysis of the Holocaust, she writes that "natural human empathy is manipulated by the powerful to produce moral indifference to the fate of marginalized groups" (Webber 2012, 14). Thus, officials are forced to bracket any feelings of sympathy or moral responsibility for those who are subject to a state's exclusionary mechanisms and to use "rational" and "technical" considerations as the basis for decisions that result in the oppression of racialized groups (see also Alexandra Hall 2010).

In Norway, Eileen Muller Myrdahl (2010) suggests that family reunification policies, in which prospective marriages are assessed on the basis of their conformity to Western standards of love and courtship, are meant to exclude racialized groups from the Norwegian national imagination. She argues that the policies contain unstated but powerful racialized logics that are meant to exclude certain individuals from Norwegian citizenship and membership in the national community. As she explains, the state's effort to link immigration control with the prevention of "forced marriages"

> reflects the ways in which discourses of gender, race, and nation congealed ... to shape an increasingly over identification of "Third World-looking people" ... with practices that places this group incompletely present in national space. The discursive placement of some citizens incompletely in national space means that the nation can be imagined as potentially "pure" – untainted by the practices that are invested with negative racializing meaning. The aspiration to this "purity" requires surveillance, policing, and maintenance of the demarcation between those belonging to, and therefore present in, the nation, and those whose extraneousness must be maintained in the face of their physical presence (Muller Myrdahl 2010, 106).

Finally, Dutch government policy requires that both prospective immigrants and those who already live in the Netherlands must pass civic integration exams, which focus on their command of the Dutch language and knowledge of Dutch society. This is justified on the grounds that knowledge of the language and an understanding of and commitment to Dutch society and culture are critical to combating extremism and promoting successful participation in Holland. The integration test for prospective immigrants applies to people who wish to migrate to the Netherlands for marriage or for family reunification. However, it is not required for EU citizens or for citizens of Switzerland, Australia, Canada, Japan, New Zealand, South Korea, and the United States (Human Rights Watch 2008). The EU citizens are exempt due to various treaty obligations, and the others are exempt because they are assumed to have "the capacity, ability, inclinations, or willingness" to integrate (ibid., 2). The real, thinly veiled, targets of the policy are family members and prospective spouses who are Muslims and who wish to migrate from countries such as Morocco and Turkey. According to Human Rights Watch (ibid.), the policy is discriminatory because it applies mainly to "non western" countries (Bonjour and de Hart 2013). During its first year of operation, immigrant applications from Turkey and Morocco "have fallen significantly" – and thus its unstated goal was achieved.

Hidden Agendas in Canada's Immigration System

Though Canada officially abandoned race, ethnicity, and nationality as immigrant selection criteria in the late 1960s, allegations that its current border control is informed by unstated biases and hidden agendas are very much alive (Simmons 1998). Three broad, but linked, agendas have been identified: they are grounded in class, gender, and race. Evidence for their existence is based on the reading of certain immigration policies or on assumptions about how visa officers and other border control officials make discretionary decisions.

The class-based agenda of immigration control, which in some ways is not very hidden, is linked to the spread of neo-liberalism (Barber and Lem 2012; Abu-Laban 1998; Fleras 2015). Yasmeen Abu-Laban and Christina Gabriel (2002, 96) argue that since the 1990s Canadian immigration policy-makers have embraced neo-liberal notions of "individual self-sufficiency, economic performance, and fiscal restraint" to prioritize the selection of self-supporting, "highly skilled, well educated and flexible workers as prospective citizens." Perceived as economic agents, these desirable immigrants "hit the ground running" and make immediate economic contributions to Canada; their sole value lies in their contribution of labour, skills, or financial capital. Sociologist Alan Simmons (2010) calls them "designer immigrants." Those who lack either valued skills or capital are deemed undesirable or unsuitable for Canada, and immigration policy is designed to keep their numbers down (see also Kirkham 1998).

This broad neo-liberal class-based agenda has intended, but unstated, consequences for the gender and racial composition of immigration flows to Canada. As Yasmeen Abu-Laban and Christina Gabriel (2002, 96) explain, the neo-liberal construction of the ideal immigrant and citizen "tends to favour male applicants from countries with extensive educational and training opportunities, thus serving to reinforce current gender and ethnic/racial exclusions within the policy."

The view that the ideal immigrant is still conceived as educated, male, and white remains a powerful theme in commentary and analysis about Canadian immigration policy and the actualization of border control mechanisms (Razack 1999). As Grace-Edward Galabuzi (2006, 8) points out, though legal restrictions against non-European immigrants were removed during the 1960s, certain administrative practices, such as the preference for skilled workers and the rules for refugee determination, put "visible minority" immigrants at a disadvantage: "These measures, largely enacted as the source countries for immigrants became predominantly countries in the global South, served to manage the flow of immigrants so as not to threaten the Eurocentric nature of the country."

In this light, various immigration policies and border control mechanisms have been interpreted as either racist in intent or as racist in their consequences because they have predominantly negative effects on visible minorities. Considerable attention has been paid to the various migrant labour schemes in which workers from abroad are permitted only temporary access to Canadian society and jobs. In her study of the Non-Immigrant Employment Authorization Program, the precursor to Canada's current Temporary Foreign Worker Program, Nandita Sharma (2006, 22) argues that the use of temporary guest-worker-type visas, beginning in the mid-1970s and increasing into this century, is meant to curb non-white immigration. As Sharma (ibid., 22–23) explains, the policy "legalized the resubordination of many non-Whites entering Canada by recategorizing them as temporary and foreign workers ... The racialized criteria of admittance in Canadian immigration policy was shifted from the pre-1967 categories of 'preferred races and nationalities' on the new category of non-immigrant (or migrant) worker."

In a similar vein, some interpret the Seasonal Agricultural Worker and the Live-in-Caregiver Programs as reflections of racism and sexism. The former program brings more than twenty thousand workers, mainly men, from Mexico and the Caribbean for up to eight months a year to labour in Canada's agricultural enterprises. That they are seen as good enough to work in Canada but not as good enough to stay is explained as arising from the perceived undesirability of Mexican and Caribbean immigrants, and hence from racism (Preibisch and Binford 2007; Satzewich 1991).

The Live-in-Caregiver Program, in which (mainly) women migrate to Canada under a probationary-type arrangement, albeit with a pathway to permanent residence, is seen as based in sexism and racism (Hallock 2009). Policies designed to bring female caregivers to Canada have changed over the years, depending in part on the source countries of workers. Before the Second World War, British women were recruited for domestic service, but by the early 1950s, women from eastern and central Europe were the main target of recruitment. Between the late 1950s and early 1980s, the focus was on Caribbean women, who were initially defined as temporary workers (Daenzer 1993). Now, most live-in caregivers are Filipinas. Historically consistent sexist notions of who is an appropriate caregiver have been overlaid by historically contingent racist understandings of the care-giving capacities of various groups of women from around the world (Stasiulis and Bakan 2005).

The administrative structure of the immigration bureaucracy, as well as the processes used to assess visa applications, generates concerns about, and allegations of, racial and other biases in border control. For example, a common criticism of the 1990s fixed on the location of overseas visa offices. At that time, most offices were in Europe and the United States, even though the majority of immigration applications were coming from Asia, Africa, and the Caribbean. The choice of location was said to serve unstated racialized processing priorities: it facilitated the migration of white Europeans and Americans to Canada while slowing that of visible minorities (Jakubowski 1997, 21).

More recent scholarship examines the micro-level decision making of visa officers, how they assess credibility and risk, and how various prejudices inform what should be universally applicable selection criteria. The literature tends to concentrate on discretion in the visa issuance decision-making process, which remains controversial among academics, NGOs, and applicants, who often see it as allowing officer biases to play a role in border control. Canadian legal scholar Sharryn Aiken (2007, 68–69) argues that "the continued role of discretion in overseas immigration decision-making permits individual, biased immigration officers to make discretionary decisions, and it allows the law, more broadly, to act as a tool for perpetrating racism." The Canadian Race Relations Foundation (2001), Evelyn Kallen (2003, 112), Yasmeen Abu-Laban and Christina Gabriel (2002), and Frances Henry and Carol Tator (2010) all assert that racial, gender, and class biases continue to creep into the immigrant selection system via discretionary decision making. Some contend that in the skilled worker selection system, white applicants are most likely to be given the benefit of the doubt and are subject to a positive substituted evaluation, whereas their visible minority counterparts are most likely to be subject to a negative substituted evaluation. In reference to variable rejection rates for family class spousal applications, Avvy Go, director of the Metro Toronto Chinese and South Asian Legal Clinic, suggests that "there's a very strong bias among officers in that they think that immigrants from certain countries ... come here using marriage as a ticket to immigration to Canada, in particular, countries such as

India and China" (CBC News 2010). And Anna Pratt (2005) asserts that the immigration officers in Canada who are responsible for detaining and deporting individuals use images of deserving and undeserving non-citizens as they decide whom to detain at the border and whom to recommend for deportation. These images are structured by ethnic and racial stereotypes, and by the officers' perceptions of risk.

Though many commentators believe that visa officers have racialized understandings of credibility and risk, which work to disadvantage racialized groups in the application process, Alan Simmons's (2010) more nuanced approach suggests that some of the biases in the system can be explained by the path-dependent nature of immigration. He maintains that though Canadian policy does not directly select immigrants on the basis of their national, ethnic, or racial origin, the selection criteria used within the policy do influence the constitution of overall immigrant flows to Canada. He posits that migration flows are structured by three interrelated determinants: the motivation to emigrate, the resources to leave, and the ability to meet a country's rules of entry. The clustering of these three factors helps to understand the broader patterns of international migration but also why some countries or regions might be "underrepresented" in immigration flows to Canada and why immigration policy appears to contain elements of race-based bias. Individuals with few resources, such as family ties in Canada, might not see Canada as a desirable destination, and thus past immigration flows or connections to it shape current patterns of motivation to come to the country. Similarly, Canada's entry rules, particularly for immigrants in the economic class, are heavily weighted in favour of high education, experience in relatively skilled jobs, and the ability to speak English or French. As a result, individuals who lack these assets are inevitably at a disadvantage in selection processes and decisions. In short, immigration outcomes, when measured by flows from various countries or regions, reveal a constellation of motivations, resources, and selection factors – not simply race (Simmons 2010, 113–37).

Taking Accusations of Bias Seriously

Claims of racial or other forms of unsanctioned bias at the meso level of immigration control, particularly in the decisions of visa officers, ought to be taken seriously. Canada's reputation for having a fair and transparent immigration system whose door is open to individuals from all over the world is continually tainted by such assertions. Moreover, individual and/or institutional-level biases are, in some ways, anathema to the workings of the ideal bureaucracy described by Max Weber (1964). After all, bureaucracies are organized to manage, standardize, and depersonalize large-scale decision making. In removing the personal element from the mix, bureaucratic decisions are supposed to apply equally to everyone, regardless of their circumstances or identity.

However, to seriously consider accusations of bias requires that visa officer decision making be understood in the context of the larger policy implementation process. Officers are obviously key agents in border control and in carrying out government immigration policy and objectives. They give life to abstract and general immigration policies and procedures, and they mediate between the large-scale social and economic conditions that propel individuals to migrate and the individual- and family-level calculus involved in deciding whether to leave or stay put. They are gatekeepers of national borders, and thus their decisions about visa issuance are simultaneously about inclusion and exclusion – to accept those whom the state defines as deserving and to reject the "undeserving."

At the same time, however, there is more to policy implementation than faceless and nameless bureaucrats who consciously or unconsciously sneak in their partialities as they follow predefined rules and procedures, check boxes, and stamp "approved" or "refused" on visa applications. The next chapter aims to advance such a broader understanding of the complexities of implementing immigration policy.

2
Delegated Discretion

Arbitrary, huh! There is a lot of pressure on us. I wish we could be arbitrary in our decision making ... Arbitrary? Wouldn't that be nice? (Field notes, December 13, 2010)

The exercise of discretion almost always evokes accusations of bias (Lipsky 2010; Cartier 2009). The normative consensus in many assessments of the hidden agendas behind border control efforts, and specifically of visa officer decision making in Canada, is that discretion is a largely negative feature. It tends to be seen as a legally sanctioned way for biases to inform decision making and to unfairly disadvantage, or favour, certain applicants on the basis of origin, gender, ethnicity, and skin colour (Juss 1997).

This way of understanding visa officer discretion reflects a long-standing perspective on the relationship between discretion and the rule of law. Ronald Dworkin (1977, 77; see also Pratt and Sossin 2009, 301) uses a "doughnut analogy" to characterize the traditional view of this relationship: "Discretion, like the hole in a doughnut, does not exist except as an area left open by a surrounding belt of restriction." In this tradition, discretion begins where the law ends, and according to Anna Pratt and Lorne Sossin (ibid., 303), "the law and discretion are negatively correlated: more law means less discretion, and less discretion means more law." In turn, the tradeoff between the rule of law and discretion is seen as a zero-sum game, where more discretion equals less fairness and less discretion equals more fairness. Discretion is a vehicle for the exercise of arbitrary might and coercion, and is contrary to "rule of law values such as certainty, objectivity and fairness" (ibid.). The implication of this view is that, if bias is to be reduced or eliminated, discretion should be either minimized and carefully monitored or completely exorcised from decision making. The solution to the problem of discretion lies in the creation of more law and more rules to constrain the ability of administrative authorities to exercise their judgment (ibid., 302).

This approach to discretion needs to be augmented with a more sociological approach that focuses on how workers in bureaucracies actually go about making their decisions and how policies are implemented (ibid., 301). This chapter presents an alternative way of conceiving the relationship between discretion and the rule of law, one that does not see the two as necessarily mutually exclusive (Pratt 2005). Discretion is not the space in administrative systems where law is absent. Rather, it is a form of administrative decision making that is governed by established rules, procedures, and appeal mechanisms. It is perfectly compatible with the rule of law because discretionary decisions, at least in visa issuance, are reviewable by various appeal bodies, must conform to wider legal and societal understandings of what is a reasonable decision, and must adhere to the norms of procedural fairness. But discretion, in this alternative perspective, is also exercised, shaped, and constrained by a number of social and organizational contingencies and exigencies. Individuals who work in bureaucratic organizations such as visa offices also face various structural limitations in how they perform their duties and make decisions in individual cases. Discretionary bias, in this perspective, involves more than individual bureaucratic agents making decisions on the basis of their own personal values, attitudes, and backgrounds: it also stems from the larger process of policy implementation and from the demands of the organizational culture in which they work.

The Policy Implementation Process

Bill Jordan, Bo Stråth, and Anna Triandafyllidou (2003b) define policy implementation "as the administrative process through which policy decisions or legislation are actualized in society with the aim of addressing and rectifying or modifying a given social situation." They argue that there are four analytically separate but interrelated dimensions to the policy implementation process: "a) the policy formation process prior to the implementation phase, b) the organizational and inter-organizational context of implementation,

c) the behaviour of street level bureaucrats, and d) the behaviour and reactions of target groups and other social actors involved in the implementation process" (ibid., 212).

This view is useful because it challenges the notion that there is a hard-and-fast distinction between "policy making" and "policy implementation." It also reminds us that implementation involves more than government bureaucrats sitting at their desks, pushing paper, mechanically applying rules, or processing endless streams of clients. Although they are undoubtedly a key link in the implementation chain, their role cannot be easily separated from other links, including the larger policy-making environment, the organizational cultures in which they work, the groups that are targeted by the various policies, and other external social and political actors that have wider interests in policy.

Creating Immigration Policy

Three major socio-political forces, along with their institutional actors, are involved with immigration policy making in Canada (Kelly and Trebilcock 1998): federal and provincial political parties and politicians; traditionally defined interest groups such as employers and their associations, trade unions, and NGO advocacy groups; and senior bureaucrats who work in various government departments. As noted in the previous chapter, broader public attitudes also play some role in the policy-making process, but this is indirect and tends to be mediated by the politicians and bureaucrats who monitor public opinion as they decide whether to revise policy (Hardcastle et al. 1994; Simmons 2010).

Clearly, federal political parties have their own priorities and concerns when it comes to immigration policy and implementation. Each party has its own emphasis and plans for immigration policy. At the same time, the three main parties see immigration as both a general good and as necessary to sustain Canada's social, economic, and demographic development (Li 2003; Simmons 2010). Since it is relatively easy for immigrants to acquire citizenship and then vote, federal politicians and political parties rather unsurprisingly take an active interest in implementation issues related to immigration. In fact, one study shows that in federal urban ridings, up to 85 percent of constituency work is related to immigration (MacLeod 2006, 11). Much of that work involves letters, emails, and phone calls from federal politicians and their staff to immigration officials about the status of visa applications for the relatives, friends, and colleagues of constituents. Though it is difficult to tell what proportion of these are for family class cases, or for cases involving visitor visas for family members, it is undoubtedly true that broadly defined family-related immigration matters are a major preoccupation of MPs in their constituency work.

Some MPs are also deeply interested in both policy and implementation. Via the legislative mechanism of Ministerial Instructions in the Immigration and Refugee Protection Act (2001), then immigration minister Jason Kenney was able to insert the Conservative Party's priorities into the visa-processing and implementation system. Though most of the nine Ministerial Instructions issued under his watch between 2008 and 2013 pertain to economic class immigrants and the selection of federal skilled workers, some apply directly to family class immigration. During Kenney's time as minister, several changes were introduced that blur the line between "policy" and "implementation" matters.

As one visa officer whom I interviewed explained, "politics," broadly defined, may have an indirect impact on the overall policy implementation process but not necessarily on how specific files are assessed:

> Politics are involved, but not at an individual level. It's more with how to process groups, or to deal with specific interests. Some ministers are more favourable to certain groups of applicants, like family class. In Canada, there's an election, and so family class becomes a priority. The same minister a few years ago was against the family class. Ministers all have their own priorities, and that's right. As long as they are requesting that we act within the act and regulations, that's okay. It is just part of the many different aspects that we consider when we look at a case.[1]

In 2011, as the next chapter will discuss in more detail, Ottawa temporarily stopped accepting new applications to sponsor parents and grandparents to Canada. However, aware that immigrant and ethnic communities rely on this mechanism to reunite with family members in Canada and anticipating a negative reaction from that quarter, the government also introduced a new ten-year "super visa." This multiple-entry visitor visa, valid for ten years, allows parents and grandparents to stay in Canada for twenty-four months. An "Operational Bulletin," which was issued to overseas visa offices to explain the visa's purpose and how applications should be processed, stated that it was meant to be "facilitative" (Pacific Immigration Canada 2011). This was probably a code word to signal that officers were to apply the rules generously and look for reasons to approve rather than refuse super visa applications. One officer interpreted "facilitative" as telling officers how to make their decisions: "They are watching us like hawks in Ottawa. They are reading our notes for every one of our decisions ... They would say they are not fettering our decision. But they have us under a microscope. They are reading our notes; they are watching us."[2] Moreover, officers were also told to consider giving the super visa to those who had applied for a temporary resident visa before the introduction of the new rules (ibid.). Normally, visa offices process applications on the basis of the rules that were in place at the time of application, so this directive speaks to the role that politicians and party interests impose on the policy implementation process.

Provincial governments also play a part in the development and implementation of immigration policy. Though immigration is a constitutionally defined area of shared responsibility between Ottawa and the provinces, most provinces took little interest in it until the 1980s (Simmons 2010; Fleras 2015). From 1978 to 1991, Quebec negotiated various agreements with the federal government that eventually resulted in the creation of its own immigration policy and selection procedures (ibid.). Since the mid-2000s, other provincial governments have taken a much more active interest in immigration matters via the Provincial Nominee Program, which was developed in Manitoba during the late 1990s to allow employers to fast-track applications submitted by workers who possessed in-demand skills. Now, every Canadian province and territory has a negotiated program agreement with the federal government, which enables them to select some of their own permanent residents. Federal immigration officials are responsible for ensuring that these decisions conform to overall federal rules and that those who are selected are not inadmissible on health, safety, or security grounds. As a result, many provinces now have their own immigration offices and officials, and their decisions eventually flow through to federal visa officers, who have the final say about whether a visa should be issued (Carter 2012; Nakache and D'Aoust 2012).

Various lobby and interest groups, employers, labour organizations, and agencies that represent immigrants have expressed concerns about both policy and implementation (Avery 1995; Goutor 2007). Employers who see immigrants mainly as workers lobby for government policies that give them easy access to offshore labour (Satzewich 1991). Employers are also interested in how policies are implemented, particularly the efficiency with which visa offices process applications. Before the April 2014 pause on the employment of temporary foreign workers in the restaurant industry, large employers such as Tim Hortons undertook overseas recruitment drives and appeared to work with visa office staff to ensure that visas were issued in a timely manner (*GMA News* 2007). The growth in "just in time" migration programs, which allow employers relatively quick access to offshore labour, also reflects their burgeoning interest in immigration policy and implementation, particularly the speed and procedures with which visa officers make their decisions (see Lenard and Straehle 2012).

Canadian trade unions, such as the United Food and Commercial Workers Union, which is seeking to organize seasonal agricultural workers who come from Mexico and the Caribbean, also lobby to change the policy that governs their work in Canada (Hanley et al. 2012). They seek to overturn the rule that bars seasonal workers from joining unions and bargaining collectively, and are also interested in how health and safety policies are enforced at workplaces and how workers are recruited into the program. Non-governmental advocacy and research organizations such as the Canadian Council for Refugees, the Maytree Foundation, the Canadian Marriage Fraud Victims Society (now disbanded), and the C.D. Howe Institute also take stands on various immigration and refugee policy issues in Canada and make recommendations on policy implementation.

There is some debate about the role that senior bureaucrats play in the policy development process (Hardcastle et al. 1994; Satzewich 2007; Paquet 2014). Though one perspective sees them as the passive recipients of policies that are developed by politicians in committees and legislatures, it seems clear that they articulate their own policy preferences, which sometimes differ from those of NGOs (ibid.). Freda Hawkins (1989, 39), for example, argues that immigration policy shifted away from the "white Canada" approach during the early 1960s partly because the new cohort of immigration officials who had moved into senior positions abhorred the racially selective features of the immigration program at the time.

Though the roles that institutional actors play in policy development are subject to debate, it is evident, as Bill Jordan, Bo Stråth, and Anna Triandafyllidou (2003b, 212) point out, that no clear line separates policy development from policy implementation. Indeed, institutional actors do not lose their concern for immigration after certain policies have been achieved: application is also of absorbing interest to them.

Inter-Organizational Contexts

Although Citizenship and Immigration is the lead federal agency when it comes to implementing immigration policy, it nonetheless works in collaboration with several other government branches, and increasingly with provincial governments, to carry out its mandate. The main federal actors are the Canada Border Services Agency, the Royal Canadian Mounted Police (RCMP), the Canadian Security Intelligence Service (CSIS), Human Resources and Skills Development Canada, and the Department of Foreign Affairs and International Trade. Other government departments with more tangential interests in immigration-related matters include the Canadian Food Inspection Agency, which deals with immigrants or visitors who wish to bring their pets into Canada, and the Canada Revenue Agency, which handles taxation.

Though somewhat oversimplified, one way to understand the differing responsibilities of the various federal government agencies and organizations is through the distinction between "selection" and "enforcement." Immigration and Human Resources generally concentrate on the selection of immigrants. Immigration officials ensure that applicants meet various admission criteria, and Human Resources screens employer requests to hire temporary foreign workers from outside of Canada and, in theory at least, ensures that offshore workers do not undermine the wages and working conditions of Canadians. (Preibisch and Hennebry 2012). Border Services, the RCMP, and CSIS are all involved with enforcement. Before Border Services was created in December 2003, the immigration department handled both selection and enforcement. In 2003, enforcement became the province of Border Services, which also took on customs enforcement and which is administered by the larger Department of Public Safety. Today, Border Services officials staff Canadian ports of entry, where they screen visitors, immigrants, and residents who return from trips abroad. They have the final authority to admit or refuse visitors and immigrants, even those who have been issued a visa by an overseas office. They are also responsible for the detention and deportation of immigrants, visitors, and refugee claimants who land in Canada and are seen as threats to public health, safety, and security.

The RCMP also works with Citizenship and Immigration on security-related issues. The mandate of the RCMP Immigration and Passport Section, for example, is "to combat and disrupt organized migrant smuggling and the trafficking of persons," and that of the Immigration and Passport Special Investigation Section is to conduct investigations at Canadian immigration missions abroad and to combat immigration-related fraud and corruption by public officials (Royal Canadian Mounted Police 2014). CSIS is involved with security-related screening of immigrant, visitor, and refugee applicants, and in cases where visa officers have concerns about an applicant's inadmissibility, it takes part in the decision-making process.

Target Groups and Other Social Actors with Interests in Implementation

The existence of multiple political actors that have an interest in immigration policy and implementation raises the question of who is the "client," or target group, of the immigration bureaucracy (Jordan, Stråth, and Triandafyllidou 2003b). At first glance, the answer seems simple: non-citizens who seek to gain entry to Canada to live, work, study, or visit. However, the bureaucracy's clientele also includes employers who wish to hire workers from outside Canada and the provincial governments that seek to nominate certain individuals under their own immigration programs. It encompasses the Canadian citizens and permanent residents who desire to sponsor relatives to visit or settle in Canada. Moreover, as the 2014 controversy over the increased use of temporary foreign workers shows, Canadian workers can also be seen as clients of the immigration program, which is supposed to protect their interests. At least in theory, the wages and working conditions of Canadian citizens and permanent residents are not supposed to be jeopardized by the arrival of permanent immigrants or temporary workers. And somewhat more abstractly, the Canadian nation as a whole is a client of the bureaucracy because the immigration program is conceived as part of a broader nation-building strategy. This means that immigration bureaucrats who implement policy and make decisions function in a broader social and political context, where they must balance the competing demands and pressures from a diverse clientele whose interests are potentially divergent (Veugelers 2000).

Though strictly speaking, they are not "clients" of the immigration program, immigration consultants and lawyers also have an interest in the implementation of policy. They have a clear stake in implementation because they represent individuals who are seeking a visa to enter Canada. Until the late 1980s, lawyers had a virtually unchallenged monopoly in representing people who needed help in applying for a visa or appealing a visa officer's refusal. Lawyers remain actively involved in advising applicants and representing them in appeal cases. The Canadian Bar Association has a National Immigration Law Section with over a thousand members. The section organizes an annual conference and provides various kinds of professional resources and supports for immigration law practitioners (Canadian Bar Association 2014). Notably, through federal access-to-information requests, it also collects and compiles a yearly government contact list, which contains the names, email addresses, and posting locations of visa officers. This list is provided to members to facilitate their contact with the officers who are processing their clients' files and whose decisions they wish to influence.

During the late 1980s, with the rise of the immigration consultant, the legal profession's monopoly began to slip. Initially, consultants were niche players, providing advice to, and advocacy for, individual applicants for permanent and temporary resident visas, but they eventually began to represent refused applicants at appeal bodies. There are now over 2,500 consultants in Canada, and they are currently in the throes of a complex professionalization process that involves, among other things, the creation of a body to regulate entry into the profession and to monitor the professional practice of members.[3]

Finally, the courts and other judicial bodies are among the most significant external institutional actors that have an interest and a say in immigration policy implementation. The amount of immigration-related jurisprudence in Canada is massive. However, among the many court decisions on the subject, two Supreme Court of Canada rulings – *Baker* and *Singh* – are widely seen as landmarks in the implementation of policy and the ability of applicants to appeal the decisions of visa offices.

According to Roger Rowe (2008, 338), the 1999 *Baker* case "set a new standard for the review of administrative discretion and the content of the duty of procedural fairness." The case focused on Mavis Baker, a single mother of four Canadian-born children who was subject to a deportation order for overstaying her original visitor visa. Baker applied to remain in Canada on the basis of "humanitarian and compassionate" grounds, but the visa officer who reviewed her case refused the application. Her appeal focused on his failure to consider the best interests of her children and to reveal his reasons for refusal. If she were deported to Jamaica, her children would either have to accompany her or be placed in care in Canada until they reached the age of majority. Prior to *Baker*, "immigration officers were not required to give reasons when refusing [humanitarian and compassionate] applications" (Rowe 2008, 339). Ruling in favour of Mavis Baker, the Supreme Court decided that immigration officers must give reasons for their decisions and must be "alive and sensitive" to the interests of children when the removal of their parents was involved (ibid., 340). Though there are debates about how well Citizenship and Immigration meets this stipulation, particularly in humanitarian and compassionate applications, *Baker* had the long-term effect of providing failed applicants with the reasons for their refusal and enabling them to address, and potentially rebut, them (Hallock 2009).

The 1985 Supreme Court *Singh* ruling also had a significant, long-term impact on how visa officers made their decisions and on how the decisions could be appealed. The case involved seven people whose applications for refugee status were initially refused. The refusals were subsequently upheld by the then existing Immigration Appeal Board. *Singh* revolved around whether refugee applicants had the right to an oral hearing as part of the adjudication of their case. Before 1985, visa officers and the Immigration Appeal Board could make decisions on their cases without giving them an opportunity to defend themselves at an oral hearing. The Supreme Court ruled that this practice was in contravention of both the Canadian Charter of Rights and Freedoms and the Canadian Bill of Rights, and that refugee applicants in Canada had the right to an oral hearing as part of the consideration of their application (Kelly and Trebilcock 1998, 414).

Singh resulted in the creation of the Immigration and Refugee Board of Canada, whose four divisions are now responsible for various types of appeals. In 2012 alone, the board rendered decisions in more than forty thousand cases; it also had a roughly equal number of cases that were pending. The board's Refugee Protection Division hears claims for refugee status made within Canada and decides whether to accept them. Anyone who is dissatisfied with its decision can appeal to the Refugee Appeal Division. The Immigration Division hears cases where individuals are deemed inadmissible to, or removable from, Canada because of health, safety, and security considerations. Finally, the Immigration Appeal Division hears appeals in refused family class sponsorship cases. Persons who are refused a visa for the various types of economic class can apply to the Federal Court of Canada for a judicial review of the visa officer's decision. Refusal decisions of the Immigration Appeal Division can also be subject to a judicial review in the Federal Court of Canada. Except for decisions rendered by the Refugee Appeal Division, applicants can appeal the decisions of these judicial bodies to the Federal Court of Appeal. In some instances, people whose appeals are denied can apply to the Supreme Court of Canada to have their case reconsidered. Generally, these judicial bodies review whether decisions were wrong in fact or law, or whether the way in which a decision was made breached the principle of natural justice. In successful appeals, courts do not normally instruct that a visa be issued: instead, the prior decision-making body is required to reconsider the case in light of the reasons for the successful appeal. It can still decline to issue the visa, but its reasons for doing so must differ from those that the court has disallowed.

Obviously, the policy implementation process is more complicated than first meets the eye. A variety of political, professional, and organizational actors and stakeholders have an interest in policy development and implementation, and such interests shape in subtle, and not so subtle, ways how visa officers make decisions.

Street-Level Bureaucrats: Understanding Discretion

Michael Lipsky (2010, 3) defines "street-level bureaucrats" as "public service workers who interact directly with citizens in the course of their jobs, and who have substantial discretion in the execution of their work." Generally, they are responsible for delivering benefits, sanctions, and/or statuses that "structure and delimit people's lives and opportunities" (ibid., 4), and they must "cope with their client's personal reactions to those decisions" (ibid., 13; see also Jordan, Stråth, and Triandafyllidou 2003b).

Lipsky's (2010, 3) list of typical street-level bureaucrats includes "teachers, police officers, and other law enforcement personal, social workers, judges, public lawyers and other court officers, health workers, and many other public employees who grant access to government programs and provide services to them." Government officials who issue visas and other travel documents are among the "other public employees" who can be considered street-level bureaucrats (Alpes and Spire 2013). Though they do not grant access to specific government programs (such as social assistance), they nonetheless control access to a highly significant public benefit: legal admission to a country for a non-citizen. In this, they are similar to other status-conferring front-line bureaucrats, such as police officers and court officials, whose decisions define clients in fundamental and highly consequential ways. The accumulated decisions of police officers and court officials end up categorizing certain individuals as, for example, "thief," "young offender," or "sexual offender." The decisions of visa officers define individuals as potential legal temporary or permanent residents in a country. Thus, border control mechanisms, in the form of visa issuance decisions, are best understood as status-conferring processes. An officer's decision to approve a visa application confers a particular status on individuals: they become legal permanent or temporary residents of a country. Alternatively, the denial of a visa also confers a type of informal status: ineligibility to legally enter a country. From a mobility perspective, the ineligible may choose to access a different country, and some may try to enter the desired country and/or remain there without state permission, in which case a visa officer's refusal is part of a path-dependent process in which they are eventually defined as "undocumented," "irregular," or "illegal" immigrants.

Although the institutional actors mentioned above all have some interest, or role, in the policy implementation process, the everyday responsibility for implementation falls to public servants, or street-level bureaucrats. But as Jordan, Stråth, and Triandafyllidou (2003b) correctly emphasize, public servants must absorb, make sense of, and manage these other interests as they go about their jobs. At the same time, the unique organizational cultures in which they work also play a role in the policy-making processes, as, no doubt, do their own personal values and beliefs.

The Delegation of Discretion

As Anna Pratt and Lorne Sossin (2009, 302) point out, laws and rules are not "self-executing." The implementation of government policy involves the work of human beings, who function in the context of bureaucratic structures, and who must apply various rules and procedures to the "real world" of clients, cases, and applicants. Inevitably, there are points in the decision-making process where "the application of the law takes one twist rather than another" (Jordan, Stråth, and Triandafyllidou 2003b, 212). As Jordan, Stråth, and Triandafyllidou (ibid., 211) explain,

> Naturally, legislative jargon aims at being clear and concrete. However, in reality, policy mandates are more often than not too complex or too vague. Their implementation requires more than technical-administrative execution ... The implementation of policy mandates entails thus a relatively high level of interpretation so that concrete individual cases are made to fit into general rules.

Fitting cases into predefined rules entails discretion on the part of street-level bureaucrats (Lipsky 2010; Juss 1997; Emerson 1994). Police officers cannot always be directed by an official handbook when they conduct a criminal investigation, decide whether to charge or warn someone for a traffic violation, or determine whether to book an unruly teenager for a relatively minor indiscretion or take him home to his parents. Social workers cannot find a rule or procedure to cover every possible scenario about whether a child requires state protection. University professors cannot always be guided by their course outlines or departmental rules and procedures in imposing late penalties for student papers. Although client "cases" exist in rule-based environments where procedures and eligibility criteria for benefits or sanctions are clearly specified, as are the policies and procedures used to assess eligibility, they are usually so diverse and complicated that policy-making authorities cannot possibly create a written rule for every contingency (Lipsky 2010; Triandafyllidou 2003). Thus, precisely because their caseloads are complex and messy, and because of the inherent ambiguities involved with finding and assessing "the facts," street-level bureaucrats are generally permitted to exercise their discretion.

As with these other rules-based environments, the policies, rules, and procedures that define who deserves a visa and who does not, and how to differentiate between the two, do not in themselves result in decisions in concrete cases. Referring to the complexity of implementing immigration policy, Jordan, Stråth, and Triandafyllidou (2003b, 211) argue that "immigration policy in particular is faced with a constantly evolving and shifting reality of population movements and a variety of strategies for entry and survival in a host country." Since the global terrain of immigration is never static, a state's immigration policy and procedures can never completely anticipate the complex strategies that individuals use to legally (or illegally) cross a border.

Most states directly and deliberately (Schneider 1992, 61) delegate discretion to their immigration and border control officials to empower them to sort through and decide who is eligible to legally enter, stay, and work in the country (Webber 2012; Eggebø 2013a; Digruber and Messinger 2006; Foblets and Vanheule 2006; Hollifield 2008). Visa officers and other bureaucratic agents must apply the general rules to individual cases and exercise varying degrees of judgment about whether an applicant meets, or does not meet, the publicly defined admission or exclusion criteria (Alpes and Spire 2013).

In Canada, the delegated nature of discretion is reflected in the concept of "satisfied." The Immigration and Refugee Protection Act (2001, section 11(1), emphasis added) specifies that a foreign national who wishes to enter Canada "must ... apply to an officer for a visa or for any other document required by the regulations. The visa or document may be issued if, following an examination, *the officer is satisfied* that the foreign national is not inadmissible and meets the requirements of this Act."

Moreover, "satisfied" permeates the Immigration Regulations and the processing manuals that visa officers use to guide their decisions. It frames the ways in which they interact with applicants and communicate their decisions to them. For instance, in the sample templates that Citizenship and Immigration provides to officers, the suggested wording of "refusal letters" almost always explicitly contains some version of the phrase "I am not satisfied that you meet the requirements of the Act and the Regulations" (Citizenship and Immigration Canada 2011c, Appendix A).

In commenting on the inherently discretionary nature of "satisfied," one immigration program manager said that "the definition of 'satisfied' is so big you can drive a truck through it ... Those kinds of words in the act are all about discretion without saying it is discretion."[4]

An additional legislated element to discretion stems from the principle that a visa officer's decision cannot be "fettered" (Waldman 2009, 14). This means that though officers may consult with colleagues or supervisors about a case, they cannot be told what decision to make. It also means that though the Immigration Regulations and the guidelines in the processing manuals should inform the decision-making process, they cannot be so narrow as to determine the outcome of an application: each case must be assessed on its own merits, and the guidelines cannot prescribe a particular outcome or decision (ibid., 15).[5]

Thus, the notions of "satisfied" and "non-fettered decision making" highlight both the delegated and discretionary aspects of the decision regarding who will receive a visa. In effect, the use of "satisfied" transforms all officer decisions into an exercise of discretion because they must apply their own judgment in determining whether an applicant meets Canada's admission criteria. The buck stops with them, at least until an applicant files an appeal.

Credibility, Risk, and Bad Decisions

The gate-keeping function of border control officials, particularly the decision to issue or refuse a visa, is ultimately linked to visa officer understandings of the linked notions of credibility and risk (Heyman 2009, 369–70; Pratt 2005; Makaremi 2009, 417). As Josiah Heyman (2009, 370) explains, though border control officials work in a "categorical world" where they must choose whether an individual can cross a border, credibility and risk exist on many shaded continua. Moreover, credibility and risk are not inherent attributes of visa applicants or applications. Nor are they objective facts. Instead, they are socially constructed variables that are "worked up" by those who are responsible for processing files and implementing policy (Pratt and Sossin 2009, 311; Hannah-Moffat, Maurutto, and Turnbull 2009).

For visa officers, credibility hinges on the interpretation of a bundle of factual questions related to whether people are eligible for, and deserve, a visa. But "facts" themselves are not self-evident. A critical element to the process of fitting individual cases into general rules involves their collection and interpretation (Juss 1997, 6). Referring generically to what he calls "first order decision makers," Carl Schneider (1992, 66) writes,

> First, someone must find facts, and fact-finding is inevitably a partly discretionary process, since it requires making complicated judgments whose components cannot be foretold and resolved in advance. Deciding what actually happened always involves some discretionary judgments about what evidence to hear, what evidence to regard as relevant, and what evidence to regard as reliable, to say nothing about drawing final conclusions about what actually happened.

In a context where the facts are themselves socially constructed, visa officers ask themselves certain questions regarding all applicants and the type of visa for which they are applying. These questions include, but are not limited to, Are applicants who they claim to be? Do they have the qualifications and resources they say they have? Do they meet the stated eligibility criteria for the visa? Are they really in the relationship they say they are in? Did they make their money legally? Do they have enough social ties back home to ensure that they will return there once they finish visiting Canada?

In practice, assessing credibility is a socially constructed process. As an immigration program manager told me, "It isn't rocket science, but you have to have sensitivity to the human condition." Elaborating, he added that officers

> have to tolerate a lot of ambiguity. In many environments, many people are lying, but it does not mean they are bad people, and not good candidates for Canada. A lot of people have to embellish in some countries. They might be lying, but they have traits I admire: respect for authority, family, things like that. Visa officers sometimes get hung up with credibility. A visa officer is trained to detect contradictions. They ask the same questions different ways. They look for logical inconsistencies. But at the end of the day, does it really matter? Sometimes, visa officers go overboard with credibility. In some societies, especially with refugees, there is the legally correct answer and there is the right answer.[6]

Whereas questions of criminal law are decided on the basis of reasonable doubt, most administrative and decision-making bodies use a considerably lower threshold of certainty. In visa issuance, the threshold tends to be based on the concept of "balance of probabilities." Ultimately, an officer's answer to the question of credibility is based on probability: "Is it likely/not likely that this applicant is telling the truth?" Balancing probabilities is an inherently discretionary process that is difficult to quantify; two officers, both acting in good faith and both assessing the same facts, might reasonably find themselves differing on the subject of their credibility.

Officers must also manage risk (Beck 1992; Giddens 1999; Ekberg 2007). This entails assessing the implications of making a bad decision and the harm that it is likely to cause to the officer, the client, and/or to Canadian society more generally. Risk is also linked to the predicting of behaviour and future actions.

In the world of visa officers, what constitutes a bad decision is complex and will be discussed in subsequent chapters. However, in deciding to issue a visa to an applicant, an officer must make two separate but interrelated decisions. Selection decisions, broadly defined, involve assessing whether applicants meet the stated criteria for the type of visa they have requested. This form of decision is followed by an inadmissibility decision. That is, officers must determine whether an ostensibly qualified applicant threatens the safety, security, and well-being of Canadians and is thus inadmissible to Canada. A negative admissibility decision tends to trump a positive selection decision. For example, a woman who speaks English well, has an engineering degree from the Free University of Berlin, and has many years of work experience in her field will be a good candidate for a federal skilled worker visa. However, if she engaged in unsavoury activities during her past – such as using her skills to build bombs for the German Red Army Faction in the 1980s – her eligibility for the visa would normally be overridden by her previous membership and participation in a terrorist organization.

As a first approximation, for visa officers, the riskiest decisions are those in which undeserving individuals are granted visas even though they are inadmissible to Canada because of some aspect of their past. They include people who have a significant medical condition and who might take advantage of the health care system, who have serious criminal pasts, who have participated in war crimes or human rights abuses, or who belonged to subversive or terrorist organizations. Visa officers tend to take such assessments seriously because the risks are perceived to be high: making the wrong decision could potentially harm the safety, security, and well-being of Canada.

Thus, they apply extra scrutiny and undertake extra "fact finding" whenever this form of risk is high. Those who work in areas where human rights violations occur, or occurred during the recent past, are concerned about admitting individuals who participated in atrocities, as, for example, in the Balkans, whose 1990s war involved human rights abuses and atrocities on all sides. Visa offices that process applications from men who live in the Balkans and who are of an age where they could have committed atrocities apply extra scrutiny because of the heightened risk. For understandable personal, professional, and career reasons, officers do not want their names attached to a file in which a foreseeable and critical inadmissibility factor was overlooked or not properly assessed. Issuing a visa to a war criminal, a major criminal, a terrorist, or someone with a record of human rights abuse is clearly a sign of faulty decision making, and depending on the circumstances, could result in formal or informal sanctions against the officer responsible.

Other instances in which an undeserving applicant may be granted a visa are regarded as lower risk; they revolve around selection decisions. "Lower risk" applies to people who misrepresent their educational credentials or job experience and are mistakenly issued a federal skilled worker visa. Other lower risk cases involve granting a spousal visa to someone who deliberately enters into a marriage of convenience to secure permanent resident status. Decisions about whether to issue a temporary resident or visitor visa involve questions about whether individuals are likely to comply with the relevant terms and conditions, and whether they are likely to go home when their visa expires. In this case, risk is defined as the probability that individuals will stay in Canada beyond the time specified in their visa or will launch a refugee claim. Though making mistakes in lower risk cases may be bruising to personal and professional pride, this form of error is generally seen as inevitable, given the uncertainties and ambiguities of visa processing. It is also regarded as causing less harm to Canadian society than admitting someone who is inadmissible for safety, security, or medical reasons.

Conversely, the other form of "mistake" that an officer can make is to deny a visa to a deserving person. The harm associated with this error is generally regarded as relatively low, though it does vary depending on the type of visa being applied for. Referring to temporary resident processing, a visa officer noted,

> The potential damage to the client is minimal if I make a mistake. If you are in refugee or family class processing, if you make a mistake and reject someone that is admissible to Canada, this is a bigger deal. A refugee can be killed, or a family can be separated. Those decisions are more consequential. The damage to a client of making a wrong decision is great in these

> cases. On the economic side, the damage is also greater ... The damage to a skilled worker of making the wrong decision is that they will go to Canada, face problems in becoming established, they might face mistreatment by an employer, have language problems. There is also the opportunity cost of staying here.[7]

Though officers understand that such mistakes may cause harm to applicants, they generally recognize that they do not necessarily completely slam shut the door to Canada. In temporary resident cases, applicants can reapply. If they choose to do so, a different officer is required to process their application, could see it in a favourable light, and would thus issue the visa. In permanent resident applications, officers are aware that their decisions can be appealed. Knowing that this is both possible and quite likely, depending on the circumstances, means that they associate these kinds of mistakes with relatively low risk.

What Goes into Discretionary Decisions?

As the first decision-makers in visa application cases, officers are essentially involved in finding and assessing "the facts" and making judgments about them (Juss 1997). As they review applications, they must ultimately choose whether to accept, reject, or dig deeper into the information that individuals supply. Whether a visa is issued or denied hinges on the "structures of meaning and contexts of decision making in the 'artful' and selective construction of realities" (Pratt and Sossin 2009, 306). In other words, officers are involved in the complex social construction of reality: as they work toward their decision, they impose their meanings on applicants and the information they provide.

It is tempting to see the process of "meaning making" as a purely individual attribute and to see discretionary decisions as based on the prior attitudes, social backgrounds, and upbringing of decision-makers (see Lipsky 2010). That is, the "baggage" that officers bring to their job, their background experiences, their personal likes and dislikes, and their attitudes and values all explain why some applicants benefit from discretionary decisions, whereas others do not. Though it is true that officers are expected to exercise discretion, and that their decisions cannot be fettered, it is inaccurate to see them as wholly autonomous decision-makers who are insulated from larger social forces and pressures or from their work environment.

Though their decisions are no doubt influenced to some extent by the baggage that they bring to their jobs, a more fruitful way of thinking about discretion is to focus on the larger contextual factors that shape the way in which policy is implemented and decisions are made. Locating the behaviour of front-line bureaucrats in the larger context of the policy implementation process enables us to reframe discretion as based on more than the attitudes, values, and perspectives of individuals. How officers understand credibility and risk, and how they make choices at various points in the decision-making process, is shaped by a complex combination of variables and processes that function at the micro, meso, and macro levels (Heyman 2009).

The micro-level variables are rooted in the previous on-the-job experiences of officers (Psimmenos and Kassimati 2003, 357), their interactions with clients, and their personal, professional, and national identities (Eggebø 2013a). Though the legal expectation is that every case will be treated on its own merits, front-line bureaucrats nonetheless regularly draw on their reservoir of job experience to make sense of individual cases (Alpes and Spire 2013). Since they do not have unlimited time or resources to make their decisions, they often use conceptual shorthand to categorize cases and simplify complexity. They develop triage techniques to differentiate "good" from "bad" cases and "easy" from "hard" ones. As well, they draw on understandings, or "typifications" (Frohmann 1991), of what is normal and abnormal in the culture and country in which they are working, and of what is normal for the visa category itself. These views of normality are used as filters, or measuring rods, against which individual applicants are judged and assessed (Waegel 1981). Conformity or non-conformity to a visa officer's understanding of what is normal does not necessarily predetermine his or her decision, but it does influence the choice to dig deeper into some files rather than others.

Micro-level decision making is also contingent on officer interaction with clients. As mentioned above, Citizenship and Immigration has a diverse client base, but direct contact with clients tends to be limited to visa applicants. In most cases, an officer's contact with applicants is solely via their "paper" application. As a result, much of the assessment of credibility and risk occurs without any face-to-face interaction. Though officers interview far fewer applicants than they did before the introduction of the Immigration and Refugee Protection Act in 2002, they still use interviews to clarify ambiguities and inconsistencies, to assess truthfulness, to gauge credibility, and to measure risk. In a face-to-face interview, credibility is determined by verbal responses but also by demeanour and body language: how individuals enter an interview booth, how they answer questions, and how they address an officer's concerns can factor into the decision to issue or refuse a visa.

As research on border control officers in other countries shows, how officials understand their personal, professional, and national identities can also shape the way in which they apply discretion (Triandafyllidou 2003). Visa officer self-conceptions as fair-minded and moral agents (Eggebø 2013b; Düvell and Jordan 2003) are important, even in highly bureaucratized work environments where the emphasis is on the strict enforcement of rules. Moreover, officers can differ from each other in terms of whether they are enforcement-minded or facilitative. Some are intent on imposing the letter of the law and look for complete conformity to the application process before they issue a visa. They arguably look for reasons to say "no" to applicants. Others are more facilitative, which can mean that they might try to understand the wider societal and biographical context from which an individual is applying; thus, they might be more understanding about why someone failed to follow the application process or cannot fully and unambiguously demonstrate that he or she deserves a visa. Where officers sit on the enforcement-facilitation continuum may stem from personal values, but as I argue in Chapter 4, it also depends on their accumulated experience and time on the job, their caseload, their recent encounters with similar types of applications, and their career pathway into their position.

Professional identities also come into play, as officers can conceive of themselves, and their jobs, as defenders of national borders, protectors of the immigration system, and as responsible for making the system work for its various clients. National-level identities are also relevant to decision making because being a "Canadian" visa officer has certain complex and contradictory meanings. Officers recognize that Canada is a country of migrants and that their job is to help it realize its objectives through immigration policy. Some also see themselves as contributing to a grand nation-building project in which they are selecting good immigrants for Canada. At the same time, some see Canadians as too naive, too trusting, too generous, and too easy to take advantage of because of their generally good nature. As a result, they see themselves as having to make the hard decisions that involve saying "no," or "stay out," to people who do not deserve a visa.

The meso-level of an officer's decision-making process includes a range of "intermediate variables of organizational culture ... that lie behind these discretionary practices and the values that justify each implementation choice" (Jordan, Stråth, and Triandafyllidou 2003b, 212). From the perspective of organizational culture, immigration department expectations about productivity and efficiency play a critical role in how decision making is organized and discretionary decisions are actually made. Citizenship and Immigration is a high-caseload department, where there are more applications for permanent resident visas than there are spaces in the immigration program. Visa officers work under time and resource limitations, and like the employees of other high-caseload bureaucratic environments, they develop various strategies to help them make decisions in the context of workload constraints.

The way in which responsibilities are assigned in visa offices also shapes discretionary decision making. Locally engaged program assistants are tasked with ensuring that files are complete, and depending on their level of authority, they also triage, or flag, certain files before an officer sees them. Assistants tend to be from the countries or regions in which their office is located, and part of their job is to bring local knowledge to bear on applications.

Larger macro-level forces also shape the social constitution of discretion and the way in which decisions are made. Decision-makers clearly absorb, or buy into, larger ideologies that drive the formation of policy (Alexandra Hall 2010). But front-line bureaucrats are not unreflexive agents who are unconcerned with, or uninterested in, how broader social forces and processes shape the behaviour of their clientele or an individual's eligibility for a public benefit (Eggebø 2013b). They have general understandings of how the world works and how macro-level forces influence an individual's past and present circumstances and eligibility for a public benefit. Their understandings are based on their education and training, their accumulated experiences on the job, and their daily interactions with applicants.

Visa officer choices and decisions are also rooted in larger macro-level variables related to the wider organizational processes of implementing immigration policy. Though visa offices, and officers, try to insulate themselves from client pressures to make decisions in certain ways, clients and others with an interest in a particular decision can nominally and indirectly contribute to the overall implementation and decision-making process. As noted earlier in this chapter, MPs often attempt to intervene on behalf of their constituents when it comes to visa officer decisions. Formal and informal pressures from headquarters in Ottawa and from immigration program managers to be either more facilitative or enforcement-minded may also subtly shape officer decisions. The activities of immigration consultants and lawyers are also part of the macro-level context for decision making, as are the interests of employers, family members, and other stakeholders.

Finally, various decision horizons (Emerson and Paley 2001) also factor into, and are invoked in, the process of decision making. As Emerson and Paley (ibid.) explain, the foreseeable reactions of courts and appeals bodies become important in the decision-making processes of street-level bureaucrats. As noted above, the fact that officer decisions are subject to appeal is also relevant to how they are shaped. Applicants, and their lawyers and consultants, are litigious and regularly challenge decisions. Many officers regard the courts as biased in favour of applicants, feel that the standard for successful appeals is too low, and believe that Canadians are being taken advantage of by legal bodies that do not understand the real-world complexities and ambiguities that they face. In this context, how they make a decision is often moulded by the knowledge that it is likely to be appealed.

3

Immigration Policy

The immigration program manager said that we work for the minister who develops policy regarding immigration, and so we have to fulfill his expectations. But I think we work for the Canadian people, to protect Canadians. (Field notes, January 16, 2012)

The specific criteria that countries use for decisions about inclusion and exclusion vary by context and over time (Joppke 2005). States tend to select permanent residents who have certain human capital attributes such as education, experience and job skills, wealth, and/or family ties and relationships with others who have already settled in the country. Some in-migration countries also select people who need protection from persecution (ibid.). Though Christian Joppke (ibid.) suggests that these are the only "legitimate" grounds for choosing immigrants in liberal democracies today, it is also true that perceived common ethnic and racial characteristics, and the possession of complementary political, ideological, and religious beliefs, sometimes condition state decisions about whom to include (Higuchi 2006; Whitaker 1987). Similarly, the criteria for exclusion, both stated and unstated, also vary. They change in response to prevailing attitudes and stereotypes, understandings of risk, and perceived threats to the economy and society. Terrorists, individuals with serious criminal records, and those with communicable diseases usually top the list of people that countries try to keep out, but exclusion criteria can also encompass the lack of human or financial capital, threatening political or ideological views, and undesirable ethnic or racial characteristics.

To understand how visa officers make their decisions, we need an overview of Canadian immigration policy. In some ways, the inclusion of "immigration" in Citizenship and Immigration is something of a misnomer because the department handles both permanent residents, or immigrants, *and* various groups of temporary residents, some of whom can eventually acquire permanent status. In fact, applications for temporary resident visas far outnumber those for permanent resident visas. Nonetheless, Canada has a long and complicated history of immigration. That history has been subject to considerable research and commentary, which will not be reviewed in detail here (but see Knowles 1992; Kelly and Trebilcock 1998; Freda Hawkins 1989; Simmons 2010; Anderson 2012). This chapter has the more modest goal of providing a brief snapshot of current immigration policy, categories, and flows to Canada.

Economic Development and Social Reproduction

Since Confederation, Canadian immigration policy has been guided by the twin exigencies of economic development and social reproduction. A carefully controlled immigration program has been seen as good for economic development. Though the definition of "good" is contested and depends on one's place in the economic system (Avery 1995), the prevailing political consensus is that various types of immigrants help drive economic development because they are a source of labour for employers and of innovation and capital for small and large businesses. They also pay taxes and help expand the domestic market for commodities and services. As a result, the ability to work in certain kinds of jobs, to bring human and financial capital, and to be self-supporting almost always determines who should be admitted as permanent residents and who should not (Kelly and Trebilcock 1998).

Immigration policy is also about social reproduction. Canadian society consists of individuals and groups who are involved in various social and familial relationships, who work in diverse settings and occupy different positions in the class structure, who partake in certain political traditions, and who have particular values and attitudes about how to live a "good life" (Howard-Hassmann 1999). It is also made up of various institutions that help to regulate and sustain social, political, and economic life. Though "social reproduction" has various meanings (Willis 1981), in this context it refers to the processes by which the social structures and relationships of society as a whole are regenerated over time (Gauntlett 2002). Recognizing that immigration is one aspect of social reproduction reminds us that immigrants are not simply "factory fodder" (Collins 1988) who are admitted solely for the purpose of feeding economic development. They also help sustain the wider set of political and social relationships that prevail in Canada.

Understanding these twin exigencies helps put into perspective the overall objectives of Canadian immigration and refugee policy, and the specific immigration categories that arise from it. The Immigration and Refugee Protection Act (2001) identifies eleven objectives of Canada's immigration program and eight objectives of its refugee program. These are listed in Appendix 1, and it is easy to see how they fit into a broad economic development and social reproduction framework. Objectives 3.(1)(c), (f), (g), and (j) speak to immigrants and temporary residents as agents of economic development: visitors are good for trade, commerce, and tourism, and will help develop a "strong and prosperous Canadian economy." Objectives 3.(1)(b), (b.1), and (d) present immigrants as agents of social reproduction: they will "enrich" the "social and cultural fabric of Canadian society" and will aid the development of "minority official languages." Some objectives, particularly 3.(1)(h) and (i), involve protecting the health, safety, and security of Canadians, and they, too, speak to social reproduction. Objectives 3.(1)(a) and (e) incorporate both economic development and social reproduction. The objectives of the refugee program tend to be defined in terms of social reproduction, such as family reunification and affirming the self-image of Canadians as fair-minded and as committed to humanitarian values and international obligations.

Of course, the extent to which the immigration and refugee protection system realizes these objectives is subject to considerable debate (Abu-Laban and Gabriel 2002; Simmons 2010; Fleras 2015). Some objectives contradict each other, or are in tension (Li 2003). Some policies and recent policy changes reflect a neo-liberal economic development agenda and ensure that the safety and security of Canadians trump family reunification and humanitarian principles (see Abu-Laban and Gabriel 2002; Sharma 2012). Nevertheless, the various categories of permanent and temporary residents reflect the qualities that the Canadian government sees as valuable and will define who deserves to receive a visa and hence be included in society.

There are three layers to the Canadian state's definition of those who are undesirable and who ought to be excluded from the country. The first is spelled out in immigration legislation. In the Immigration and Refugee Protection Act, "inadmissibility" is a formal-legal construct that refers to people who are generally barred from entering, visiting, or living in Canada. Although the criteria for inadmissibility are complex, sections 33 to 43 of the act list the various categories of inadmissible individuals. They include people who pose a threat to security by engaging in, or having engaged in, terrorism, espionage, or subversion against a democratic government or institution, or in acts of violence that might endanger the lives or safety of persons in Canada (section 33). Members of an organization that has engaged in subversion or terrorism or plans to do so are also excluded (section 34). People who misrepresent themselves or withhold material facts that could induce an error in the administration of the act are inadmissible (section 40), as are those who have been convicted of serious criminality (section 36), who belong to an organized criminal group (section 37), who are unwilling or unable to support themselves or their dependants (section 39), or who have violated human or international rights (section 35). The latter includes engaging or having engaged in terrorism, war crimes, or crimes against humanity. Finally, individuals are generally inadmissible on health grounds if their medical condition is likely to endanger public health or safety or to put an excessive demand on health or social services in Canada (section 38). In some cases, individuals may "overcome" their inadmissibility if the immigration minister deems that their presence in Canada "is not contrary to the national interest" (section 42.1).

Individuals who do not meet the admission criteria for one of Canada's permanent or temporary resident categories form the second layer of undesirability. And, as noted in the previous chapter, the third and much contested layer of undesirability consists of those who are denied a visa because of extra-legal, informal, unsanctioned, and not-publicly-stated ideologies, practices, and biases.

Immigration

Nearly every year since 2001, Canada has admitted about a quarter of a million new immigrants. Today, immigrants make up about 20 percent of its population. Among developed nations, only Israel and Australia outperform us (on a per capita basis) when it comes to admitting permanent immigrants. Though the United States admits nearly four times as many immigrants as we do every year, they make up only about 13 percent of the US population (OECD 2013, 37).

Nearly every country in the world contributes to the flow of immigrants to Canada. In the recent past, some countries, such as Guadeloupe and

Slovenia, have consistently contributed only a dozen or two immigrants a year. Other countries, such as St. Lucia and Switzerland, tend to contribute a few hundred every year, and Vietnam, Taiwan, and Germany send one or two thousand a year. A few other countries are the heavy hitters of our immigration program. In 2012, the Philippines, India, and China were the top three sources of permanent residents, and each contributed more than twenty-eight thousand migrants. Seven other countries – Pakistan, the United States, France, Iran, the United Kingdom, Haiti, and the Republic of Korea – round out the top ten sources of immigrants. They each contributed between five and ten thousand immigrants to Canada in that year (Citizenship and Immigration Canada 2012c).

Jason Kenney, who was immigration minister from 2008 to 2013, was the longest-serving minister in the history of the department. He was also a particularly hands-on, active administrator, who embraced his portfolio and seemingly put his personal stamp on both immigration policy and the way in which the department operated. During his term in office, a number of reforms were introduced to create new visa categories, to redefine the eligibility criteria for certain types of visas, and to reshape how individuals applied for, and the department processed, various types of visas (Kenney 2013a; Fleras 2015). His activism was facilitated by amendments to the Immigration and Refugee Protection Act (2001), introduced as part of the controversial omnibus budget Bill C-50 in February 2008. Bill C-50 was notable for its concept of Ministerial Instructions. These empower the immigration minister to establish the eligibility requirements to apply for a visa, set processing priorities for various types of applications, limit the number of applications for specific types of visas during any one year, and institute temporary pauses on the acceptance of new applications. Since November 2008, no less than twelve sets of Ministerial Instructions have been issued (nine under Kenney's watch), most of which have to do with how individuals apply as federal skilled workers and how the department processes their files (Citizenship and Immigration Canada 2014n). The immigration regulations have also been revised, and further changes have been made through the introduction of new legislation. Whereas it is usually too simplistic to reduce policy changes to the personal attitudes of politicians, many of the 2008–13 revisions to the immigration system seem to reflect Kenney's, and the wider Conservative Party's, interest in ensuring that the system was employer friendly, economically beneficial for Canada, and not abused by the undeserving (Citizenship and Immigration Canada 2014a).

Due to numerous policy changes introduced since the mid-2000s, Canada's immigration system is now far more complex, dynamic, and differentiated than it was a decade ago. There are now more than fifteen streams by which individuals can apply for either permanent or temporary resident status in Canada. For permanent residents, these pathways are generally grouped around the broad categories of "family class," "economic immigrants," "refugees," and "others." In 2012, a total of 257,895 individuals were admitted to Canada as permanent residents: 65,010 (25.2 percent) were admitted under the family class, 160,821 (62.4 percent) were admitted as economic immigrants, 23,099 (9.0 percent) as refugees, and another 8,965 (3.5 percent) were accepted under various other categories (Citizenship and Immigration Canada 2012c).

Economic Immigrants

Economic immigrants are admitted to Canada because they are expected to make a mainly economic contribution to it. There are no fewer than eight categories of them: federal skilled workers, Quebec skilled workers, live-in caregivers, investors, the self-employed, entrepreneurs, the Canada experience class, and provincial nominees.

Skilled Workers

The skilled worker component of Canada's immigration program is made up of federal skilled workers and Quebec skilled workers. In 2012, the 91,464 skilled workers and their family members made up 35.5 percent of all migrants admitted to Canada and 57.0 percent of all economic immigrants (Citizenship and Immigration Canada 2012c, 6).

Through a series of federal-provincial agreements in the 1980s and 1990s, Quebec now has its own immigration program. It broadly mirrors that of the federal government but has minor differences in emphasis, particularly regarding French-language abilities. Quebec selects its immigrants and refugees, including skilled workers, and Ottawa determines whether they are inadmissible on the grounds outlined in the Immigration and Refugee Protection Act.

Skilled workers are selected because they possess high levels of human capital, such as education, training, experience, and skills that are in demand in the labour market and are critical to their successful establishment in the country. The federal skilled worker selection system employs a points system to assess human capital. As will be discussed in Chapter 7, the points

TABLE 1
Selection grid for federal skilled workers

Selection criteria	Maximum points
Education	25
English and/or French skills	28
Experience	15
Age (18–35 at time of application, less 1 point for each year over 35)	12
Arranged employment in Canada	10
Adaptability	10
Total	100
Pass mark	67

Source: Citizenship and Immigration Canada (2014q).

system was introduced in 1967 to make the selection process more fair and transparent. Currently, there are six selection factors, each of which is accorded a weight: education, fluency in an official language, work experience, age, the existence of arranged employment, and adaptability. Table 1 shows an abridged version of the points system. The "pass mark" is 67 out of 100 points.

Historically, the Federal Skilled Worker Program has been "oversubscribed," which is one reason why Minister Kenney paid so much attention to its application stream: many more individuals requested this type of visa than could be processed in any one year, and there were not enough yearly spaces in Canada's immigration program to accommodate the demand. Prior to the introduction of Bill C-50, Canada accepted unlimited numbers of applications in every permanent resident category. Once the associated fee had been paid, Citizenship and Immigration was under an obligation to process an applicant's paperwork through to a "final decision." The department could not possibly keep up, with the result that, by 2008, the processing queue was backlogged by more than 640,000 people. The underlying principle of visa processing was essentially first-come, first-served, and paperwork was processed on the basis of its "lock-in" date – the day on which the department received the completed application. For these federal skilled workers, whom the department terms "pre-C-50," the backlog was so enormous that some waited for more than seven or eight years before being processed. In October 2013, Ottawa announced that it would return the fees (without interest) paid by the pre-C-50 applicants who had applied before February 27, 2008, and who had not yet received a decision about their application. The refund essentially terminated the department's obligation to process the application, and those who wished to become permanent residents had to reapply under one of the currently existing immigration categories (Citizenship and Immigration Canada 2013c).

There is not enough space here to fully describe each set of Ministerial Instructions for the federal skilled worker stream. Ultimately, they enable the minister to limit the number of applications that are accepted each year, shift priorities to accelerate the processing of certain types of applications, control eligibility requirements, and create new immigration categories that are in effect for a specified time. The Ministerial Instructions in place for federal skilled workers as of May 1, 2014 (MI 12), put a twelve-month cap of twenty-five thousand on new complete applications that will be considered for processing, with sub-caps of a maximum of one thousand applications in each of fifty listed "eligible" occupations (Fleras 2015). The occupational list is heavily weighted toward engineering, health care, and management. Five hundred application spaces are reserved for international students who are currently enrolled in a PhD program in Canada. Before they enter the processing queue, applicants are "prescreened" and must demonstrate a certain proficiency in English or French. Anyone who applies in the "occupation list stream" must have at least one year of full-time or equivalent part-time paid experience during the last ten years in the skilled occupation (Citizenship and Immigration Canada 2014g). The Federal Skilled Trades Program, established under the auspices of MI 6 (announced on January 2, 2013), augments the Federal Skilled Worker Program. It focuses on admitting those who are skilled in a trade. The May 2014 Ministerial Instructions put a cap of five thousand applications in ninety skilled trades (ibid.). To further speed up processing in the skilled worker category, the department launched a new Express Entry application process in January 2015. This allows individuals to submit an online profile that the department will assess and rank. Top-ranked candidates will then be invited to apply under either the Federal Skilled Worker Program, the Federal Skilled Trades Program, or the Canada experience class. The department has made a commitment to process their applications within six months.

Provincial Nominees

Canada's Constitution gives the federal and provincial governments shared jurisdiction over immigration. Although Ottawa is responsible for overall policy making, provinces can have a say in immigration, provided that their policies do not contradict those of the federal government. In the late nineteenth and early twentieth centuries, British Columbia was one of the few provinces to actively involve itself in immigration policy, in part because its xenophobic politicians felt that Ottawa was not doing enough to curb migration from Asia (Roy 1989). Generally, however, the provinces remained relatively quiet on immigration until about 1975. As noted above, Quebec slowly expanded its control over immigration during the late 1970s. The other provinces had their first taste of immigration policy making in the late 1980s, when business immigration programs started to sprout around the world to capitalize on the fear in Hong Kong that the city's 1997 handover to China would spell the end of its free enterprise and private wealth accumulation. Provinces started by tweaking their rules for selecting business immigrants: those with relatively little immigration lowered their thresholds for investment commitments to below those of Ontario and British Columbia, provinces that had historically attracted migrants (Wong and Netting 1992). Since the late 1990s, the provinces have steadily become more involved in immigration. All provinces outside of Quebec, as well as Yukon and Northwest Territories, now have their own Provincial Nominee Programs, as negotiated with Ottawa, that help them fast-track immigrants to work in industries where labour is in short supply (Carter 2012).

Since the first cohort of 477 workers was admitted to Manitoba in 1999, the Provincial Nominee Program has expanded dramatically. In 2012, 40,829 people were admitted as provincial nominees (Citizenship and Immigration Canada 2012c, 5), and employers seem increasingly to rely on the program to bypass the cumbersome skilled worker selection system, which is slow, responds poorly to their needs, and does not admit immigrants with low skills or education (Nakache and D'Aoust 2012).

The rules and regulations for Provincial Nominee Programs vary by province. Basically, though, they allow provinces to develop their own selection criteria for immigrants. Provincial nominees must have the "skills, language abilities, education, and work experience needed to make an immediate economic contribution to the province or territory that nominates them" (Kukushkin 2009, 6). The provinces are not required to use the federal points system to identify qualified individuals. The nominee programs are essentially employer-driven (ibid., 17); employers can request that certain workers be fast-tracked to fill job vacancies. For its part, Ottawa has agreed to prioritize provincial nominee requests, thus pushing other applications further back in the queue. Like Quebec, the provinces make "selection" decisions, whereas federal immigration officials make "inadmissibility" decisions. A visa officer whom I interviewed highlighted the way in which provincial governments can shape visa processing: "A strict enforcement approach is not the approach they want us to take. The provinces want them [provincial nominees] to come and work. They go to the provinces and they will work hard. They are a good clientele and they make good immigrants."[1] However, federal visa officers do occasionally overturn a province's selection decision, which may lead to certain tensions between federal and provincial immigration officials.

Business Immigrants

Canada created a business immigration program during the mid-1980s to capitalize on the fear created in Hong Kong by the British government's transfer of authority to China. Many Hong Kong business people anticipated that the Chinese authorities would be less business friendly than the British, and thus they sought to invest their resources overseas and to secure permanent residence status for themselves and their families. As a result, Canada's business immigration program grew dramatically during the late 1980s and early 1990s. In 1994, the 27,404 business immigrants (investors, entrepreneurs, the self-employed, and their families) who came to Canada represented 12.4 percent of all migrants admitted that year. By 2012, their numbers had declined, though not to the point of insignificance (Satzewich and Liodakis 2013): in that year, the 10,080 business immigrants and accompanying family members represented less than 4 percent of all migrants to Canada (Citizenship and Immigration Canada 2012c, 6).

The business program is currently in flux, and the federal government is revamping its approach to this immigration stream (Citizenship and Immigration Canada 2014d). As a result of MI 12, introduced in May 2014, the immigration department extended its "temporary pause" on the receipt of new applications in the investor and entrepreneur categories (Citizenship and Immigration Canada 2014n). The pause on investors dates from July 2012 (under MI 5) and that on entrepreneurs from June 2010 (under MI 2). As with other visa categories affected by the new Ministerial Instructions, the pause was meant, in part, to give visa offices a chance to process the backlog of applications that had built up over the years and to give the department time to rethink the objectives of the program (Citizenship and Immigration Canada 2014a). Citizenship and Immigration still accepts applications in the self-employed category, and overseas officers continue to process the investor and entrepreneur backlog under the rules that were in place when an application was received.

At the same time that a temporary pause on investor and entrepreneur applications was in place, in March 2013, the immigration minister released MI 7, which established a new Start-Up Visa Program. This was designed to attract individuals who planned to start a new business in Canada. To qualify, they must obtain a letter of support from one of three designated "angel investor groups" in Canada or one of twenty-five Canadian venture capital funds (Citizenship and Immigration Canada 2014n).

Applicants in the self-employed category must have relevant experience in cultural activities, athletics, or farm management. They must have the intention and the ability to establish a business that, at minimum, will create employment for themselves. They must also qualify under a revised points system, but the bar is much lower for them than for skilled workers: their pass mark is 35 out of 100 points.

Live-In Caregivers

Live-in caregivers constitute another small but important plank in the economic class. Initially, they receive temporary work visas but can apply for permanent residence once they have worked in Canada for twenty-four months within a forty-eight-month period or if they have 3,900 hours of "authorized" full-time employment. In 2012, 3,690 live-in caregivers, along with their 5,322 spouses and dependants, were admitted to Canada as permanent residents (Citizenship and Immigration Canada 2012c, 6). However, in October 2013, an estimated 50,000 caregivers were waiting in the processing queue to have their status upgraded to permanent resident (Mas 2013).

Various versions of the Live-in-Caregiver Program have featured in the Canadian immigration system for well over a hundred years (Daenzer 1993). Since the turn of the twentieth century, immigration officials have made special efforts to recruit women from overseas to work as housekeepers, nannies, and domestic servants for middle-class families in Canada. British women were targeted during the first half of the twentieth century, eastern and central European women in the early 1950s, and Caribbean women from the late 1950s to the early 1980s (Kelly and Trebilcock 1998). Today, nearly all live-in caregivers are female, and the vast majority of them are Filipinas.

The Canadian Experience Class

The Canadian experience class was introduced in 2008 to facilitate the permanent resident applications of individuals who live and work in Canada on various types of temporary resident permits. In 2012, 9,359 Canadian experience class visas were issued to applicants and their spouses and dependants (Citizenship and Immigration Canada 2012c, 6). To qualify for this visa, individuals must have at least twelve months of full-time (or equivalent part-time) skilled work experience in the three years before they apply. Managerial, professional, and technical jobs, and skilled trades are defined as skilled work (Citizenship and Immigration Canada 2014g).

The Family Class

In 1994, the 93,019 family class immigrants who came to Canada represented about 42 percent of the immigrants admitted during that year (Satzewich and Liodakis 2013). Though the family class remains highly significant, its numbers have nonetheless dropped since the 1990s. For example, the 65,010 family class immigrants who were admitted in 2012 made up a quarter of all Canada's immigrants in that year (Citizenship and Immigration Canada 2012c, 6). In part, the decrease is due to government perceptions that immigrants in this class make fewer positive economic contributions than other types of permanent residents. As a result, the rules were changed so that sponsoring relatives became progressively more difficult.

Although the family class is diminishing, Canadian citizens and permanent residents who live in Canada may nonetheless sponsor spouses, partners, parents, grandparents, and dependent children and children whom they intend to adopt. Under very narrowly defined circumstances, they may also sponsor non-dependent children and orphaned brothers, sisters, nephews, nieces, and grandchildren. Like the economic immigrants discussed above, sponsored family members are subject to complex eligibility rules and application procedures.

Generally speaking, though, sponsors must promise to financially support a family member for between three and ten years. The intent of this is to prevent the sponsored person from drawing on federal or provincial government benefits. How long the support provisions remain in effect depends on the nature of the relationship to the sponsor. For example, sponsored partners or spouses will be supported for three years after they become permanent residents in Canada, and dependent children are supported for ten years (or until they turn twenty-five, whichever comes first). Further, sponsors must support their parents and grandparents for ten years, during which time they will not be able to claim public benefits (Citizenship and Immigration Canada 2014h). Sponsors who default on these conditions may become ineligible to sponsor other family members. Except for the elderly, all sponsored individuals in the family class must sign an undertaking in which they "agree to make every effort to become self-supporting in Canada," though it is unclear how this promise will be enforced (ibid.).

Since the introduction of the Immigration and Refugee Protection Act (2001), family class immigration policies have undergone at least four major modifications. First, Canadian citizens and permanent residents may now sponsor their same-sex partners (LaViolette 2004). Second, due to changes introduced in November 2011, persons who have been convicted of an offence causing bodily harm cannot sponsor certain family members (Citizenship and Immigration Canada 2014h). Third, new regulations were introduced in October 2012 to curb marriages of convenience, to address what the government regards as a widespread form of fraud. "Marriage of convenience" once denoted a marriage entered into for reasons other than love; in the context of immigration, its "sole purpose is for the sponsored spouse to immigrate to Canada." This applies to common law relationships, regardless of whether the sponsor in Canada colluded in the fraud. Couples are now required to live together "in a legitimate relationship" for two years after a spouse arrives in Canada. If this does not occur, the permanent resident status of the sponsored spouse may be revoked. If a relationship breaks down after two years, sponsored spouses can retain their permanent resident status, but they are barred from sponsoring a new spouse for three more years, or five years from their date of arrival in Canada (Citizenship and Immigration Canada 2014h).

Finally, though most Ministerial Instructions deal with economic immigrants, MI 4, issued on November 5, 2011, imposed a twenty-four-month pause on new sponsorship applications for parents and grandparents. As for federal skilled workers, the processing backlog for parents and grandparents was considerable, and people could wait for as long as ten years before a visa office processed their application. The pause was meant to enable offices to clear their backlog. As noted in the previous chapter, the immigration department anticipated that this measure would be unpopular, so it created the new super visa to damp down the controversy. Valid for ten years, the super visa allows parents and grandparents to remain in Canada for twenty-four months without renewing their status (Citizenship and Immigration Canada 2014b).

Refugees

In 2012, Canada admitted 23,099 refugees, who made up 9.0 percent of its total flow of immigrants (Citizenship and Immigration Canada 2012c, 6). As with family class immigration, the yearly flow of refugees has dropped significantly in less than a decade: in 2005, Canada admitted 35,768 of them, 13.6 percent of its total immigrants. Individuals can become officially recognized as refugees, and hence as permanent residents, via two mechanisms: resettlement from outside of Canada and the in-Canada refugee protection process.

The first mechanism applies to people who are not yet in Canada. These applicants are divided into two categories – the convention refugee abroad class and the country of asylum class.[2] The convention class encompasses people who cannot return to their home country because of a well-founded fear of persecution for reasons of race, religion, political opinion, nationality, or membership in a particular social group. Individuals in the country of asylum class have left home because they are seriously and personally affected by civil war, armed conflict, or massive human rights violations (Satzewich and Liodakis 2013).

Canada works with the United Nations High Commission for Refugees, which determines the legitimacy of individual claims for refugee status under one of the two categories mentioned above. In 2014, the commission estimated that the number of refugees, asylum seekers, and internally displaced people exceeded 50 million (United Nations High Commissioner for Refugees 2014). About 12 million of these are under the care of the commission, and these UN-certified refugees constitute a pool from which Canada and other countries select people for resettlement.

Some refugees are sponsored by the federal government, which resettles them in Canadian communities and provides a year of financial and other assistance, including training in English or French. Others are privately sponsored by individuals, groups, certain charitable organizations, and provincial governments, a form of sponsorship that Ottawa encourages. Sponsors must agree to "provide financial and emotional assistance" for between one and three years for the people whom they sponsor (Citizenship and Immigration Canada 2015, 2.6).

The in-Canada refugee protection process applies to people who are already in Canada. As with other immigration categories, the rules, procedures, eligibility criteria, and case adjudication procedures that apply to them have changed considerably since 2002. The refugee determination system is yet another place where the broader interests of the federal Conservatives, and the activism of Jason Kenney, are evident. Many recent changes have been highly controversial, and charges of being "anti-refugee" have been levelled at both the Conservatives and the immigration department.

Four recent modifications have been particularly contentious. First, in October 2011, Ottawa narrowed what it calls the "source country class" of refugee, which includes people who are still in their countries of origin but who nevertheless meet the definition of a convention refugee. This subcategory also encompasses people who were detained or imprisoned and are suffering serious deprivation of their right to freedom of expression, to dissent, or to engage in trade union activity. Now, citizens or residents of only six countries (the Democratic Republic of Congo, Sudan, El Salvador, Guatemala, Colombia, and Sierra Leone), which have a record of human rights violations, are eligible to come to Canada under this provision.

Second, Canada implemented a safe third country agreement with the United States in December 2004. Under the safe third country rule, individuals who have already found a safe haven in the United States cannot make a refugee claim in Canada and vice versa. The rule is intended to deter so-called asylum shopping, and so far, the agreement applies only to Canada and the United States. There are some exceptions to the rule: people who have family members in Canada; unaccompanied minors; holders of a valid Canadian visa, work permit, or study permit; and individuals who have been charged with or convicted of an offence that could subject them to the death penalty in the United States or elsewhere (Satzewich and Liodakis 2013, 104).

Third, the federal government has tightened the rules for the in-Canada refugee determination process. In June 2012, it passed Bill C-31, the Protecting Canada's Immigration System Act (2012), which changed the way in which in-Canada refugee claims are processed. The act allows the minister to define certain countries as designated countries of origin, which "do not normally produce refugees but do respect human rights and offer state protection" (Citizenship and Immigration Canada 2012b). As of May 2013, there were thirty-seven of these, including the United States, Mexico, Australia, New Zealand, Japan, Israel (excluding Gaza and the West Bank), every country in western and central Europe, and several in eastern Europe. Individuals from these countries who claim refugee status in Canada are expected to have their Immigration and Refugee Board hearing within thirty to forty-five days; failed claimants have no avenue of appeal. Nor can these refugees apply for a work permit in Canada. Refugees who do not come from a designated country of origin are expected to have their Immigration and Refugee Board hearing within sixty days after they submit their claim. They cannot appeal "manifestly unfounded" claims to the Refugee Appeal Division (Citizenship and Immigration Canada 2012b). Finally, the government also aims to deport failed refugee claimants during the year following the Immigration and Refugee Board's final decision (Immigration and Refugee Board 2014).

Lastly, and perhaps most controversially, in June 2012, Ottawa announced changes to the eligibility of refugees and refugee claimants to access certain state-funded health care benefits. Differing categories of refugees and refugee claimants were affected in particular ways, but the general intent of the measure was to restrict the range of medical conditions covered by the Interim Federal Health Care Program for individuals who were being processed through the refugee determination system. The change was expected to diminish costs and deter individuals from making a refugee claim solely to gain access to Canadian health care (Canadian Doctors for Refugee Care 2014).

Humanitarian and Compassionate Cases

The final permanent resident category consists of individuals who are admitted on humanitarian and compassionate grounds. In 2012, the 8,890 people who were granted permanent resident status on these grounds made up just over 3 percent of all immigrant arrivals in Canada (Citizenship and Immigration Canada 2012c, 6). The Immigration and Refugee Protection Act (2001, section 21) enables the immigration minister to approve "deserving" individuals who fall outside the selection criteria, as specified in legislation, or who are otherwise inadmissible to Canada. Broadly speaking, people who have been refused a visa may nonetheless be issued a permanent resident visa if there are humanitarian and compassionate reasons for doing so. About a third of humanitarian and compassionate cases involve family class applications in which "the best interests of the child" are taken into consideration. The remainder relate to other immigration categories or situations in which a person is granted permanent residency for reasons of "public policy." In some instances, the minister will delegate the decision to staff in an overseas visa office (Citizenship and Immigration Canada 2014m, 19–23).

Temporary Residents

Although Canada admits a quarter of a million permanent residents every year, and "immigration" is part of our self-definition as a nation, it also admits a large number of temporary residents (Sharma 2006). Many have no desire to remain in Canada, but many others hope that their temporary status will eventually lead to permanent residence. In fact, several temporary resident visa categories contain pathways to permanent residency.

There are four types of temporary residents: visitors, students, temporary foreign workers, and those who are issued a temporary resident permit. Like permanent residents, they are subject to differing visa application procedures, eligibility criteria, and conditions of stay.

Visitors and tourists are often overlooked in wider debates about the Canadian immigration program. A significant and publicly stated objective of the program is to facilitate the entry of "visitors" (which include tourists, students, and temporary workers) "for the purposes of trade, commerce, tourism and international understanding and cultural, educational and scientific activities" (Immigration and Refugee Protection Act 2001, section 2). International tourism is a small but important part of the engine that drives Canada's economic activity. In 2012, 16 million overnight visitors came to the country and spent an estimated $12.3 billion during their stay (Canadian Tourism Commission 2012).

Visitors brush up against the immigration bureaucracy in two main ways. First, some must secure a visa before they arrive, as Chapter 8 discusses in more detail. Visa officers who assess their applications must determine whether they are genuine visitors and whether the true purpose of their trip differs from their stated intentions. Visitors who hold passports from countries that are "visa exempt" can simply board a plane (or drive across the border) and come to Canada without giving the government notice or receiving prior permission via a visa. Canada imposes visa requirements on nationals of some countries, in part to exclude visitors who could potentially harm Canadians or could try to circumvent the permanent resident visa process.

Second, the immigration department and Canada Border Services Agency are jointly responsible for enforcing the conditions under which individuals can visit the country. Regardless of whether they require a visa, visitors must comply with immigration rules, which generally do not permit them to work in Canada, access public benefits such as health care or social assistance, and stay in the country beyond certain prescribed limits.

Post-secondary institutions in Canada and other countries are increasingly looking to recruit students from abroad (Marginson 2014). In 2012, 328,672 international students were studying in Canada (Citizenship and Immigration Canada 2012c, 53). The government plans to increase this number to 450,000 by 2022 and estimates that these students could generate up to eighty-six thousand new jobs and add $10 billion to the economy

(CBC News 2014a). Universities have jumped onboard international student recruitment. Some have defined it as an "internationalization strategy" that enables local students to rub elbows with international students and become better global citizens, but there is no doubt that cash-strapped universities also eye international students as sources of revenue (Marginson 2014). International students who attend post-secondary institutions pay significantly higher fees than their Canadian counterparts, so they are clearly good for a university's bottom line (CBC News 2014a).

Individuals who have been accepted to study at a school, college, university, or other educational institution in Canada must obtain a study permit before they arrive. They must also show that they have enough money to pay their tuition fees, living expenses for themselves and accompanying family members, and return transportation to their country of origin. They must also "satisfy" a visa officer that they will "leave Canada at the end of ... [their] authorized stay." Though the immigration department wants most international students to leave Canada upon completing their studies, it also wants to encourage some of those who earn a PhD in Canada to stay permanently. Thus, it has created a special stream within the Federal Skilled Worker Program to permit these students to stay permanently (Citizenship and Immigration Canada 2014g).

Canada has a dizzying array of programs, schemes, and agreements with other governments that enable individuals to come and work on a short-term, "temporary" basis (see Lenard and Straehle 2012; Citizenship and Immigration Canada 2012c, 64). Seasonal agricultural workers from Mexico and the Caribbean, intra-company transfers, exchange professors, spouses of foreign workers and students, information technology staff, and low-skilled labourers are collectively termed temporary foreign workers. They make up an increasingly large component of Canada's temporary residents, and on a yearly basis they now far outnumber the economic immigrants who are admitted as permanent residents. In 2002, Canada had about 180,000 temporary foreign workers, a figure that reached nearly half a million by 2012 (ibid., 53). This prompted concerns that the immigration program was increasingly being transformed into a "guestworker" program (Alboim 2009) and that employers were using temporary foreign workers to undercut the wages and working conditions of Canadians (Stanford 2014).

Temporary foreign workers differ from immigrants in that they generally do not have the right to permanent residence. Some, such as seasonal agricultural workers, are tied to specific employers and cannot quit or change their jobs without permission from the federal government. Should they do so without authorization, they are deemed to be in violation of their work permit rules and are subject to deportation. Seasonal agricultural workers from the Caribbean and Mexico can work in Canada for up to eight months a year, after which they must return home (Preibisch and Hennebry 2012). Those who come under the "low-skilled pilot program" are initially granted a one-year "open" work permit and are not required to work for a specific employer. Though they can renew their permits for several years, they do not have a clear pathway to permanent resident status (Lenard 2012). However, some temporary foreign workers, such as live-in caregivers, can apply to become permanent residents. In addition, highly skilled individuals may apply for permanent residency via the Canadian experience class of the Federal Skilled Worker Program, as described above.

Finally, individuals who are otherwise inadmissible or who are not genuine visitors can be issued a temporary resident permit if "justified reasons" exist for doing so (Citizenship and Immigration Canada 2014s). The permit is granted at the discretion of a visa officer, Border Services official at a port of entry, or the immigration minister (Citizenship and Immigration Canada 2014c). These permits can be issued in a variety of circumstances. For example, Jacob Zuma, the current president of South Africa, would be inadmissible to Canada because he was a member of the African National Congress in the 1970s and 1980s, when it was working to overthrow the South African government. Ottawa does plan to remove the African National Congress from its list of subversive organizations whose members are inadmissible to Canada (York 2012), but until that occurs, Zuma would have to apply for a temporary resident permit to enter the country. In other scenarios, certain high-ranking government officials or influential businesspersons would be inadmissible due to their criminal records. In these cases, MPs reportedly lobby the immigration minister to issue a temporary resident permit (Ditchburn 2013). The minister can issue a "do it" to a visa office, which is a general exception to the non-fettering of decision making noted in the previous chapter. The visa officer is absolved of responsibility for the file, and the minister's office takes formal responsibility for the decision. In 2012, 13,564 temporary resident permits were issued to people who would not normally be admissible to Canada (Citizenship and Immigration Canada 2012c, 23).

Linking Policy and Administration

Everyone who seeks permanent resident status in Canada must apply in advance for a visa, as do most categories of temporary residents. Though the line between the temporary and permanent migration streams has become somewhat blurred because temporary migration can sometimes lead to permanent residence, the two streams do have differing implications for the way in which applications are processed. Obviously, visa officers do not make their decisions in a policy or organizational vacuum, and so this snapshot of how Canada defines desirable and undesirable permanent residents and visitors helps set the context for understanding how they go about their work.

The other important context for officer decisions is the organizational structure of the immigration department and its overseas operational environment. The department is currently modernizing its office procedure to improve processing efficiency and enhance client service (Citizenship and Immigration Canada 2014a). Moreover, it is a bureaucratic organization with a complex division of labour and dynamic and evolving relationships between in-Canada and overseas offices, and between overseas offices and the Department of Foreign Affairs and International Trade. Though Foreign Affairs does not make visa issuance decisions, it administers the immigration department's physical space and some of its staffing decisions. Though visa officers are responsible for visa issuance decisions, they work at the end point of a much broader series of decisions, processes, and structures that directly and indirectly shape how they make their own decisions and exercise their discretion.

4

Visa Offices and Officers

I don't agonize over decisions ... If you agonize over decisions, this is not the right job for you. (Field notes, April 25, 2011)

Like other federal government departments, Citizenship and Immigration is subject to budgetary pressure. In a retrenchment era initiated under the Liberals during the late 1990s and continuing into the present, it is expected to do more with less (Government of Canada 2014a). From 2012 to 2015, its overall budget is expected to decline by $52.0 million, dropping from $1.545 billion in 2012–13 to $1.492 billion in 2014–15. The department also anticipates a decrease of 342 full-time equivalent employees, from 4,637 in 2012–13 to 4,295 in 2014–15 (Citizenship and Immigration Canada 2012–13, 11). To better manage its increasingly scarce resources, it is currently undergoing a process of "modernization" (Clement 2013). The far-ranging modernization agenda includes a number of initiatives, but two central aspects of it involve the development of new methods for sharing and storing information about visa applicants and officer decisions, and shifting more application-processing functions to offices in Canada (Citizenship and Immigration Canada 2014a).

The Modernization Agenda

To modernize its management of information, the immigration department introduced a new Global Case Management System (GCMS) in 2011 to replace the old Computer Assisted Immigration Processing System (CAIPS) and Field Operations Support System (FOSS) databases, both of which were designed during the 1970s. Essentially the department's "selection" database, CAIPS stored information about temporary and permanent resident visa applications. Visa officers also entered their notes regarding individual files and their decision outcomes into CAIPS. The notes recorded the decision-making process. FOSS, on the other hand, was the "enforcement" database. Shared by the immigration department and Border Services, it tracked applicants after they arrived in Canada and included information about deportation orders, visa overstays, and failure to appear at an immigration hearing or voluntary departure. It also stored data about individuals who were refused at ports of entry, warrants issued for immigration violations, and suspected and known terrorists (Meurrens 2013). The new GCMS is a complicated merger of the information previously stored separately in CAIPS and FOSS. Since not all the information in CAIPS and FOSS can be transferred into GCMS, visa officers must use all three until the transition to GCMS is complete.

Because the use of official records "extends beyond the individual who produces them" (Meehan 1986, 73), the information in CAIPS, FOSS, and GCMS has both an internal and external "projected career." Internally, in cases of individuals who have previously attempted to immigrate to Canada, visa officers use CAIPS and GCMS to see what information they gave about themselves at the time and what concerns their own colleagues raised, if any. Previous information is often compared with the current visa application to determine credibility. Discrepancies regarding education, places of residence, marriages, relationships, and the existence of dependent children are typically a cause for concern: they raise questions about the reliability of the application and commonly prompt a visa officer to dig deeper.

In a sense, FOSS (and now GCMS) provided "life cycle" information about individuals whose visa applications were approved and who came to Canada. For example, FOSS tracks whether someone who entered Canada on a visitor visa subsequently applied for refugee status, what decision the Immigration and Refugee Board made in the case, and whether a deportation followed if the board rejected the claim. FOSS (and now GCMS) can also contain information about applicants' criminal records in Canada (if any), whether they sponsored a family member for permanent residence, and whether they defaulted on the support commitments. Visa officers also check past migration history and subsequent events in an immigrant's life in Canada while they make their decisions about the application before them. Information in the databases can also be factored into their assessment of applications from family members who seek temporary or permanent residence in Canada. If, for instance, an Estonian woman applies for a visa to visit her brother in Canada, an officer might search GCMS for the brother's immigration history. If it reveals that he initially came on a visitor visa but then claimed refugee status, the officer might choose not to issue a visa to the sister. Because the brother did not get into Canada by "the proper" way, there is a risk that she will do the same. In short, the databases provide a very full picture of people's visa applications and migration history in Canada. Through these record-keeping practices, the "sins" from applicants' pasts can catch up with them, and so can those of their relatives.

The immigration department also uses the GCMS/CAIPS case notes to improve future decision making. In situations where individuals receive a temporary resident visa but claim refugee status after arriving in Canada, officers are often asked by a superior to review their decision to determine whether they missed anything. If they did, they use this informal reassessment to improve their investigative techniques or strategies. The office can also use the information to detect broader patterns and profiles of queue jumpers, which Chapter 8 discusses in more detail.

Immigration department records also have an external career, as information in CAIPS, FOSS, and GCMS is subject to federal access-to-information rules. Acting on their own, or with the help of a consultant or lawyer, individuals have the right to access the department's information about their file. Some simply wish to learn where their application stands in the processing queue. Those whom an officer has summoned to an interview to address certain concerns hope to determine in advance what those concerns might be. Though they normally receive a "concerns" letter, they see accessing their case notes as a way of discovering what the officer is thinking about their file. Finally, those whose visa application is refused can employ the information to support their appeal. They may use the notes to argue that the officer made an error in fact or in law, or violated the rules of procedural fairness. In such cases, the notes are also read and considered by Immigration and Refugee Board adjudicators or by Federal Court judges.

The immigration department's modernization agenda also entails shifting more visa-processing functions to offices in Canada. These are generally cheaper to operate than their overseas equivalents, so part of the long-term plan is to reduce reliance on the latter. The department's operational activities are organized under the purview of the assistant deputy minister of operations. The "operations" side of the department includes International Region, which is responsible for overseas visa office decision making, as well as the Health Management, Case Management, Operational Management and Coordination, and Foreign Credentials Referral Branches. Each branch is administered by a director general, who reports to the assistant deputy minister of operations, as do the regional directors general of Quebec, Ontario, Atlantic, the Prairies and Northern Territories, and British Columbia and Yukon.

The department organizes visa issuance decision making though a network of offices in Canada and overseas (Citizenship and Immigration Canada 2014e). It operates four types of offices in Canada – Multicultural Program, In Person, Centralized Intake, and Case Processing Centres. Of these, the Multicultural Program offices play no role in visa issuance decisions and are mainly responsible for the delivery of programs and issues related to people who are already settled in Canada (ibid.).

Canada's twenty-five In Person offices have minimal application-processing functions. Except for Nunavut, which is served from Manitoba, every Canadian province and territory has one of these offices, and several provinces have more than one. Although the offices mainly organize settlement services for newcomers and liaise with settlement agencies, they do handle a very narrow range of visa-processing tasks. Individuals may contact them only if they submitted their application within Canada (usually for a visa extension), if the normal processing time has passed, and if they cannot verify the status of their application online. They may also contact an In Person office to report a change in their status and can make an in-Canada refugee claim at some In Person offices. None are "open to the public." Once an application for one of these services is received, the office contacts the individual and decides whether seeing him or her in person is necessary (Citizenship and Immigration Canada 2014e).

Canada has just one Centralized Intake office, which is located in Sydney, Nova Scotia. It handles the initial eligibility review of all economic class applicants, including federal skilled workers, provincial nominees, Quebec skilled workers, the Quebec business class, the Canadian experience class, and the investor and self-employed classes. The office vets applications to determine whether they meet the predefined eligibility criteria. In the case of a federal skilled worker application, for example, the office determines whether the individual fits the criteria specified under Ministerial Instructions, and it does a first assessment of whether he has the requisite number of points to achieve a pass mark on the selection grid. If he is deemed eligible to apply for the visa, his application is forwarded to an overseas office for the final selection and admissibility decisions (Citizenship and Immigration Canada 2014e).

Canada has four Case Processing Centres, in Vegreville (Alberta), Mississauga, Sydney, and Ottawa. Each is responsible for a different category of visa application. The Vegreville office deals with extensions to visitor and other temporary resident permits, and sponsorship applications for family members who are already in Canada. Mississauga processes applications for the sponsorship of family members who live abroad. Like the Centralized Intake office, it handles the initial eligibility assessment, in this case for Canadian citizens and permanent residents who wish to sponsor family members from abroad. The Case Processing Centre in Sydney deals with applications for permanent resident cards and those related to citizenship issues. Ottawa's Case Processing Centre, called the Case Processing Pilot-Ottawa, has been in operation only since 2012 and thus is relatively new. It processes temporary resident visa applications from within Canada and permanent resident visa applications from persons within Canada and the United States that have been prescreened by the Mississauga office or the Centralized Intake office in Sydney. It took on many of the functions of the Buffalo visa office, which was closed in May 2012, and is part of the effort to shift more final decisions about certain kinds of visas to Canada (Citizenship and Immigration Canada 2014e).

Except for the Case Processing Pilot-Ottawa, which does conduct some interviews with visa applicants, these offices are off-limits to the public. Applications must be submitted by mail, and any that are dropped off in person are generally not accepted. The only way to communicate with these offices is via a generic email address or fax (ibid.).

International Region coordinates the operations of Canada's network of overseas visa offices. It is responsible for staffing, setting and monitoring immigration targets, and providing various kinds of support services to decision-makers overseas. It tends to work closely with the Case Management Branch, whose role is to provide "effective management of high profile, complex, contentious and sensitive cases" (Citizenship and Immigration Canada 2011b).

Currently, there are forty overseas visa offices, which administer four regions: the Americas, Africa and the Middle East, Europe, and Asia and the Pacific. Individual offices are Full Service Processing Centres, Regional Processing Centres, or Satellite offices. The Full Service Centres issue visas for all categories of application but only from a single country. The office in Havana, for example, deals with the full range of temporary and permanent resident visas, but only for applications submitted in Cuba. Regional Processing Centres handle the full range of visa applications from two or more countries or regions. For instance, the Vienna office takes applications from Austria, Bosnia and Herzegovina, Croatia, the Czech Republic, Germany, Hungary, Kosovo, Macedonia, Montenegro, Netherlands, Serbia, the Slovak Republic, and Slovenia. Satellite offices, which are usually small, process limited types of visa applications. The office in Chandigarh, India, takes applications only for visitor, student, and temporary worker visas.

In addition to shifting more visa-processing functions to Canada, the immigration department has entered into agreements with a private-sector company, VFS Global Group, which specializes in "visa and passport issuance-related administrative and non-judgmental tasks" (VFS Global Group 2014). VFS Global works with forty-five client governments in 110 countries, operates 2,012 Visa Application Centres for these governments, and as of May 2014, claimed to have helped process over 77 million visas worldwide (ibid.). The Visa Application Centres that work in conjunction with Canadian visa offices generally help to process applications for various categories of temporary resident visas; they answer questions about the application process in local languages, ensure that applications are complete, transmit them and their supporting paperwork to visa offices, and return passports and decision documents to applicants (Citizenship and Immigration Canada 2014i). Some also offer tracking services to inform applicants of where their file sits in the processing queue. The agreements with VFS Global Group are a cost-saving measure that are intended to spare visa offices the burden, and expense, of interacting with people when they submit a visa application, particularly short-term visitors and temporary residents. This form of outsourcing enables the immigration department to conserve its scarce and expensive embassy-based resources. Most staff whose offices have relationships with Visa Application Centres are relieved that they no longer receive applications. As Chapter 8 discusses in more detail, the Visa Application Centres eliminate the routine and time-consuming aspects of receiving a properly completed and documented application, and they allow offices to put more resources into evaluating credibility and risk.

Because labour is divided between immigration offices in Canada, overseas visa offices, and Visa Application Centres, the procedure for submitting a visa application and the way in which it flows through the decision-making process depend on the type of visa one is applying for and one's country of residence. A concrete example will help illustrate the complexity of the situation: If a woman in Belize wishes to visit Canada, she must send her visitor visa application to the Guatemala City Visa Application Centre because her own country does not have a Canadian visa office. After ensuring that her application is complete, the Guatemala City Visa Application Centre turns it into a PDF and sends it electronically to Ottawa, where a formal file is created. Ottawa then forwards the PDF to the visa office in Guatemala City, which reviews and makes a decision about the application. If its officer has concerns and needs to interview the applicant, she must normally travel to Guatemala City. (In instances where application volumes justify the expense, officers will sometimes go to countries that have no visa office to interview several applicants.) Alternatively, if her application is accepted, a visa is placed in her passport, and this is returned to the Visa Application Centre in Guatemala City, which forwards the passport and visa to her. If, however, the same woman decides to apply as a federal skilled worker, she must send her application to the Case Processing Centre in Sydney. If the Sydney office concludes that she meets the relevant criteria, her application is forwarded to the Canadian visa office in Mexico City. If the office wishes to interview her, she must travel to Mexico City, again at her own expense. If it accepts her application, it returns her passport, with the visa, directly to her.

Embassies, Consulates, and Visa Offices

Though the immigration department's modernization agenda includes a long-term plan to shift more visa processing to Canada, most selection and admissibility decisions are still made in overseas offices. These are housed at Canadian embassies, high commissions, or consulates, which, as the face of Canada abroad, normally host a mix of federal and provincial government departments and Crown corporations. In 2009, Canada had 173 diplomatic missions in 107 countries (some countries have an embassy or high commission as well as one or more consulates), which employed over 7,600 people, both Canadians and locally engaged staff. About two-thirds of staff worked for the Department of Foreign Affairs and International Trade, and the remaining third were employed by thirty-two other departments, Crown corporations, provincial governments, and other organizations (Foreign Affairs and International Trade Canada 2009, 1–2).

Though visa officers work for Citizenship and Immigration, they are also foreign service officers, and thus their compensation falls under the policies crafted between Foreign Affairs, the Treasury Board of Canada, and the Professional Association of Foreign Service Officers.[1] In 2010, entry-level visa officers who had just completed the three-year Foreign Service Development Program earned $61,047. A top-end immigration program manager's annual salary was $112,512 (Treasury Board of Canada Secretariat 2012). Foreign service officers are also eligible for a number of allowances that compensate them for living and working abroad (Mosey 2004). One of these is the post differential allowance, which is a measure of the "hardship" entailed in working at various missions abroad. The allowance is also intended to encourage officers to put in for postings at missions that are difficult to staff. As one immigration program manager explained, speaking of the now closed office in Damascus, "Some people won't come to Damascus for family reasons, which is why we have so many young, single staff. The allowances are higher here, so people can actually make some money by working here. There are extra trips home. And some people like working in a place like Damascus because it sounds exotic."[2]

Offices that are difficult to staff are distant from Canada and are subject to various health, safety, and security concerns (Mosey 2004). Foreign Affairs classifies its missions abroad on a five-point "hardship scale" (ranging from "1," which signifies lowest hardship, to "5," which stands for greatest hardship). For example, as of July 2012, postings in Singapore and Hong Kong were rated as level 1; Abu Dhabi and Buenos Aires were at level 2; Kyiv and Port of Spain were level 3; Nairobi, Delhi, and Beijing were level 4; and Islamabad and Guatemala City were level 5 (National Joint Council 2012b). An officer who is single and is posted to a level 1 mission receives a post differential allowance of $3,178. At a level 5 mission, the allowance goes up to $12,719. If an officer is accompanied by three dependants, the allowance at a level 5 posting increases to $19,712 (ibid.; National Joint Council 2012a).

Foreign Affairs is responsible for the overall operation of embassies and consulates; it provides and maintains office space, official residences, and staff accommodation, it organizes information technology, security, and transportation, and it hires locally engaged staff (Foreign Affairs and International Trade Canada 2009, 2). The physical space and many day-to-day aspects of the immigration department's overseas operations thus fall within the provenance of Foreign Affairs. Like other departments and agencies that have an overseas presence, the department leases its space from Foreign Affairs. Space is paid for by the department, and the money goes into covering the overhead expenses associated with running the office (see ibid.). A deputy program manager told me that the department pays about $200,000 to cover the overhead costs of one new visa officer position.[3]

Immigration must compete for space with other federal government departments that have, or want to have, an overseas presence. To achieve this, it negotiates with the Committee on Representation Abroad, a branch of Foreign Affairs (Foreign Affairs and International Trade Canada 2009). A deputy program manager described how the process works:

> We go to the committee and say we need to expand our office, or put an office somewhere. They say, "Show me the money. Where is the money coming from?" They look at whether there is space to accommodate the extra staff members that are being requested. They look at the cost of the extra space. They look at competing demands in the embassies. They might have requests from Border Services, the RCMP, CSIS, or Agriculture Canada for space at the embassy. People say, "If we are backlogged in a certain office, just put more people there." It's not that simple. There are a finite number of visa officers. We can't operate that quickly. In that case, we have two options. One, we can use secondments to backfill, or two we can hire new officers, but that takes time.[4]

Whereas some critics suggest that the location of overseas visa offices reflects racialized biases in processing priorities (Jakubowski 1997), siting arises from complex resource management decisions that must be negotiated with other government branches and so are not entirely within the department's control.

Its operational guidelines specify that its physical space should be separate from other offices and departments in an embassy or consulate (Citizenship and Immigration Canada 2013b). A layer of security normally prevents employees of other government departments, including the ambassador or high commissioner, from freely accessing the workspace of visa officers (ibid.). The intent of this is to maintain the security of the department's confidential files. It also protects the legally constituted autonomy of officers, ensuring that their decisions are not fettered or influenced by other individuals, either within or outside the department.

In practice, visa offices vary in how closely they enforce the boundaries between themselves and other embassy staff. Some take a strict approach.

In one instance, the immigration program manager had to politely "explain" to an ambassador that it was inappropriate for him to drop by and chat about individuals who were applying for a visa. At the same time, completely enforcing the boundary between offices is often a challenge (Citizenship and Immigration Canada 2013b). In some embassies, the physical layout is such that completely walling off the visa office is difficult. Although doing so is inappropriate, ambassadors, high commissioners, and other high-ranking officials do sometimes pressure offices to issue a visitor visa to individuals, commonly diplomats or government officials from the country where the mission is located. As one officer explained, "I will get pressure from the ambassador to let some diplomat in, but you have to look at the file. You always have to consider Canada's interest."[5]

In situations where credibility and risk are difficult to assess, some offices accept representations by embassy staff on behalf of a visa applicant whom they know, though this is not exactly encouraged. One large office accepts informal representations regarding applicants who wish to visit Canada for business or other purposes. Officers will not approve a visa solely on the basis of the recommendation, but it might help tip the scales if an officer is sitting on the fence. Alternatively, an informal inquiry or representation by a colleague might involve simply extracting a file from the queue to speed up its turnaround time.

The Visa Office Workforce

Canadian overseas visa offices vary in size. For example, the small Tokyo office (now closed) had only thirteen employees in 2009, the medium-sized Singapore office had thirty-six in 2010, and the large Beijing office had ninety-two in 2007 (Citizenship and Immigration Canada 2009b, 2010c, 2008).

Figure 1 shows how the visa office in Kingston, Jamaica, was organized in 2008. It is headed by an immigration program manager. Larger offices also have a deputy immigration program manager. Beyond these two upper management positions, both of which must be occupied by Canadians, the office staff is further categorized into Canada-based officers and locally engaged staff. The former are further subdivided into what I will refer to as "visa officers" and migration integrity officers, both of whom are considered as foreign service officers. Some offices also have a medical officer. Except for the locally engaged positions, all are open only to Canadians. Locally engaged staff are nationals of the country in which the office is

FIGURE 1 Kingston mission organization, 2008

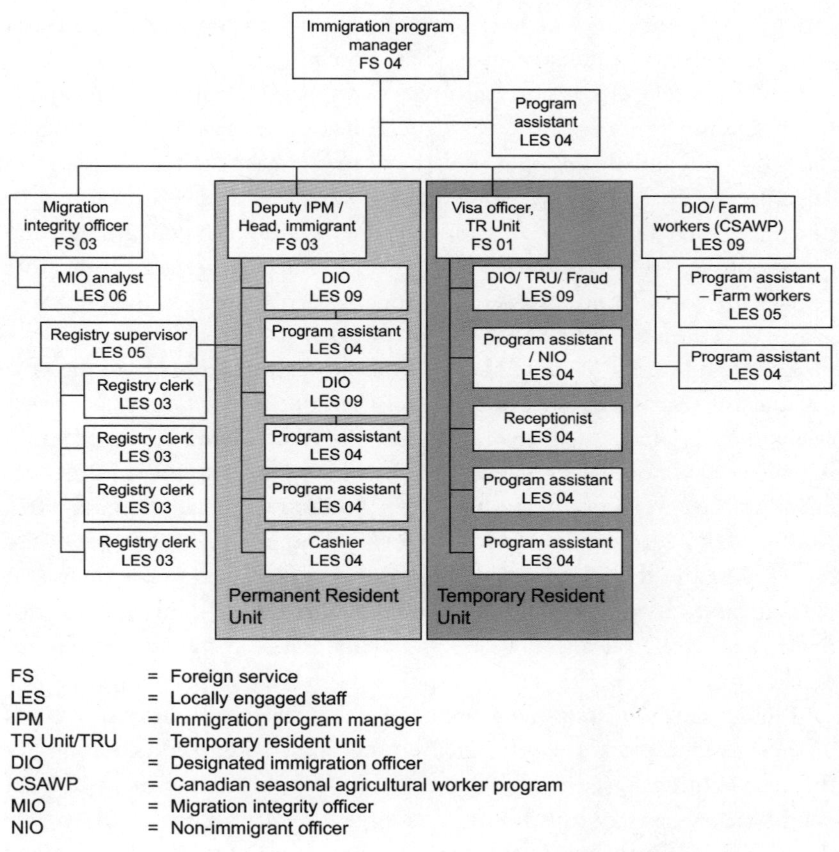

Source: Citizenship and Immigration Canada (2010b).

located, third-country nationals, and Canadian expats. They have varying responsibilities. Most handle clerical or support duties, but some can make decisions in certain types of visa issuance cases.

Large offices are often subdivided into units. At minimum, an office is usually split between a Temporary Resident Unit and a Permanent Resident Unit. Depending on volumes and caseloads, the latter can be subdivided into an Economic Class Unit, a Family Class Unit, and a Refugee Unit. In such cases, a unit manager oversees the work of the visa officers and program assistants who process that category of file.

Immigration Program Manager

Visa offices are headed by immigration program managers, usually senior foreign service officers who have worked their way up and who have several years of overseas field experience. Like other foreign service officers, they normally rotate overseas postings every two years, with stints at headquarters in Ottawa mixed in. However, depending on the size and complexity of the office and global staffing needs, they can stay longer than two years in one posting. They are responsible for organizing the decision-making process, based on country- and mission-specific conditions; managing staff and the various external relationships of the office; and reviewing decisions that require the concurrence of a senior officer. Most also process their share of visa applications.

Although International Region in Ottawa closely monitors both the productivity of visa offices and the quality of their decisions, it does not necessarily micro-manage their organization or the flow of work. Thus, program managers have some degree of autonomy in these areas. One manager referred to the seventeenth-century British Admiralty in describing how this worked: "The admirals in London set overall direction and policy but the ones sailing the ships for years without direct contact had to use their own wits and assessments to figure things out. The immigration missions are not really run from Ottawa, and we are given a lot of leeway to figure things out on the ground."[6]

Though newly posted managers inherit the decision-making structures of their predecessors, they do set the tone in an office and often modify those structures, based on their own experiences and assessment of local conditions, resource constraints, and operational challenges. They also shape broader office culture and cue staff regarding how to think about certain processing issues or kinds of cases, particularly those that require their concurrence. One officer commented, "We always have firm management here. Management gives us strong direction. We are briefed on the office goals, the targets, and the priorities for specific units."[7] However, as a manager suggested, managers must tread a fine line between expressing their views and fettering officer decisions:

> You talk with the staff, to explain why it is important to you. I am not trying to fetter discretion, but you try to come up with a meeting of the minds about what constitutes humanitarian and compassionate. Sometimes we have training sessions; in Delhi, we had the "Delhi Academy." We talked about expectations in processing, things like humanitarian and compas-

> sionate, authority to return to Canada, [criminal] rehabilitation cases. It was a conversation about what will convince me. It was also about what I wanted to see procedurally.[8]

Program managers are also responsible for undertaking quality assurance exercises in their office. These are essentially retrospective reviews of decisions or decision-making procedures for specific kinds of visa applications. Reflecting the tension between the demand for productivity, which is measured by meeting processing targets and deadlines, and the demand for good decisions, the exercises involve in-depth reviews of sample applications to check whether individuals were truly eligible for the visa they received, whether they engaged in fraud or misrepresentation, and whether they conformed to their conditions of entry once they arrived in Canada. International Region expects that offices will regularly undertake quality assurances, but departmental audits suggest that the ability of a program manager to comply is sometimes hampered by resource constraints (Citizenship and Immigration Canada 2011a).

Like their counterparts in other large, complex organizations, program managers must not only shepherd the flow of work, but must also monitor a variety of external relationships and how the office's performance is perceived in Canada and abroad. As one manager explained, "An immigration program manager's concerns are different from that of an immigration officer. They have to be concerned about how the host country receives their work. They are worried about cases that blow up under their jurisdiction, and media reactions in Canada."[9] Like senior immigration officials more generally, managers are concerned about how their work is perceived in Canada and about specific cases that might attract negative public attention. The latter tend to involve individuals who were denied a visa despite their seemingly legitimate reasons to travel to Canada. Managers must therefore subject potentially controversial decisions to what one described as "the *Globe and Mail* test," which for him, meant phrasing his written statements in such a way that they would embarrass neither him nor the department if they appeared in the newspaper.[10] One manager described having "his hand slapped" by International Region because his office's definition of humanitarian and compassionate grounds was too narrow to override an otherwise legally correct and justifiable refusal decision.

Depending on the office and the caseload, managing external relationships can involve liaising with bodies such as the International Organization for Migration or the United Nations High Commission for Refugees. But program managers can also be drawn into the more mundane, micro-level external relations of the office. In an example drawn from my own experience, I was walking to the mission to begin my day's work when I noticed that a man had set up a small table and a chair in the middle of the sidewalk near the embassy. This seemed odd, and I wondered why he was there. I guessed that he belonged to the country's security services and was keeping a not-too-subtle eye on the comings and goings at the embassy. Later, as the program manager and I went down the street to get a coffee, we passed the man and I asked the manager what he might be "up to." The manager explained that the man was a "consultant" who hired himself out to visa applicants. As he sat at his little table, he helped them fill out their applications in English. The manager added, "He does a terrible job. He will put the wrong information down on forms, say that someone is single when someone is married and things like that." Though he could not be stopped from plying his trade, the manager was able to convince the local authorities to "move him down the street."[11]

In handling the larger external relationships, managers also concern themselves with the appearance of conflicts of interest. Some immigration consultants who work in Canada today are retired foreign service officers who hope to capitalize on their experience by offering advice to prospective applicants for admission to Canada. Some whose foreign service work included immigration advertise this fact because it implies that they have special insider knowledge and access to visa offices. Some consultants seem to believe that their past experience provides them with social capital among currently serving officers. As a manager explained, they try to use their past connection with the department as an "opening" with the person who is making decisions about their client's case. Referring to one of these, a manager remarked, "He tries this folksy stuff. He writes to people ... saying 'Hey [Alice, pseudonym], ... [Jeff Eldridge, pseudonym] here, former foreign service officer, I have this client –.' He does that all the time, with everybody. It's really unprofessional."[12]

Certainly, program managers are sensitive to the appearance of conflict of interest with their former colleagues, regardless of whether they know them personally. As the same manager pointed out, "You have to be careful of the optics. I can't go to lunch with former colleagues or lawyers. Some former colleagues are now consultants. Sometimes they call up and say, 'Hey, I'm in town, want to go for lunch?' and I say, 'I can't.' I don't want to be seen to be in a conflict of interest."[13]

The manager added that conflict of interest concerns extended beyond consultants to wider business and community contacts in the mission's country of operation. He mentioned a long-standing series of corruption allegations at the Hong Kong office during the late 1980s and early 1990s that had attracted considerable press attention, including a W5 television documentary (Federal Accountability Initiative for Reform 2014):

> There was a real problem in Hong Kong a few years ago ... There are lots of wealthy business people in Hong Kong, and they were wining and dining the head of the mission and others. A lot us were thinking, what are they doing? These business people are not your friends. Obviously they are going to want favours. The head of the mission didn't seem to realize that.[14]

As a result, program managers often attempt to avoid meeting influential people in their country of operation, simply to forestall the appearance of a conflict of interest.

Visa Officers

Most Canada-based officers are career foreign service officers. However, depending on the office and the workload, they are supplemented by Canadian public servants who are on temporary duty assignments, usually from Border Services, a Citizenship and Immigration office in Canada, or the ranks of retired visa officers. A secondment to International Region from another government department usually lasts for two years, after which individuals normally return to their previous job in the public service. Retirees fill in for a few weeks or months at a time.

Newly minted visa officers must have completed the three-year Foreign Service Development Program. New recruits to the immigration department and Foreign Affairs tend to be university graduates from various disciplines. Some have worked for a few years with immigration-related international organizations such as the UN High Commission for Refugees, in legal settings, in other federal government departments, or elsewhere in the public sector, such as education. After they take the highly competitive post-secondary recruitment tests, the department selects a small yearly cohort of about twenty-five candidates to undergo Foreign Service Development Program training. The first year of this involves six weeks of classroom instruction on topics such as the interpretation and application of the Immigration and Refugee Protection Act, cross-cultural issues, and interview skills. Students also engage in role-playing exercises with refugees who have gone through the admissions process and with former visa officers, "who know all of the tricks."[15] They are given jobs at department headquarters in Ottawa, and they visit airports, border ports of entry, and various department and Border Services offices. Also during the first year, they are posted overseas for six weeks to gain experience in application processing, and though they may be in training, the expectation is that "they produce."[16] They return to headquarters for further classroom training and are then posted overseas on a probationary basis for two years.

International Region assesses recruits during the second year of their overseas posting, and they are released from government employment if they are deemed unsuitable as foreign service officers: "The first posting is going to make or break them."[17] As a deputy manager explained, "Sometimes it is clear that an officer is a hiring mistake. Usually it is a judgment issue. Can you look at a case and in a very short time can you make a decision, 'yes or no?'"[18] An officer who had trained new recruits at headquarters noted that though they failed the program for various reasons, the ability to make quick decisions is critical during the early phase of their career trajectory:

> They get all kinds of coaching. But they have to pass the overseas component of the training. If they do not pass, then they are out. Some can't pass the exams because they don't really know how to apply the law. Sometimes, they self-select out. There is a personal suitability for the job really. Some people are not able to manage in an overseas environment; they can't take the stresses of living in a different culture. But also, they might fail because they can't get along with others, they say inappropriate things to clients in interviews; those kinds of things could make them fail out of the program. Some people have a hard time making decisions.[19]

Once recruits pass through their probationary period and are made permanent, Canada-based foreign service officers normally do two-year rotations. They usually rotate in the summer, between July and August when most offices are in the thick of processing visitor and student visas. Canada-based officers submit their request for their next posting during the autumn prior to their scheduled rotation. They have three options: they can ask to remain where they are, to go back to headquarters in Ottawa, or to stay overseas but at a different office.[20]

Posting preferences are shaped by personal and professional factors. Some officers choose their locations due to workload considerations. For example, an officer who wishes to gain experience with refugee applications will choose an office that processes large numbers of them. Others may see certain locations as exotic or are attracted by the special allowances that come with high-hardship postings. Some marry a local resident or develop a love for a country or region and wish to remain there. As one officer confided, "Asia is infectious"; she limited her choices to Asian countries.[21]

Opportunities for spousal employment also factor into posting preferences. As in Canada more generally, dual-income couples are the norm among visa officers, and considerable stresses accrue to juggling two careers. In fact, spousal employment is a key issue in the Canadian foreign service, and the challenges associated with two-career households are a major source of attrition (Mosey 2004). As one deputy program manager noted, "There is a high attrition rate in the foreign service. It is hard to be a two career couple."[22]

In cases where a partner is not a foreign service officer, Canada has reciprocal agreements with some countries that allow Canadian spouses to work there. Normally, however, they receive no preferential access to work visas, or the labour market, in the country where their partner is posted. Thus, they must go through the same channels as other foreigners to secure a temporary work visa and must also learn the dynamics of the local labour market. Their job search may be assisted by staff at the embassy, who may know of an opening, and they sometimes secure low-level clerical employment there.

In cases where partners both work for the foreign service, their posting preferences are guided by how difficult it is to get posted near each other. Couples who work for the foreign service but in different departments (usually Immigration and Foreign Affairs) and who have secured positions at the same mission sometimes request to stay there for more than one rotation rather than trying to find two openings elsewhere.

Actual posting decisions are made centrally by International Region in Ottawa and are based on seniority, family, and age considerations. Immigration program manager vacancies and unattractive postings are filled first, whereas young and single Canada-based officers are the last to be placed. Though postings are based on a combination of officer preferences and anticipated needs and vacancies, program managers also play an informal role in staffing decisions. Because they work with a variety of officers during their careers, they know many of them personally and are thus familiar with their strengths and weaknesses, and how well they get along with people, which can play an informal part in their postings. In the absence of first-hand knowledge, a manager might also call a senior colleague to learn more about a particular officer. A manager might object to having a certain officer posted to his or her mission because of negative past experiences. Conversely, in anticipation of a rotation, a manager might pursue "good" officers, encouraging them to rank his office first on their posting preference form. However, International Region knows that managers can try to stack the deck with "stars." As one deputy manager suggested,

> Some managers try to do an end run around International Region by trying to get specific people. But you don't always get who you want. There are always underperformers. They are plodders. They produce, but they will never be management material. One office can't have all the stars. The managers get to know officers because they worked with them in other offices. But managers can't fire them, and you can't have them go home. International Region has a vested interest in making an employee happy.[23]

Elaborating on what makes a star, the same person said,

> It is an officer who understands the laws, who understands file flow, who can process cases, who has integrity, who deals with staff effectively, has a handle on the work, has good people skills, and can supervise staff. It is more than the ability to make decisions. You need to have people skills. Some produce amazing numbers but are horrible to work with.[24]

A long-serving manager in another office expressed similar sentiments. "Knowing the job" and making "good defensible decisions" were mandatory, but so were broader interpersonal and interpretive skills:

> They have to have very good interpersonal skills to deal with the staff, especially the locally engaged staff. You have to remain open to the possibility that you are wrong. You are self-aware, self-critical. You are open to the possibility of bias. You don't like to hear them claim that they are right all the time. They are concerned about others' experience, mainly that of the clients. You have to have a kind of sensitivity. You have to be able to work as a team. You have to be able to work in a context where things are ambiguous. You cannot be so worried about making a decision. You can't be too programmatic. You have to be curious about other cultures. You have to take an interest in the nuances of how things are done. A seasoned foreign service officer can see the bigger picture. They have to display a flexibility

> where and however they are needed. Last week we were preparing for an emergency trip to the Congo, in case problems broke out there during the elections. You have to have a willingness to help out.[25]

Using an analogy that most Canadians would understand, another deputy manager explained that handling staffing issues is not unlike coaching hockey:

> A visa office is like a hockey team. You have your first line, second line, third line and fourth line. Your first liners are the superstars. They are the ones who make good decisions quickly and can do everything. Then the second liners are like your defencemen. They have specific skills and you can throw them in to stop the puck or to solve a problem. The third liners are the basic players; they can do the job but there is nothing spectacular about them. The fourth liners, the coach throws them in and closes his eyes and hopes for the best.[26]

When I asked what made for a fourth liner, he replied that it was "someone who can't make decisions; they are just not comfortable making decisions. They take too long, or they try to make too many notes. They might sit on a file, and keep requesting more documents; meanwhile the documents are piling up and they still can't make a decision."[27]

A manager in another office made similar comments; while discussing the qualities of officers, he remarked, "Some are just not comfortable with decision making. Yes, some are slow. It might be a training issue, but some are just slow. Getting a decision is like pulling teeth. They are never satisfied. They are always requesting more docs. This can come from seeing too many angles of a case."[28]

Clearly, making good decisions quickly, in a context of uncertainty, is a hallmark of a good visa officer, at least in the minds of senior managers, a belief that is not lost on the officers themselves. As one pointed out, "Citizenship and Immigration hires people to demonstrate judgment; they hire people to make decisions."[29]

Migration Integrity Officers

All overseas visa offices have at least one migration integrity officer, but offices that deal with high levels of fraud often have two. Through the 1990s and early 2000s, there were fewer than twenty integrity officers, most of whom dealt with overseas airport interdiction. Since 2003, they have been formally employed by Border Services, and their numbers were augmented in 2006 by anti-fraud migration integrity officers, whose job is mainly to detect broader patterns of fraud (Canada Border Services Agency 2009).

The integrity officers who handle airport interdiction tend to be stationed in cities that offer direct flights to Canada or at major international hubs in which significant volumes of passengers are Canada-bound. Their job is to prevent individuals who lack valid visas and/or passports from catching a flight to Canada, so they often stand at boarding gates, checking travel documents alongside airline staff. In describing his job, one officer touched on the efforts of in-migration countries to extend their borders:

> I do visits and interception at three airports where there are direct flights to Canada. I show up for three days at a time and do interception work. Usually I find four to five cases per flight. I can ask questions of travellers about their admissibility based on their bona fides. The boarding gate is considered as a port of entry to Canada, which allows me to ask these questions. I cannot stop a person from boarding a flight, but I can say to airline staff, "If this person boards the flight, your airline will be subject to a $3,200 fine." That usually works.[30]

The $3,200 fine is an airline sanction, discussed in Chapter 1, a layer of extra-territorial border control designed to prevent undeserving individuals from setting foot on Canadian soil. As noted in Chapter 3, once someone enters Canada and claims refugee status, he or she is subject to an adjudication process that, until recently, had many layers of appeal and which allowed claimants to access various health and social services while their cases were heard. To avoid the cost of removing ineligible individuals, Canada, like many other in-migration countries, imposes sanctions on airlines for carrying passengers without proper documentation.

In this outward expansion of the Canadian border, a major part of the migration integrity officer's job is to train airline staff to detect fake passports and visas, and to identify "imposters" (Canada Border Services Agency 2009). As one integrity officer explained,

> There are two types of fraud I am concerned with: forged documents and imposters. The trend is for imposters to be a bigger problem than forged documents. We are getting better at training airline staff at detecting forged

> documents, but they are less likely to check pictures to see that the person holding the passport is the one on the picture ... It is harder to get airline staff to do this, but it is not that hard. You break the face down into components – eyes, nose and mouth. And their ears, the ears are the key. They are like fingerprints.[31]

Many integrity officers have cultivated cooperative relationships with their counterparts who work for other Western countries, particularly those who are stationed in airports. For example, when officers cannot be at an airport, their colleagues from other countries reportedly pitch in to help airline employees check passengers travelling to Canada. The migration integrity officers will return the favour.

Because the consequences of a wrong decision can be relatively serious, integrity officers who work in airports often keep unorthodox hours. Always "on call," one officer said,

> I have four cell phones on all the time. I tell airline staff to call me at any time of day or night. If they have a concern, I can, within minutes, run a check on a name and a document to see if it is fraudulent. There is a twenty-four-hour National Risk Assessment number I call in Ottawa, and they can tell whether the visa has been issued properly or not.[32]

Though he was sensitive about the word "profiling," he did state that profiles are used to frame credible and non-credible travellers to Canada. They also shape how officers deploy their time. As he put it, "Istanbul is a difficult airport to do interdiction work. Istanbul is a busy hub because it is a transit point between Canada and Asia. I can't say the word profiling, but passengers are in bound from Pakistan, India, Bangladesh, Sri Lanka, Azerbaijan and Georgia, and those are my biggest challenges."[33]

According to one integrity officer, fraudsters and people who help individuals use false documents tend to choose direct flights to Canada. As airlines expand their operations, and as their capacity increases to fly ever longer distances without refuelling, direct flights to Canada from overseas are becoming more frequent. An integrity officer explained that "new routes are targeted by smugglers. They are vulnerable. They know that a new route means that an airline might not be that sophisticated in detecting document fraud and so the new routes are targets of fraud."[34]

A 2009 evaluation of the Border Services admissibility screening apparatus found that since 2002, integrity officers had intercepted a yearly average of 5,500 "illegal migrants" before they departed for Canada. As the cost of filing a refugee claim and removing a person from Canada is estimated to range from $4,768 to $41,085, Border Services calculates that its interception activities "result in a potential cost avoidance" to Canada of between $26 and $225 million per year. It regards this as a "cost-effective component in the Agency's multi-border strategy" (Canada Border Services Agency 2009, 22).

All visa offices now have at least one anti-fraud migration integrity officer. Although visa officers are also responsible for detecting fraud and misrepresentation in applications, they have neither the time nor the resources to analyze whether individual cases reflect broader patterns of deception. As a result, anti-fraud integrity officers attempt to link particular cases to the individuals, organizations, or processes that help to perpetuate the fraud (Citizenship and Immigration Canada 2010e). As one anti-fraud officer explained, much of her work involved verifying the identity-related documents submitted in support of visa applications: "It is quite challenging work. The workload is quite high. We have sixteen countries ... I am doing country reports, which are reporting on processes in countries regarding how they issue documents. I need to know a lot about the context of various countries. How do people hold genuine documents from their countries?"[35]

In war-torn countries with a history of instability and conflict, and where government infrastructure has been destroyed, assessing identity documents is often difficult. In such cases, individuals who have, and do not have, certain identity-related documents are both potentially challenging for anti-fraud officers:

> With family reunification of refugees, there are few identity documents to prove the relationship. In Somalia, there has been no central government. If someone comes to you with a document supposedly issued by the central government of Somalia, you know it is suspicious. You can find documents sold on the street. It is always a challenge to determine the truthfulness of documents. Anything can be bought because of corruption in the area ... In some countries, there is identity and nationality fraud ... Here we have people passing off as being someone from a war zone.[36]

Like other migration integrity officers, this anti-fraud officer cultivated relationships with authorities in a number of countries in her region, and with immigration authorities from other immigrant-receiving states, to help visa office staff understand what genuine documents look like and how they are generated (Salter 2011):

> I build contacts with local authorities. I try to get samples of genuine documents ... It takes a long time to understand these countries. So I need to share knowledge and build up information. I try to detect patterns of fraud that we find. I share it with my colleagues from other countries, the US, the UK, Australia, Norway. For example, we have counterfeit airline letters. Letters saying that someone is an employee of an airline, and they need to go to Canada for something. But each country has its own rules about privacy and what it can share.[37]

Anti-fraud officers also conduct site visits and field investigations to verify the information on visa application forms: "This year we have been doing more anti-fraud work here in the office. We try to do more digging into the files. I assist with document verification. Sometimes, I do site visits to verify information like letters indicating experience."[38] According to the Citizenship and Immigration manual for anti-fraud work (Citizenship and Immigration Canada 2010e, 17), site visits can include interviews with "managers, employees, employers or others present who are able to address questions related to an applicant's *bona fides* or questions about the organization in question." Interviews and visits can involve the verification of schools, business invitations, businesses alleged to be employing skilled or other workers, or individuals undertaking to assist or sponsor a relative.

Locally Engaged Staff

There are nine grades of locally engaged staff, but the basic distinction is between those who have the authority to make decisions in certain kinds of visa application cases and those who do not. Those who can make decisions are the non-immigrant officer and the designated immigration officer. The former, who is at level 7 or 8 of the job grade, can make decisions on temporary resident applications, whereas the latter, at level 9, can make decisions on both temporary and permanent resident applications. Though the decision-making powers of designated immigration officers are similar to those of Canada-based officers, certain types of cases are off-limits to them, such as an individual who is suspected of being criminally inadmissible to Canada (see Citizenship and Immigration Canada 2009a).

Lower-grade locally engaged staff work as receptionists, data entry clerks, registry clerks, and cashiers. Their jobs are routine, and they play no role in decision making. Mid-grade locally engaged staff are either program assistants or case analysts. Program assistants, who tend to work for the decision-making officers, ensure that applications are complete, schedule interviews, and follow up with applicants if additional information is required or submitted (see Government of Canada 2014b). They also act as interpreters in interviews between Canada-based officers and applicants. When they work for a specific Canada-based officer, they are also conduits for local knowledge about the reputation of educational institutions, intergroup tensions, the credibility of banking, tax, and identity documents, manners and customs, courtship and marriage traditions, and patterns of crime in communities. When they conduct the initial review of a visa application, they use their experience, training, and local knowledge, often flagging unusual aspects that might be of concern to the officer for whom they work.

Case analysts, who do not work under a specific decision-maker, work in pools in various units. They assess the credibility of specific types of applications, such as family class spousal and partner sponsorships. They identify inconsistencies in applications, alerting decision-makers in their unit to potentially fraudulent documents or identifying aspects of an application that are not typical of the country or region.

Non-immigrant officers and designated immigration officers normally work their way up the ranks of locally engaged staff. Their positions are highly coveted, in part because they involve six months of training in Ottawa. The training is a compressed version of the Foreign Service Development Program. They do not rotate between visa offices.

In some countries, becoming locally engaged staff is like winning the lottery because the position is a good job and is "a job for life."[39] Staff turnover is often low, and competition is stiff for higher-grade jobs. Where turnover is higher, employment with the Canadian embassy looks good on a resumé and allows ambitious individuals to find more lucrative jobs with international organizations, NGOs, or private-sector companies that are looking for English- and/or French-speakers who have professional and interpersonal skills.

Most locally engaged staff are nationals of the country in which the visa office is located, but some are third-country nationals or Canadian expats. How far they proceed up the decision-making chain depends on the perceived security risks in their country and the past history of malfeasance in their office. In some countries, Canadian risk assessments indicate that staff are under pressure to report on their activities, and those of the Canadian embassy itself, to local security services. Rather than putting them in this uncomfortable position, Foreign Affairs "manages risk" by keeping them out of the higher-grade decision-making jobs. In other instances, past malfeasance in an office limits how high current staff can climb. Visa office malfeasance is rarely made public, so how big a problem it is remains unclear. Immigration program managers whom I interviewed were reluctant to discuss it, but the potential for malfeasance seemed ever present in their minds. However, there is some evidence that past incidents of misbehaviour could taint all the locally engaged staff in an office, which was frustrating for those who showed initiative and wanted to get ahead. In one office, a program assistant told me tearfully that because a locally engaged colleague had been involved in malfeasance a few years earlier, her office no longer promoted staff to decision-making positions. It was obvious that she was working hard to impress the manager and the Canada-based officers with her initiative and abilities in hopes that if a designated immigration or non-immigrant position did eventually open up, she would be well placed for a promotion.

The relationship between the decision-making officers and the case analysts and program assistants is quite close, and the former often rely on staff to flag concerns about an application. However, as in any hierarchical relationship, tensions sometimes arise between decision-makers and staff. Some Canada-based officers can be somewhat dismissive of the local knowledge that staff bring to application assessments. Asked whether his program assistant helped with fraud detection, one Canada-based officer stated simply and without elaborating, "Not so much." Conversely, many staff work with a variety of Canada-based officers during their careers and thus are aware of differences in style. They quickly learn whether officers are receptive to their knowledge and input. As two staff members stated in a joint interview,

> All Canada-based officers are different, but there are two types. Some are anal. All they want is a word-for-word translation of what the person says. They do not want our input, or us to explain that even though they said something, in this context that meant something else. Other Canada-based officers are more interested in the meaning of what the person will have to

> say. Some ask us, "So what do you think of what he said?" They still have the decision to make, but at least they ask us for our opinion. They may not act on the opinion, but at least they ask.[40]

***

Before we explore the ways in which visa officers make their decisions, it is important to understand what choices they make to either issue or refuse a visa. Approval rates vary from office to office, but as the next chapter suggests, the pattern of variation is not necessarily what one might expect, given the lingering suspicion that officer discretion and decision making are racialized.

5

Approval and Refusal Rates

People have this idea that we are here to refuse people. No, we are here to approve people within what the act and regulations allow. They think our lives are all about making people miserable. (Field notes, April 25, 2011)

To put it baldly, the job of a visa officer is to exercise a rather simple binary choice – to approve or to refuse a visa application. This chapter employs a quantitative approach to examine the choices that officers make. In particular, it analyzes approval rates for family class spousal and federal skilled worker permanent resident visas. Focusing on organizational culture, it delves into how officers make their decisions and how their discretion is socially constituted. Like most employees of bureaucratic organizations, officers must manage competing demands at work, and though these may be complementary in theory, they often clash in practice. Officers are expected to uphold the goals of the Immigration and Refugee Protection Act and to maintain certain service standards, but productivity tends to take priority when caseloads are high. The demand for efficiency means that officers must ration their time and vary the intensity with which they scrutinize each application. Thus, for a visa officer, a typical day at work entails negotiating multiple goals.

Family Class and Skilled Worker Approvals

This chapter focuses on visa office approval rates for the two largest components of Canada's immigration program: family class spousal and partner, and C-50 federal skilled worker applications. The tables give information on the number of applications processed, accepted, refused, and withdrawn in 2012. Applicants were refused because they did not meet the selection criteria for the visa and/or were deemed inadmissible because of health, security, or criminality considerations. Approved applicants met the selection criteria for the visa and were determined to be "not inadmissible" for health, safety, or security reasons. Some individuals, however, withdrew their application before it was fully processed. Since considerable time often elapses between the submission date of an application and the point when the office begins to work on the file, withdrawals probably occur for one of three reasons: applicants expect to be refused and prefer not to have that recorded in their file, their circumstances have changed and they believe they are no longer eligible for the visa, or they simply decide not to move to Canada. For administrative purposes, Citizenship and Immigration counts "withdrawals" as "cases processed" but does not factor them into its calculation of approval rates. The approval percentages that appear in the tables are therefore calculated as approvals divided by approvals plus refusals times one hundred.

Table 2 provides an overview of approval rates by application category. It shows that in 2012, visa offices in Canada and overseas processed 351,678 permanent resident applications. Of those, 275,451 were approved, 57,563 were refused, and 18,664 were withdrawn. The 22,251 "C-50 MI Refused" individuals applied for federal skilled worker visas but were deemed ineligible under the Bill C-50 amendments to the Immigration and Refugee Protection Act. Since they were refused due to ineligibility, they are not counted as having been "processed" by a visa office. Table 2 shows that the overall approval rate for all categories of permanent resident applications was 83 percent, which generally suggests that Canadian immigration policy is more oriented toward immigrant inclusion than to exclusion. For economic applications, the overall approval rate was 84 percent, with considerable variation between types of application. The approval rate for Quebec skilled workers was 97 percent, the highest for all economic visas. Federal skilled workers are divided between those who applied before the introduction of Ministerial Instructions under the auspices of Bill C-50 (called "pre-C-50" cases) and following the introduction of Bill C-50 (called "C-50" cases). Approval rates

TABLE 2

Permanent resident visa application approval rates, all categories, 2012

Category	Approved	Refused	Withdrawn	Total processed	Approval rate, excluding withdrawn and C-50 refused (%)	C-50 MI refused
ALL PERMANENT RESIDENTS	275,451	57,563	18,664	351,678	83	22,251
ECONOMIC (TOTAL)	164,499	32,197	11,752	208,448	84	22,251
Skilled workers (total)	97,641	26,171	7,874	131,686	79	22,251
Federal skilled workers (C-50)	52,639	21,392	3,375	77,406	71	22,251
Federal skilled workers (pre-C-50)	8,658	3,684	4,125	16,467	70	0
Quebec skilled workers	36,344	1,095	374	37,813	97	0
Entrepreneurs	499	347	267	1,113	59	0
Self-employed	283	171	211	665	62	0
Investors	8,752	964	2,099	11,815	90	0
Provincial nominees	38,658	2,135	455	41,248	95	0
Live-in-Caregiver Program	9,195	336	687	10,218	96	0
Canadian experience class	9,471	2,073	159	11,703	82	0
NON-ECONOMIC (TOTAL)	110,660	25,281	6,872	142,813	81	0
Family class (total)	78,307	12,341	4,424	95,072	86	0
Spouses, partners, and children (total)	46,116	9,387	3,318	58,821	83	0
Spouses and partners	42,502	7,619	2,772	52,893	85	0
Children and other family class	3,614	1,768	546	5,928	67	0

TABLE 2

Category	Approved	Refused	Withdrawn	Total processed	Approval rate, excluding withdrawn and C-50 refused (%)	C-50 MI refused
Parents and grandparents	32,191	2,954	1,106	36,251	92	0
Refugees (total)	23,619	4,055	1,943	29,617	85	0
Government-assisted refugees	5,162	604	297	6,063	90	0
Privately sponsored refugees	5,102	2,285	1,116	8,503	69	0
Protected persons landed in Canada	9,542	275	58	9,875	97	0
Refugee dependants	3,813	891	472	5,176	81	0
Humanitarian and compassionate	8,662	8,862	494	18,018	49	0
Permit holders' class	68	22	2	92	76	0
Others	4	1	9	14	80	0
MISSING OR INVALID	292	85	40	417	77	0

Source: Citizenship and Immigration Canada (2012f).

in these two categories were 70 and 71 percent respectively. The approval rate for Quebec skilled workers was considerably higher than for federal skilled workers, but as noted in Chapter 3, federal visa offices do not "select" them. The applications selected by Quebec immigration officials are forwarded to federal visa offices for final approval, so the data in Table 2 do not provide any indication of Quebec's original selection approval rate. In the Quebec case, federal visa officers make "inadmissibility" decisions only, which hinge on health, security, and criminality considerations. As a result, the 1,095 cases listed as "refused" are likely on the grounds of inadmissibility.

The overall approval rate for business-related applications was 87 percent, with considerable variation between specific categories. The approval rate for entrepreneurs and the self-employed was relatively low, at 59 and 62 percent respectively, whereas the approval rate for investors was 90 percent. The provincial nominee and live-in caregiver categories both had high approval rates: 95 and 96 percent respectively. Provincial nominees are selected by provincial governments, and live-in caregivers who apply for a visa must have a written employment contract and a positive labour market opinion (issued by Human Resources and Skills Development Canada, the labour market opinion affirms that no Canadian worker is available for the job). These high approval rates indicate that though federal visa officers are required to review provincial selection decisions and scrutinize labour market opinions and job contracts, they may be reluctant to oppose the choices of provinces and private employers. This speaks to the potential informal influence of third parties on the policy implementation process (see Stasiulis and Bakan 2005, 87).

In the non-economic categories of permanent residence, the overall approval rate was 81 percent, although again there was considerable variation by category. Protected persons landed in Canada and government-assisted refugees had the highest approval rates, at 97 and 90 percent respectively. Privately sponsored refugees, on the other hand, had an approval rate of 69 percent. Parent and grandparent applications also had a relatively high approval rate of 92 percent, whereas spouse and partner applications had an approval rate of 85 percent. Persons who applied for permanent resident status on the basis of humanitarian and compassionate grounds had the lowest approval rate for all categories: 49 percent. These cases tend to be dealt with mainly by visa offices in Canada that review applications from people who are already living in the country but are subject to removal orders and who claim that they should be allowed to stay for humanitarian and compassionate reasons.

Table 3 shows that in 2012, 280,168 of 351,678 (80 percent) applications were processed by overseas visa offices, which approved 84 percent of

TABLE 3

Permanent resident visa application approval rates, all visa categories, by office location, 2012

Office	Approved	Refused	Withdrawn	Total processed	Approval rate, excluding withdrawn and C-50 MI refused (%)
All points of service	275,451	57,562	18,664	351,677	83
Total abroad	221,092	42,093	16,983	280,168	84
Africa and Middle East	31,581	6,005	3,065	40,651	84
Asia and Pacific	90,184	16,088	8,650	114,922	85
Europe	51,475	13,365	2,194	67,034	79
Americas	47,852	6,635	3,074	57,561	88
Total Centralized Processing Region	47,528	6,301	1,402	55,231	88
CIO Sydney	5	2,438	35	2,478	0
CPP Ottawa	25,593	2,084	480	28,157	92
CPC Mississauga	57	595	253	905	9
CPC Vegreville	21,873	1,184	634	23,691	95
Total Backlog Reduction Office	696	2,953	110	3,759	19
BRO – Niagara Falls	1	1,382	3	1,386	0
BRO – Vancouver	569	1,271	105	1,945	31
BRO – Montreal	126	300	2	428	30

Total Inland	6,135	6,215	169	12,519	50
Ontario Region	3,737	3,587	116	7,440	51
Atlantic Region	72	50	2	124	59
Quebec Region	1,156	2,009	19	3,184	37
Prairies/NT Region	654	268	20	942	71
British Columbia/Yukon Region	516	301	12	829	63

Source: Citizenship and Immigration Canada (2012f).

applications. Processing in Canada occurs mainly at one of four offices in what is called the Centralized Processing Region. Their functions are discussed in Chapter 4. The immigration department has also recently created three backlog reduction offices, in Niagara Falls, Vancouver, and Montreal, whose roles are to review applications for pre-removal risk assessment and those made on humanitarian and compassionate grounds. These offices have relatively low approval rates; in fact, the Niagara Falls office approved just 1 of the 1,386 cases that it processed in 2012. Regional offices also make some decisions in permanent resident cases, where applicants already live in Canada. Their approval rates vary from 37 percent in Quebec to 71 percent in the Prairies and Northwest Territories.

For administrative purposes, Canada's overseas network of visa offices is divided into four regions: Africa and the Middle East, Asia and the Pacific, Europe, and the Americas. The offices in Taipei, Damascus, and Buffalo were all closed in 2012, albeit for different reasons. Buffalo succumbed to the modernization agenda noted earlier, Damascus for security reasons related to the civil war in Syria (its caseload was transferred to Beirut), and Taipei because of small processing volumes (its caseload was transferred to Hong Kong). Table 4 shows that in 2012, the overseas approval rate was 84 percent for the economic class, 85 percent for the family class, and 79 percent for refugees. Offices in the Americas had the highest approval rate for economic class applications (90 percent), whereas those in Europe had the lowest rate (77 percent). For family class, this pattern was reversed: European offices approved 91 percent, and the Americas approved 82 percent. Europe approved 89 percent of refugees, whereas the Americas approved 73 percent. Approval rates in Africa and the Middle East, and Asia and the Pacific, fell between those of Europe and the Americas for all three categories.

These broad geographical approval rates can be further broken down by visa office and application category. Table 5 provides information on overall approval rates by visa office for spousal and partner applications. It shows that overseas offices processed about 43,000 of the 53,000 (81 percent) applications submitted for spousal sponsorship. The European offices had the highest regional approval rate: 92 percent. However, rates varied from 85 percent in Rome to 97 percent in Berlin. Six of the ten European offices had approval rates in excess of 90 percent. Ankara also had a notably high rate, 92 percent, though much of its caseload came from the European "borderlands" of Turkey, Turkmenistan, Iran, Azerbaijan, and Georgia.

European offices, however, dealt with only 7,126 (or 16.5 percent) of the 42,984 spousal cases processed abroad. Most were handled in Asia and the

TABLE 4
Approval rates, by overseas region and general admission category, 2012

Location	Percentage of applications approved		
	Economic class	Family class	Refugees
Africa and the Middle East	88	82	78
Asia and the Pacific	85	85	77
Europe	77	91	89
Americas	90	82	73
Total abroad	84	85	79

Source: Citizenship and Immigration Canada (2012f).

TABLE 5
Spousal and partner application approval rates, by overseas visa office, 2012

Office	Approved	Refused	Withdrawn	Total processed	Approval rate, excluding withdrawn and C-50 MI refused (%)
All points of service	42,502	7,619	2,772	52,893	85
Total abroad	34,664	6,305	2,015	42,984	85
Africa and Middle East	**5,023**	**1,039**	**354**	**6,416**	**83**
Abu Dhabi	407	84	58	549	83
Accra	518	377	46	941	58
Amman	169	24	25	218	88
Beirut	326	29	42	397	92
Cairo	519	48	21	588	92
Dakar	677	112	31	820	86
Damascus	86	3	7	96	97
Nairobi	1,100	160	83	1,343	87
Pretoria	135	52	8	195	72
Rabat	938	115	28	1,081	89
Tel Aviv	148	35	5	188	81

►

TABLE 5

Office	Approved	Refused	Withdrawn	Total processed	Approval rate, excluding withdrawn and C-50 MI refused (%)
Asia and Pacific	**16,121**	**3,236**	**775**	**20,132**	**83**
Beijing	1,794	156	70	2,020	92
Colombo	685	108	26	819	86
Delhi	3,861	978	69	4,908	80
Hong Kong	2,628	736	86	3,450	78
Islamabad	2,255	543	238	3,036	81
Kuala Lumpur	52	4	1	57	93
Manila	2,410	136	121	2,667	95
Seoul	466	23	21	510	95
Singapore	1,139	508	119	1,766	69
Sydney	586	38	17	641	94
Taipei	0	1	2	3	0
Tokyo	245	5	5	255	98
Europe	**6,306**	**563**	**257**	**7,126**	**92**
Ankara	920	81	61	1,062	92
Berlin	144	5	9	158	97
Bucharest	264	22	12	298	92
Kyiv	320	38	26	384	89
London	1,265	63	27	1,355	95
Moscow	465	70	24	559	87
Paris	1,843	126	42	2,011	94
Rome	272	49	9	330	85
Vienna	515	86	32	633	86
Warsaw	298	23	15	336	93
Americas	**7,214**	**1,467**	**629**	**9,310**	**83**
Bogota	321	188	31	540	63
Buenos Aires	88	21	8	117	81
Buffalo	2,419	198	207	2,824	92
Caracas	55	3	2	60	95
Guatemala City	375	146	40	561	72

Havana	819	119	38	976	87
Kingston	870	168	98	1,136	84
Lima	278	56	22	356	83
Mexico City	565	87	82	734	87
Port-au-Prince	312	178	12	502	64
Port of Spain	433	182	39	654	70
Santiago	55	6	7	68	90
Santo Domingo	450	84	38	572	84
São Paulo	174	31	5	210	85

Source: Citizenship and Immigration Canada (2012f).

Pacific, which collectively managed nearly half of overseas spousal and partner applications. Asia and the Pacific, Africa and the Middle East, and the Americas all had approval rates of 83 percent. However, closer examination shows that twelve offices in these three regions had approval rates of 90 percent or higher. This included high-volume offices such as Beijing and Manila, medium-volume Cairo, Beirut, Sydney, and Seoul, and small-volume Santiago and Caracas. Accra (58 percent), Bogota (63 percent), Port-au-Prince (64 percent), and Singapore (69 percent) had the lowest approval rates for spousal applications.

Finally, Table 6 provides data on approval rates for federal skilled worker applications since the 2008 introduction of Ministerial Instructions under Bill C-50 (Citizenship and Immigration Canada 2012f). Table 6 shows that the overseas visa office approval rate for C-50 federal skilled workers was 73 percent, twelve points below the rate for spousal applications. In contrast to their record for spousal applications, European offices collectively had the lowest approval rate (63 percent) for C-50 federal skilled workers. The approval rates of Ankara (48 percent), Warsaw (49 percent), Moscow (63 percent), and London (68 percent) were considerably below average.

Conversely, the region-wide approval rate in Africa and the Middle East was 79 percent, as was the case in Asia and the Pacific, followed closely by the Americas at 78 percent. In Africa and the Middle East, only Accra (67 percent) had an approval rate below the global average of 73 percent. In Asia and the Pacific, the approval rates of Colombo (66 percent),

TABLE 6
Approval rates for C-50 federal skilled worker applications, by overseas visa office, 2012

Office	Approved	Refused	Withdrawn	Total processed	Approval rate, excluding withdrawn and C-50 MI refused (%)
All points of service	52,639	21,392	3,375	77,406	71
Total abroad	51,999	18,914	3,256	74,169	73
Africa and Middle East	**6,108**	**1,599**	**441**	**8,148**	**79**
Abu Dhabi	0	0	1	1	0
Accra	1,501	755	28	2,284	67
Amman	0	0	0	0	0
Beirut	0	0	0	0	0
Cairo	2,186	414	50	2,650	84
Dakar	364	55	72	491	87
Damascus	18	3	18	39	86
Nairobi	907	271	195	1,373	77
Pretoria	641	70	25	736	90
Rabat	93	4	36	133	96
Tel Aviv	398	27	16	441	94
Asia and Pacific	**20,697**	**5,400**	**857**	**26,954**	**79**
Beijing-RPC[a]	1,722	194	46	1,962	90
Colombo	459	233	49	741	66
Delhi	7,975	2,462	285	10,722	76
Hong Kong	2,355	203	42	2,600	92
Islamabad	61	45	17	123	58
Kuala Lumpur	45	6	0	51	88
Manila	4,734	926	65	5,725	84
Seoul	961	192	65	1,218	83
Singapore	1,512	767	182	2,461	66
Sydney	807	372	103	1,282	68
Taipei	0	0	3	3	0
Tokyo	66	0	0	66	100

Europe	**15,943**	**9,294**	**761**	**25,998**	**63**
Ankara	732	802	40	1,574	48
Berlin	73	10	13	96	88
Bucharest	150	10	4	164	94
Kyiv	159	53	7	219	75
London	10,481	4,830	461	15,772	68
Moscow	813	485	83	1,381	63
Paris	303	26	17	346	92
Rome	120	50	14	184	71
Vienna	217	26	15	258	89
Warsaw	2,895	3,002	107	6,004	49
Americas	**9,251**	**2,621**	**1,197**	**13,069**	**78**
Bogota	126	280	38	444	31
Buenos Aires	18	3	2	23	86
Buffalo	7,325	1,820	548	9,693	80
Caracas	74	81	54	209	48
Guatemala City	207	36	349	592	85
Havana	19	2	25	46	90
Kingston	455	37	55	547	92
Lima	38	0	8	46	100
Mexico City	445	183	65	693	71
Port-au-Prince	0	38	4	42	0
Port of Spain	253	71	15	339	78
Santiago	3	0	0	3	100
Santo Domingo	40	5	2	47	89
São Paulo	248	65	32	345	79

[a] Regional Processing Centres (RPC) and some other visa offices are responsible for processing permanent resident applications for more than one country. They also oversee operations and manage the permanent resident targets of satellite offices within the region they serve.

Source: Citizenship and Immigration Canada (2012f).

Singapore (66 percent), and Sydney (68 percent) were below the average. The Islamabad office, which processes C-50 federal skilled worker applications from Afghanistan only, also had a below-average rate. In the Americas, Bogota (31 percent), Caracas (48 percent), and Mexico City

(71 percent) were below average. Port-au-Prince scored zero, but it processed only forty-two applications in 2012.

The ten offices with the highest approval rates were Tokyo (100 percent), Rabat (96 percent), Tel Aviv (94 percent), Bucharest (94 percent), Hong Kong (92 percent), Paris (92 percent), Kingston (92 percent), Havana (90 percent), Beijing (90 percent), and Pretoria (90 percent).

It is worth exploring the implications of these data. As noted in Chapter 1, some commentators have suggested that visa officers exercise their discretion in a racialized manner to favour white over non-white applicants. If this were so, permanent residence approval rates for white applicants would be higher than those for visible minorities. Unfortunately, the data to test this pattern are limited. Citizenship and Immigration does not collect statistics on the race of people who apply for a visa or who land in Canada. The department does publish statistics regarding applicants' "country of last permanent residence" but does not connect this information with approval rates.

An alternative but imperfect way to measure the racialization of discretion is to examine the outcomes of decisions by location of visa office. If a pattern of race-based bias does exist, it should reveal itself in differential approval rates at differing offices. In particular, offices in countries whose applicant pools are predominantly "non-white" should have consistently lower approval rates than offices in countries whose populations are largely "white." Considerable caution is needed in applying this approach. Race is, of course, a social construction, not a biological attribute, which means that all racial categorizations are inherently problematic (Miles and Brown 2003). Moreover, many visa offices process applications from more than one country. As a Regional Processing Centre, the office in London, England, for example, handles permanent resident applications (both economic and family class) from Britain and several northern European countries. But it also processes economic-related applications (such as federal skilled workers, Quebec skilled workers, and entrepreneurs) from Pakistan and the Gulf states. Thus, London takes in a mix of economic applications, which means that interpreting its decisions in terms of racialization is difficult.

In addition, many countries are ethnically and racially diverse, so imputing ethnic or racial origin solely by country of residence is difficult. In the past, the populations of many western European countries were predominantly "white," but today they are multi-ethnic and multi-racial. For instance, Britain, France, Holland, and Germany have substantial populations of racialized minorities, so data on decision-making outcomes by visa office cannot capture within-country differences in the race or ethnicity of applicants and whether they matter in terms of how applications are processed.

As a result, interpreting office approval rates in light of race must be done carefully. However, detailed comparisons between visa offices and visa categories suggest that approval rates do not square with an effort to keep Canada white and to stem the flow of visible minorities. As Table 5 shows, European offices had the highest average approval rate for family class spousal applications, but the two large-volume offices in Asia and the Pacific, Beijing and Manila, had approval rates that were over 90 percent and were comparable to those of Paris and London, the two-high volume European offices.

Furthermore, approval rates differed notably within regions. Beijing's approval rate of 92 percent was fourteen points higher than Hong Kong's 78 percent, yet both offices processed applications from Mainland China (the latter also takes applications from Hong Kong, Macau, and Taiwan). If the decision-making process were racialized, it is unclear why Beijing's approval rate would be so much higher than Hong Kong's, or why it was comparable to that of London and Paris. Similarly, the approval rate was relatively low in Accra, at 58 percent, but relatively high in Dakar (86 percent) and Nairobi (87 percent). Again, if the decision-making process were race-based, it is difficult to explain the nearly thirty-point discrepancy between these African offices. Nor is it clear why the Nairobi and Dakar rates were comparable to those of Kyiv, Moscow, Rome, and Vienna.

In relation to C-50 federal skilled workers, inter-office comparisons also question whether the selection process favours white applicants. The office in Sydney, Australia, had a relatively low approval rate of 68 percent, lower than every office in Africa and the Middle East (except for Accra, but only by one point). The Sydney office also processes applications from small Pacific island states, but they contribute relatively few migrants to Canada, so one can safely assume that most of its applicant pool is from Australia. Though Australia is diverse, it has historically defined itself as white, so its comparatively low approval rate seems to run counter to what might be expected if the selection process were race biased.

Similarly, Warsaw, a relatively high-volume office that also processed applications from Estonia, Latvia, Lithuania, and Belarus, had the third-lowest approval rate for C-50 federal skilled workers of all overseas visa offices. Caracas and Ankara had about the same approval rate, and only Bogota scored significantly lower. Presumably, the Warsaw applicant pool was mainly white, so the low rate would seem to suggest that whiteness was not a universal discretionary benefit. Moreover, the approval rates of the large-volume Beijing, Hong Kong, and Cairo offices were higher than those of London, Kyiv, Moscow, Rome, Ankara, and Warsaw.

As with spouses and partners, the variability in C-50 federal skilled worker approval rates within broad geographical regions also suggests that race plays less of a role in decision making than might be expected were the process racialized. Kingston, Jamaica, had an approval rate of 92 percent, compared to the Port of Spain rate of 78 percent. Though Kingston and Port of Spain differ somewhat in their respective demographic makeup, and perhaps in their applicant pools, Kingston's high approval rate suggests that its applicant pool is not necessarily disadvantaged because of race. And in South and Central America, the Bogota office had the lowest approval rate for all overseas visa offices (31 percent), whereas Guatemala City had an 85 percent approval rate. This discrepancy, which is greater than fifty points, seems unlikely to be explained by presumed racial differences in the two applicant pools.

Finally, variations in approval rates within the same office cast further doubt on the idea that the decision-making process is racialized. The Sydney, Ankara, and Warsaw offices all had relatively high approval rates for family class spousal applications (94 percent, 92 percent, and 93 percent respectively) but relatively low approval rates for C-50 federal skilled workers (68 percent, 48 percent, and 49 percent respectively). Hong Kong and Pretoria, on the other hand, had relatively high rates for the skilled workers (92 percent and 90 percent respectively) but relatively low rates for spouses and partners (78 percent and 72 percent respectively).

Organizational Cultures and Competing Goals

If visa office approval rates do not reflect a pattern of race-based bias, what are officers really looking for, and how do they go about making their decisions?

To answer these questions, it is important to understand that like all front-line bureaucrats, they must manage competing goals (Lipsky 2010, 40). At the most basic level, they must handle the demands of efficient, mass client processing while treating each individual application as unique and deserving of fair consideration. And they must do this in a manner that is consistent with departmental policies and the constraints of the organizational culture in which they work.

As noted in Chapter 3, the Immigration and Refugee Protection Act (2001) lists nineteen objectives of Canada's immigration and refugee program. These broadly defined objectives no doubt inform the approach of overseas visa officers, most of whom probably align their goal orientations with those of the immigration and refugee protection program. At the same time, each may place different emphasis on each of these goals. Moreover, most officers probably choose their profession because their own values are broadly consistent with those of the immigration program. Some see themselves as part of a critically important nation-building project in which their job is to select the good immigrants that Canada needs and to keep it safe from undesirables. Many, if not all, also hold to professional client service goals where they aim to make fair, objective decisions based on the merits of an individual's case. These goals are reinforced by the Immigration Appeals Division and the Federal Court, adjudication bodies that hear appeals of refusal decisions and that, generally speaking, consider issues of procedural fairness and reasonableness in an officer's decisions.

These goals, however, inevitably bump up against the organizationally driven goal of the efficient mass processing of applications. Michael Lipsky (2010, 44) argues that "the fundamental service dilemma of street level bureaucracies is how to provide individual responses or treatment on a mass basis." Large caseloads significantly shape the way in which decision making is organized and how discretion is socially constituted. They demand efficiency and the ability to work swiftly. They also compel organizations to monitor the productivity of those who implement policy, deliver services, and make decisions (Waegel 1981, 265). The obsession with productivity forces front-line bureaucrats to ration the amount of time they devote to specific cases and to interacting with clients. It also determines how deeply they dig into applications and what techniques they use to scrutinize some applications more than others.

By any measure, Citizenship and Immigration is a high-caseload department. There are many more people applying for permanent resident status in Canada than there are places in the annual immigration program. Before 2008, applications were processed on a first-come, first-served basis. As a result, in 2012 there was a backlog of about 600,000 applications awaiting a decision, which was down considerably from two years earlier, when the backlog was in the neighbourhood of 1 million (Kenney 2013b).

At an organizational level, the department's modernization agenda, driven by the need to do more with less, means that many features of the application process are designed to minimize interaction with applicants. Doing more with less also means that International Region invests considerable time and resources in monitoring the productivity of visa offices and officers. Citizenship and Immigration uses two mechanisms to achieve this: it specifies standard processing times for applications, and it establishes yearly targets for the number of permanent resident visas to be issued by each office. The department's website publishes the standard processing times for various types of permanent and temporary resident visas – how long the office will take to process a "normal" application. This period is measured by the processing time for 80 percent of all applications. Standard processing times vary considerably by visa office and visa category. For example, Islamabad's standard processing time for family class spouse, partner, and dependent children cases is thirty-five months, the longest of all offices. Dakar, Singapore, Guatemala City, Kingston, New York, and Los Angeles take two years or longer to process this type of application. Offices that take less than one year include Rabat, Tel Aviv, Hong Kong, Sydney, London, Paris, Warsaw, Havana, and São Paulo (Citizenship and Immigration Canada 2014p).

Applicants naturally want to know how long they will wait for a decision, so publishing standard processing times is certainly a nod to better client service. However, it also enables the department to manage expectations and to discourage applicants, as well as their lawyers, consultants, and in some cases MPs, from contacting visa offices for an update on their position in the processing queue. Fielding such queries takes time and organizational resources, and offices generally do not respond to individuals whose applications fall within the published processing time. Thus, revealing the processing period gives offices a cushion in which they can safely ignore ordinary queries from people who wish to learn how their file is progressing through the system.

But in another way, the publication of standard processing times also helps International Region hold a visa office's feet to the fire. An office that misses its deadline, particularly in temporary resident applications, can cause consternation among applicants and interested stakeholders in Canada regarding the apparent inefficiencies in the visa issuance system. Though offices counsel applicants not to book their travel arrangements until they have a visa, some people probably ignore this advice, end up missing or cancelling a flight, and then complain that their visa was not processed in time. Relatives, friends, and business colleagues in Canada are unhappy when travel arrangements go awry because a visa was not issued on time, which can prompt them to complain to their MP. The department's reputation may be tarnished if a high-profile business deal falls through or students miss their first week of classes because an office took "too long" to process visas. No doubt, the political stature of a community in Canada also plays some role here. Immigrant and ethnic communities that are politically organized often complain about visa processing and try to pressure MPs and the immigration department to put more resources into temporary resident processing to speed things along. Thus, revealing processing times is a way of encouraging public vigilance over the visa issuance process.

However, visa offices themselves also have good organizational reasons for keeping up with the processing times. If they fail to do so, queries from applicants and their MPs will increase, and replying will simply consume resources. Offices also have structural incentives for processing applications, particularly for temporary resident visas, as quickly as possible. They can predict certain seasonal variations in application volumes, and most overseas offices process large numbers of visitor visa applications during the late spring and early summer because these are peak travel times to Canada. However, what an office cannot predict is the daily volume of temporary resident applications that it receives. In a single day, a busy office such as Beijing can receive as many as a thousand visitor applications from its Visa Application Centres, and these consistently high volumes could persist for days or even weeks at a time. If a large-volume office falls behind on visitor visa processing, it can quickly dig itself into a backlog hole, which leads to more queries from applicants and MPs, and has knock-on effects for processing other visa applications.

Citizenship and Immigration's other strategy to manage productivity is to assign processing targets for each category of permanent resident visa. The targets form an essential part of the Annual Immigration Plan, which the immigration minister announces in Parliament every November. In 2014, the minister expected that between 240,000 and 265,000 permanent residents would be admitted to Canada (Citizenship and Immigration Canada 2013a). To reach this figure, the permanent resident visa categories are assigned specific targets and are then distributed to individual visa offices.

The immigration department has recently changed the way in which it defines its category and visa office targets. Before 2013, when I was conducting the fieldwork for this project, targets were defined as the number of visas that were issued. Now, however, targets are defined as the number of applications that are finalized. This change means that refused applications and those withdrawn by applicants are also included in the target. Under the previous system, the targets did not take into account that acceptance rates differed from office to office. Offices with low approval rates had to process more applications to meet their target than offices whose approval rates were higher. The new method of defining targets gives offices slightly more flexibility because the number of visas that it needs to issue in each category each year is not predetermined. At the same time, the department probably uses past rejection and withdrawal rates when it calculates the finalized targets for the upcoming year, so targets still undoubtedly contain implicit expectations regarding how many visas an office should issue every year.

Table 7 gives the overall 2014 processing targets for all categories of permanent resident visas and shows that visa offices were expected to reach final decisions regarding 328,945 applications. Due to the modernization efforts described in the previous chapter, 41,285 (or 13 percent) of the 328,945 finalized applications were to be processed in Canada. Nonetheless, most applications (287,660, or 87 percent), were to be handled by overseas offices. Table 7 also shows that overseas offices were expected to finalize 183,760 economic applications (including federal and Quebec skilled workers, various categories of business immigrants, live-in caregivers, provincial nominees, and Canadian experience class), 79,000 family class applications (including spouses, partners, and dependent children, and parents and grandparents), and 24,600 refugee applications.

These targets are in turn distributed among the now thirty-nine visa offices around the world. Table 8 provides information on the 2014 targets for economic visas at each office. It shows, for example, that London had the highest target for federal skilled worker visas: 12,500 finalized applications. Other offices with federal skilled worker targets in excess of 1,000 were Delhi (8,100), Warsaw (7,800), Manila (2,200), Singapore (2,180), Ankara (1,550), and Accra (1,400). Together, these seven offices were expected to process 35,730 (71 percent) of all federal skilled worker applications. Several offices, including Beirut, Rabat, Islamabad, Rome, Bogota, Guatemala City, Havana, Lima, Santiago, and São Paulo, have federal skilled worker targets of less than 100. The targets for other economic immigrants are also listed in Table 8.

Table 9 provides the 2014 targets for non-economic cases, which include family class and refugee applications. It shows that Delhi (6,000) had the highest target for spouses, partners, and dependent children. Other offices with spousal, partner, and dependent children targets of 1,000 or greater

TABLE 7

Permanent resident operational targets, applications finalized, 2014

Immigration category	In-Canada applications finalized	Overseas applications finalized	Total applications finalized
TOTAL ECONOMIC	16,715	183,760	200,475
Federal skilled workers	–	50,000	50,000
Quebec skilled workers	–	29,000	29,000
Federal business	–	12,400	12,400
Quebec business	–	6,300	6,300
Live-in-Caregiver Program	16,715	6,060	22,775
Provincial Nominee Program	–	55,000	55,000
Canadian experience class	–	25,000	25,000
TOTAL NON-ECONOMIC	24,570	103,900	128,470
Spouses, partners, and children	9,710	53,800	63,510
Parents and grandparents	–	25,200	25,200
Total family	**9,710**	**79,000**	**88,710**
Government-assisted refugees	–	8,300	8,300
Privately sponsored refugees	–	10,500	10,500
Visa-office referred refugees	–	600	600
Protected persons landed in Canada	8,000	–	8,000
Dependants abroad of protected persons	–	5,200	5,200
Total refugee	**8,000**	**24,600**	**32,600**
Humanitarian and compassionate	6,800	–	6,800
Public policy	–	300	300
Permit-holders	60	–	60
Total others	**6,860**	**300**	**7,160**
GRAND TOTAL	41,285	287,660	328,945

Note: The "total applications finalized" column includes all positive final decisions, all negative decisions at all stages, and all withdrawn applications.

Source: Citizenship and Immigration Canada (2014j).

TABLE 8

Permanent resident overseas operational targets by office, economic applications finalized, 2014

	Economic							
	Quebec skilled workers	Quebec business	Provincial nominees	Live-in caregivers (dependants abroad)	Canadian experience class	Federal business	Federal skilled workers	Total economic target
Africa and Middle East								
Abu Dhabi	275	400	800	58	–	–	–	1,533
Accra-RPC[a]	236	30	800	3	–	150	1,400	2,619
Amman	–	–	150	–	8	–	110	268
Ankara-RPC[a]	600	1,000	200	–	–	550	1,550	3,900
Beirut	400	125	75	–	–	–	34	634
Cairo	250	125	150	–	–	300	200	1,025
Dakar	2,378	88	27	8	–	12	126	2,639
Nairobi	650	30	180	15	2	125	171	1,173
Pretoria	30	15	93	2	–	25	134	299
Rabat	1,350	20	6	4	–	5	5	1,390
Tel Aviv	200	4	900	2	–	20	114	1,240
Asia and Pacific								
Beijing-RPC[a]	50	14	40	150	–	3	695	952
Colombo	–	–	900	10	–	2	103	1,015

Delhi-RPC[a]	200	400	5,000	30	–	450	8,100	14,180
Hong Kong	650	3,000	2,000	2,000	–	5,575	250	13,475
Islamabad	4	17	19	4	–	21	80	145
Manila	190	80	9,625	3,550	–	300	2,200	15,945
Singapore-RPC[a]	75	130	1,000	43	–	300	2,180	3,728
Sydney, Australia	10	8	350	1	–	46	355	770
Europe								
Bucharest	1,800	5	850	2	–	30	36	2,723
Kyiv	300	20	750	18	–	60	90	1,238
London-RPC[a]	350	350	2,575	2	–	850	12,500	16,627
Moscow	334	150	500	10	–	350	594	1,938
Paris-RPC[a]	9,400	100	350	6	–	57	506	10,419
Rome	300	11	150	14	–	61	33	569
Vienna-RPC[a]	85	6	300	5	–	50	500	946
Warsaw	15	3	450	3	–	2	7,800	8,273
Americas								
Bogota	20	–	20	10	–	4	37	91
Buenos Aires	20	–	15	–	–	–	–	35
Guatemala City	–	6	3	–	–	58	5	72
Havana	229	2	15	–	–	–	27	273
Kingston	8	2	59	36	–	20	468	593

▸

◂ **TABLE 8**

	Economic							
	Quebec skilled workers	Quebec business	Provincial nominees	Live-in caregivers (dependants abroad)	Canadian experience class	Federal business	Federal skilled workers	Total economic target
Lima	40	10	10	10	–	12	2	84
Mexico City	3,340	80	380	7	–	395	300	4,502
Port-au-Prince	139	–	–	7	–	–	–	146
Port of Spain	9	20	37	6	–	123	214	409
Santiago	26	–	5	–	–	–	3	34
Santo Domingo	40	–	10	–	–	9	47	106
São Paulo	700	9	40	6	–	115	35	905
US offices	83	11	354	71	90	31	399	1,039
Centralized Processing Region	**7,000**	**30**	**25,800**	–	**25,000**	**150**	**8,600**	**66,580**
Overseas allocated targets	**29,000**	**6,300**	**55,000**	**6,060**	**25,000**	**12,400**	**50,000**	**183,760**

[a] Regional Processing Centres (RPC) and some other visa offices process permanent resident applications for more than one country. They also oversee operations and manage the permanent resident targets of satellite offices within the region they serve.

Note: The "total applications finalized" column includes all positive final decisions, all negative decisions at all stages, and all withdrawn applications (in persons).

Source: Citizenship and Immigration Canada (2014k).

TABLE 9

Permanent resident overseas operational targets by office, non-economic applications finalized, 2014

	Non-economic								
	Spouses, partners, and children	Parents and grandparents	Dependants abroad of protected persons	Government-assisted refugees (other than Quebec)	Government-assisted refugees (Quebec)	Visa-office-referred refugees	Privately sponsored refugees	Public policy	Total non-economic target
Africa and Middle East									
Abu Dhabi	550	120	43	91	–	–	199	–	1,003
Accra-RPC[a]	1,500	100	277	135	32	–	165	–	2,209
Amman	600	100	100	463	–	80	515	–	1,858
Ankara-RPC[a]	1,100	750	166	1,510	82	80	155	–	3,843
Beirut	750	300	50	990	20	54	1,375	–	3,539
Cairo	950	125	104	345	–	60	1,065	–	2,649
Dakar	1,500	100	281	170	360	–	16	–	2,427
Nairobi	2,200	346	1,075	1,555	680	250	3,225	–	9,331
Pretoria	130	57	183	–	315	–	909	–	1,594
Rabat	1,000	175	–	–	20	–	–	–	1,195
Tel Aviv	200	150	21	10	–	–	65	–	446

▸

◂ **TABLE 9**

	Non-economic								
	Spouses, partners, and children	Parents and grandparents	Dependants abroad of protected persons	Government-assisted refugees (other than Quebec)	Government-assisted refugees (Quebec)	Visa-office-referred refugees	Privately sponsored refugees	Public policy	Total non-economic target
Asia and Pacific									
Beijing-RPC[a]	2,000	500	149	8	–	–	3	–	2,660
Colombo	850	700	188	72	–	–	10	–	1,820
Delhi-RPC[a]	6,000	5,200	500	62	–	–	120		
Hong Kong	2,000	750	122	15	–	–	5	–	2,892
Islamabad	377	524	139	33	–	–	1,320	–	2,393
Manila	4,500	1,550	16	4	–	–	41	–	6,111
Singapore-RPC[a]	3,000	850	30	990	83	26	484		5,463
Sydney, Australia	1,000	150	4	–	–	–	–	–	1,154
Europe									
Bucharest	400	250	29	–	–	–	3	–	682
Kyiv	500	152	38	15	4	–	10	–	719

London-RPC[a]	4,000	390	390	6	–	–	32	–	4,818
Moscow	650	290	54	140	15	–	590	–	1,739
Paris-RPC[a]	1,800	260	19	5	5	–	30	–	2,119
Rome	300	160	36	–	–	–	60	–	556
Vienna-RPC[a]	1,000	100	20	10	–	–	10	–	1,140
Warsaw	150	50	10	5	–	–	–	–	215
Americas									
Bogota	400	50	128	–	300	50	59	–	987
Buenos Aires	125	57	1	–	–	–	–	–	183
Guatemala City	86	25	28	–	–	–	–	–	139
Havana	400	29	31	15	–	–	–	–	475
Kingston	2,000	150	45	26	–	–	–	–	2,221
Lima	202	209	12	–	–	–	–	–	423
Mexico City	1,900	570	300	4	–	–	5	–	2,779
Port-au-Prince	830	163	263	–	–	–	–	–	1,256

◂ **TABLE 9**

	Non-economic								
	Spouses, partners, and children	Parents and grandparents	Dependants abroad of protected persons	Government-assisted refugees (other than Quebec)	Government-assisted refugees (Quebec)	Visa-office-referred refugees	Privately sponsored refugees	Public policy	Total non-economic target
Port of Spain	1,100	350	125	–	–	–	–	–	1,575
Santiago	140	13	7	–	–	–	1	–	161
Santo Domingo	500	30	25	4	–	–	–	–	559
São Paulo	330	55	1	–	–	–	–	–	386
US offices	590	96	191	–	–	–	2	–	879
Centralized Processing Region	**6,500**	**9,250**	–	–	–	–	–	–	**15,750**
Overseas allocated targets	**53,800**	**25,200**	**5,200**	**6,460**	**1,840**	**600**	**10,500**	**300**	**103,900**

[a] Regional Processing Centres (RPC) and some other visa offices process permanent resident applications for more than one country. They also oversee operations and manage the permanent resident operational targets of satellite offices within the region they serve.

Note: The "total applications finalized" column includes all positive final decisions, all negative decisions at all stages, and all withdrawn applications (in persons).

Source: Citizenship and Immigration Canada (2014l).

were Manila (4,500), London (4,000), Singapore (3,000), Nairobi (2,200), Beijing, Hong Kong, and Kingston (2,000 each), Mexico City (1,900), Paris (1,800), Dakar and Accra (1,500 each), Port of Spain and Ankara (1,100 each), and Rabat, Sydney, and Vienna (1,000 each). These seventeen offices were expected to process 37,600, or 70 percent, of all spousal, partner, and dependent children applications.

Table 9 also shows that only a few offices process refugee applications. Nairobi, Ankara, Beirut, Cairo, Pretoria, Islamabad, and Singapore do the bulk of refugee processing and are collectively expected to tackle 15,606 applications, or 62 percent of all overseas refugee applications. Other visa office and category non-economic targets are also listed in Table 9.

Though they are meant to set productivity expectations for visa offices and officers, the targets also have consequences for the decision-making process for permanent resident applications. As one immigration program manager remarked during our interview, "the target is king" for International Region.[1] Indeed, the auditor general of Canada noted that the department's "performance, among others, is measured by its success in achieving the annual target immigration levels" (Auditor General of Canada 2009, 9). To some extent, the reputation of the department and the minister depends on how closely offices meet their targets. A deputy program manager explained how this works in practice: "International Region has to go in front of the deputy minister if it has not met its targets. Like any production line, if you can't do it, you have to have a reason."[2] Not meeting the target also makes the program and unit managers look bad, and will form part of the departmental assessment of how well both are performing. As another deputy manager commented, "If we don't meet our targets, then it is regarded as bad management. Then it is represented in our appraisals all the way down the line. If you are over- or undershooting on your targets, it is bad management. You should never let that happen."[3] As another immigration program manager explained, a guiding principle in immigration is "you don't want to embarrass the minister."[4]

Failing to meet a target means that another office will be asked to make an unexpected last-minute adjustment to its own target and perhaps scramble to issue more visas at the end of the year. Dealing with this situation became easier when the Global Case Management System database was introduced in 2011, because it enables offices to process files originally earmarked for another office. Nonetheless, last-minute adjustments and negotiations undoubtedly become a point of embarrassment and of friendly and not-so-friendly mockery among program managers about how well they run their offices.

International Region monitors decision making at its overseas visa offices to ensure that they are on track to meet their targets. As the director general of International Region wryly commented after authorizing me to do the research for this project, "Now you will see how the offices have to dance to ... [my] targets."[5] At the time, I did not appreciate the full significance of his words, but by the end of my first site visit, I had learned that dancing to targets was a major preoccupation in overseas offices. As a deputy manager explained,

> We have become number freaks. We have to meet our targets, within +/– 3 percent. But you don't want to exceed your target either. If you reach your processing target by September, you can't issue any more visas, and that is a problem. And if you go over your target ... they will say next time you can process the target numbers with fewer resources, or increase the targets.[6]

Pressure to meet targets trickles down to the visa officer level. Officers are expected to make decisions that conform to Canadian law, and to make them quickly. Indeed, as noted in Chapter 4, from a program manager's perspective, a good officer is one who can make decisions quickly. Depending on the style of program and unit managers, individual officers are assigned specific visa issuance targets. In smaller offices, the expectations surrounding targets are more informal, but the program manager and officers always keep targets in mind. One of my site visits occurred during December, and the program manager explained that she was reluctant to have me come at that time because the staff were busy trying to meet their targets, and she was concerned that my presence would slow them down. On two occasions, the program manager implored officers and locally engaged staff to keep processing files while I interviewed them.[7] In another office, a designated immigration officer explained that she had a "constant three hundred bring forward" cases in her name, which meant that she was juggling three hundred cases at a time, and that as soon as she cleared one case with a final decision, another was added to her pile.[8] In a large-volume office, the program manager said that though his officers did not have specific targets, he nonetheless had to "keep an eye" on overall productivity and watch for variations between officers:

> Some are more efficient than others. Some are more risk averse, and so they take more time. But you have to keep an eye. If someone issues two thousand visas and the rest of the staff are issuing about nine hundred, you have

> to wonder about whether that person is really doing their job and being too lenient. On the other hand, the person who only issues four hundred visas is also a concern. We can't have people agonizing over decisions. So, numbers rule us.[9]

One consequence of the pressure to meet targets is that visa offices and officers limit their direct contact with applicants and reduce the number of interviews with them. Interviews slow the decision-making process, so International Region encourages officers to "waive interviews whenever possible" (Citizenship and Immigration Canada 2011c, 40). As a result, they are used sparingly and only if an officer has concerns about the credibility of an application or if the risks of making a wrong decision are high.

The fact that officers conduct interviews only in problematic cases may negatively affect their attitude to their applicant pool. In a rather frank discussion about how time pressures had slowly been ratcheted up, and how application processing had changed since the introduction of the Immigration and Refugee Protection Act, a program manager lamented,

> There are so many things we miss. We only interview if we are leaning towards a refusal. We don't interview good applicants. This can make an officer sour. We don't get the sense of nation building that we used to have. It cuts into job satisfaction. There is no way of talking to clients, we don't counsel them any more. In face-to-face circumstances, we are only dealing with likely refusals. This can lead to the development of a negative mindset. You start the whole interview process with a set of concerns that you have identified on the basis of the paper screening. The old way, you could come in having a visa, and in the interview you could talk yourself out of it! Young officers have not done that kind of interview. They tend to have an enforcement mentality. The system is set up to kind of sour your worldview.[10]

A Canada based-officer thoughtfully described the long-term implications of not interviewing applicants:

> In family class processing, it is very hard not to become cynical. When all you interview are the problematic cases, that influences your view of the applicants. It's easy to say they are all bad, and what happens is that you start refusing for all of the wrong reasons. But the positive side effect of the quality assurance is that you get to see the good cases and the bad cases. When you bring someone in for an interview, you can tell right away, you

> get a gut feeling that there is something wrong here, or that it's good. At the end of the day, you have to ask yourself whether you would want this person to be your neighbour. It's hard to put a finger on it but when you strongly feel that there is something about an applicant, there usually is. The positive thing about the quality assurance is that it helps an officer get around the idea that "everyone's a liar" attitude. It's easy to become cynical. You become immune to the hardship of local conditions.[11]

Though quality assurance exercises help reintroduce a sense of balance into decision making, it is easy to see how the lack of face-to-face interaction can colour the worldview of visa officers.

This negative dynamic is counterbalanced by the fact that officers must generally work harder to refuse an application than to approve it. Interviews take time away from processing other files, and since officers know that their decisions can be appealed, they may devote extra time to refusals, which can be reviewed by a Federal Court judge or an Immigration Appeal Division adjudicator. Thus, the notes that officers create and enter into the database are arguably more thorough, involved, and detailed for refusals than for approvals. Because they must work harder to refuse an application, one could suggest that this tends to favour applicants. Citing the potential of an appeal and the general tone of an office, a Canada-based officer elaborated: "Sometimes I ask myself if it is worth the trouble to refuse, because I know it will be appealed, and they will probably win. Sometimes, the department wants us to make a decision a certain way. Sometimes it's not worth the trouble to say no."[12]

Though somewhat reluctant to talk about how target-driven time pressures affected their own decision making, several officers did discuss more abstractly how they could influence elements of an overall selection decision. A Canada-based officer explained that "the targets generally work to the advantage of the client. If we didn't have the demands that are on us, the refusal rate would be much higher. If I had enough time, I would at least triple my refusal rate."[13] Another Canada-based officer said much the same thing: "In some cases, you are 'feeding the target beast.' The big buzzword is 'risk management.' You just can't take the time to verify every document. Sometimes you have to overlook things to get the program numbers. That is why quality assurance exercises are very important. Risk management means closing your eyes."[14]

A third Canada-based officer argued that the pressure to meet targets could affect approvals but did not believe that targets influenced inadmissibility decisions:

> I could see how pressure to meet the target might tip a decision in someone's favour. You have to work a lot harder to say no, and if someone is under pressure of time, they might make a selection decision that might give an applicant the benefit of the doubt. I could see that, but not on an admissibility issue. If there is criminality or medical grounds, I can't see that.[15]

It is important to tease out the implications of the demand to meet targets. From an organizational point of view, officers have little incentive to go out of their way to look for reasons to reject an application because doing so will take more time, and they know that their decision will probably be appealed. Further, under the pre-2013 dispensation, when operational targets were defined as the number of visas issued, not the number processed, racially biased officers would have had to process more applications than their colleagues did to find the "good" cases that deserved a visa. If they systematically rejected more applications due to racist bias, they would tend to issue fewer visas than their colleagues and would have a harder time meeting their target. This would inevitably attract the attention of the program manager and result in a review of how they made their decisions. It is hard to see how a racist immigration officer could survive in a context where the pressure is on to issue visas and to issue them quickly.

The Racialization of Bias?

Though commentators still believe that visa officers have racialized understandings of credibility and risk, and that these work to disadvantage racialized groups in the application process, there is a need for a more nuanced and sophisticated understanding of both officer discretion and the nature of bias in the Canadian immigration system along the lines suggested by Alan Simmons (2010) and which was discussed in Chapter 1. He argues that though Canadian policy does not directly select immigrants on the basis of their national, ethnic, or racial origin, the selection criteria used within the policy do influence immigrant flows to Canada.

It is clear that, for differing categories of visa, and for visa offices, approval rates vary. Though the pattern of approvals discussed above is not conclusive, it does not suggest that decisions are grounded in a racist bias. Visa officers may indeed bring their own prejudices to their thinking about credibility and risk, and it is certainly possible that these do inform some aspects of their decisions. At the same time, however, discretion is more than an individual attribute. As the literature on street-level bureaucracy shows

(Lipsky 2010), organizational culture and contextual factors shape how discretionary decisions are made. Focusing on the social constitution of discretion reveals that though productivity goals do not necessarily trump the other goals of visa officers, they do affect how they make decisions. The need to meet a target is unlikely to result in the issuance of a permanent resident visa to an obviously undeserving applicant. However, in ambiguous cases, it may help produce a positive decision, particularly if it comes at the end of the year when pressure to meet a target is greatest. At the same time, the pressure to be efficient undoubtedly shapes how intensely officers scrutinize some applications and not others. Visa offices and officers must ration how much time they spend on an application. As a result, they use various mechanisms and broader understandings of the macro-level forces that shape migration to frame applications as credible or not credible.

6

Spousal and Partner Sponsorships

> *In immigration, we kind of have this joke: you can marry for love, you can marry for sex, you can marry for money, but you can't marry for immigration.* (Field notes, December 14, 2010)

In March 2012, the federal government introduced the notion of "conditional status" as a disincentive for individuals who seek to gain permanent residency in Canada by entering into a "marriage of convenience." Under the new regulations, they must live with their sponsor for two years or face the possibility that their permanent resident status will be revoked. In addition, if they wish to sponsor a new spouse, they must wait for five years after the date that they became a permanent resident (Citizenship and Immigration Canada 2012e). The victims of what Ottawa sees as marriage fraud are the naive and unsuspecting Canadian sponsors who are hoodwinked by foreign nationals into entering into relationships that will end as soon as they arrive in the country (Aulakh 2010). But Ottawa also sees Canadian society and its "generous" immigration system as victims. In introducing these measures, then immigration minister Jason Kenney explained that "Canadians are generous and welcoming, but they have no tolerance for fraudsters who lie and cheat to jump the queue ... This measure will help strengthen the integrity of our immigration system and prevent the victimization of innocent Canadians" (ibid.).

Citizenship and Immigration's overseas visa officers constitute a longer-standing bulwark in the efforts to curb the entry of individuals who are involved in sham marriages. As they decide whether to issue a spousal or partner visa, officers must assess whether a relationship is genuine, or real, and whether its primary purpose is immigration. If the officer concludes that it is not genuine, or that its primary purpose is to secure immigration status for an applicant, he or she has the authority to refuse the application.

Canada is not alone in its concern over marriages of convenience, or "marriage migration." Many other in-migration countries attempt to uncover false marriages and thus to prevent fraudsters from securing a permanent resident visa. These efforts generally involve intrusive investigative regimes in which the everyday details of courtship, relationship development, and family life are subject to scrutiny (Abrams 2007; Bhabha and Shutter 1994; Digruber and Messinger 2006; Eggebø 2013a, 2013b; Webber 2012; Foblets and Vanheule 2006; Khoo 2001; Europa 2013). Whether they are police officers, civil registration authorities, or overseas visa officers, the state agents who conduct investigations and form judgments about relationships use various combinations of flags and indictors to sort through individual cases and decide to dig deeper into some applications as opposed to others.

Digging Deeper

Though treating each application on its own merits is both a legal requirement and an ideal to which most, if not all, visa officers aspire, the demand to process files quickly means that this goal cannot be achieved by spending equal time on all applications. Officers cannot afford to approach every application as a blank slate. Nor can they question every aspect of every applicant's background. The tension between the desire to provide good client service and the need for speed necessarily prompts officers to budget their time, to take shortcuts in evaluating credibility, risk, and an applicant's eligibility for a visa.

The literature on discretion recognizes that "non-actions" are just as important as "actions" when it comes to understanding decision making (Heyman 2009; Keith Hawkins 2002). Actions and non-actions relate to what Norbert Cyrus and Dita Vogel (2003) term "the intensity of investigations," or what visa officers refer to as "digging deeper." Visa offices and officers develop ways to triage applications that allow them to simplify the world and informally map individual cases into deserving and undeserving categories, and to differentiate between credible and non-credible and low- and high-risk applications. The mapping process leads them to look more closely at some applications rather than others.

This decision is not made at random and is shaped by forces at the macro and micro levels – an officer's understanding of the larger macro-level conditions that prompt people to move to Canada and his or her micro-level perception of what a normal application looks like. Officers have general, quasi-sociological understandings of why people move and how global inequalities, push forces, and visa regimes in Canada and abroad form their decisions. They also recognize the patterns of fraud in their region of operation. Their perception of the macro forces leads them to view some applicants as more desperate than others to emigrate. In turn, this helps them define individuals from some countries or regions as more likely to engage in fraud to secure permanent residence in Canada, including entering into a fake relationship with a Canadian.

Officers' micro-level understandings of normality also enable them to differentiate between applicants. From their point of view, normal cases come in certain types and have certain common features. These typifications of normality are like measuring rods against which individual applications are assessed (Waegel 1981); they allow officers to transform and map complex cases into credible/non-credible categories. A deviation from the norm will not automatically result in a visa refusal, but it does encourage officers to probe further. Upon doing so, they may discover that their reservations were justified and will thus refuse the visa; or they may be satisfied that the application is genuine and will therefore approve it. Conversely, adherence to the norm does not automatically lead to an approval, but in the absence of conflicting evidence, the more an application conforms to perceived norms, the greater its chances of success.

Typifications of normality are, however, inherently problematic for officers. Unlike other street-level bureaucrats who function in relatively homogeneous cultural and socio-political contexts, they deal with applicants from all quarters of the globe and from places where the religious and cultural norms, expectations, and behaviours depart significantly from those of Canada (Juss 1997). As any first-year sociology or anthropology student knows, what is normal in one cultural context can seem abnormal or odd elsewhere. As a result, visa officers consider normality in light of three frameworks: Canadian cultural standards, universally applicable human standards, and the standards of the applicant's country, region, or culture. They must sift through and take into account these competing standards of normality.

This approach to understanding the social constitution of discretion builds on that of Robert Baldwin and Keith Hawkins (1984, 581), who view decision making as "complex, subtle and woven into a broader process." Though they are analytically distinct, officers' macro- and micro-level understandings of applicants and their circumstances are invoked simultaneously and shape how they map individual applications into deserving and undeserving categories. Definitions of normality and understandings of how structural contexts influence migration are best conceived as part of the social context within which officers make decisions. But in recognizing the importance of context for the decision-making process, Robert Emerson and Blair Paley (2001, 232) argue that it is not an objective and fixed entity that stands outside of discretionary decisions and directly determines their nature. In other words, views of normality and wider understandings of migration are not contextual factors that "cause" visa officers to make one kind of decision over another. Instead, context is better understood as interactionally and situationally emergent. As Emerson and Paley (ibid.) put it, context is "the processes whereby particular traits are invoked or made relevant to specific decisions." Thus, when officers make their decisions, macro- and micro-level factors are not used as checkbox, categorical variables but instead to work up the definition of some applications as credible and others as not credible.

The Family Class Spousal Application Process

Anyone who applies for a permanent resident visa for a spouse or partner who lives outside of Canada embarks on a complicated process. Citizens and permanent residents must first submit their application to the Case Processing Centre in Mississauga. The centre conducts an initial assessment to determine whether the sponsorship eligibility criteria are met. Individuals cannot be sponsors if they cannot financially support a spouse, have been convicted of certain types of sexual or violent crime, or failed to honour a past sponsorship agreement (Citizenship and Immigration Canada 2014r). After the initial assessment, the file is transferred to an overseas visa office where the applicant's spouse or partner must submit a completed application form and questionnaire. He or she must fill out a six-page "Sponsored Spouse/Partner Questionnaire," which solicits detailed information about the couple's relationship (Citizenship and Immigration Canada 2012d). It asks when and where the couple met, if they were introduced by a third party, whether gifts were exchanged, how they communicate, whether friends or family are aware of their relationship, and what ceremonies and receptions formalized and celebrated their marriage.

A key part of the questionnaire focuses on "the development of the relationship." The question reads, "Describe how your relationship developed after your first contact/meeting with your sponsor and if you and your sponsor dated or went on any outings or trips together" (ibid., question 9). Couples are encouraged to submit a variety of documents, including photographs, letters, emails, web chat logs, telephone bills, bank statements, insurance policies, wills, school certificates, and anything else that might support their story.

An officer can issue a visa solely on the basis of the paper application, the written answers to the questionnaire, and the supporting documents. However, if the officer is leaning toward a refusal, the spouse must be given an opportunity to address his or her concerns. The officer can send a "concerns letter" to the spouse, asking for additional information and/or clarification of certain aspects of the application. If the response "satisfies" the officer, the visa will be issued. If it does not, the spouse can be called in for an interview, during which he or she has the chance once again to address the officer's doubts. If the sponsor cannot travel overseas, only the spouse will be interviewed. If the sponsor can attend, both can be interviewed, either separately or together. Interviews normally last about an hour, though some that I observed were almost two hours long.

Chapter 9 discusses the interview dynamics and how the answers to questions, as well as demeanour and body language, provide additional information that officers use to assess credibility. After the interview, the officer either accepts or rejects the application. A refusal can be appealed to the Immigration Appeal Division of the Immigration and Refugee Board.

The standard of proof used by officers is based on the balance of probabilities, which, as already noted, is an inherently discretionary threshold. As a designated immigration officer explained,

> My decision is based on a balance of probabilities. That is the key word – the balance of probabilities. That is how I interpret the law. I have the docs, and whatever is on the table, if there is a 51 percent chance that they are telling me the truth then I will give the ... doubt in favour of the applicant.[1]

Another officer claimed that in his region, "immigration always plays *some* role in the reasons for the marriage. My job is to determine whether it was *primarily* for immigration."[2]

In this context, officers who differentiate between deserving and undeserving applicants engage in a complex process of risk management. Though they are motivated by the general goal of maintaining the immigration system's integrity, in spousal sponsorship cases risk applies to the long-term consequences of making a wrong decision. Emerson and Paley (2001, 234) refer to the trajectory and consequences of a decision as a "decision-making horizon." In this case, officers issue or deny a visa on the basis of the available information, but their choice is also conditioned by their understanding of how a wrong decision will play itself out for the couple, for themselves, and for Canadian society.

In theory, officers can make two kinds of mistakes in spousal sponsorship cases. First, they can reject a couple whose relationship is genuine. This error will greatly delay the couple's reunification in Canada, but officers are relatively untroubled by it, in part because it can be appealed (Kingwell 2008). When they work with family class spousal and partner cases, they typically keep the possibility of an appeal in mind. Since they know that couples have another opportunity to make their case, and that appeals often succeed, they tend not to worry about denying a visa to people whose relationship could be genuine. Moreover, since they see appeals as inevitable regardless of the merits of the case, and since at least some believe that the appeal process favours applicants, an appeal is not necessarily taken as proof of faulty decision making.

They can also make the mistake of admitting someone whose relationship with a sponsor is not genuine or who has entered into it primarily for the purpose of immigration. This type of error risks harming both the Canadian sponsor who is being cheated by someone overseas and Canadian society in general. In reviewing a family class application, one Canada-based officer remarked that though she wished there were more photographs to document the development of the relationship and was still not entirely convinced that it was real, she had nonetheless decided to issue the visa because doing so posed little threat to Canadian society or the wider objectives of the immigration program:

> I would like to see more pictures but you know, this looks real. I am going to accept the application. Even if the marriage is not genuine, or it falls apart after a few years, the mother and her daughter are going to be assets to Canadian society. They are not going to do bad things. You can just tell that Canadian society will benefit from their presence. So that makes me even more comfortable with the decision.[3]

Enforcement-minded officers define "harm" to Canadian society somewhat more broadly. For them, maintaining the integrity of the immigration system is a priority, and it is undermined by wrong decisions in which cheats are rewarded and would-be migrants are simply encouraged to copy their deceitfulness.

Invoking Macro Contexts

Visa officers must make a discretionary choice to dig deeper into applications. Non-action, or refraining from closer scrutiny, is structured at the macro level and is informed by an officer's understanding of the broader relationship between socio-economic development and migration, and by an understanding of the socio-legal contexts within which applicant biographies are formed. Conversely, action, or digging deeper, is structured by their understandings of patterns of fraud in their country or region of operation.

Migration Opportunities and Development

Visa officers' initial mapping of spousal relationships as genuine or non-genuine is guided by their understanding of the broader migration opportunities that are available to applicants. In turn, these opportunities are seen as conditioned by the visa regimes of Canada and other countries, and by patterns of global inequality.

Though the visitor visa and the spousal visa are distinct migration streams, there is an indirect relationship between the two when it comes to their processing. As Chapter 8 discusses in more detail, some visitors to Canada must obtain a visa before they arrive, whereas others do not. In countries whose nationals do not need a visa to visit Canada, officers perceive little incentive for an individual to enter into a false marriage. As one Canada-based officer said,

> When I was in Korea, there was no visitor visa requirement. A Korean could just get on a plane and come to Canada. As a result, there were no marriages of convenience. There was no need for Koreans to enter into a marriage of convenience because if they wanted to get to Canada, they could just jump on a plane.[4]

At the same time, officers also consider global visa regimes as they decide whether to probe more deeply into a file. Specifically, visa policies of other countries, and the extent to which nationals can legally migrate elsewhere, shape how fully Canadian visa officers scrutinize certain relationships. For example, the Philippines is well known as a major source of global migrants

(Castles and Miller 2003). Since Filipinos can legally leave and return to the Philippines with relative ease, Canadian visa officers believe that they experience little pressure to enter into a fake relationship as a way of reaching Canada: "Marriage of convenience cases are very rare here. I've seen maybe ten or fifteen cases in the whole time I have been here. Part of the reason for that is that there are other avenues for Filipinos to work abroad. This reduces the pressure to enter into a marriage of convenience in order to get into Canada."[5]

As migration scholars have observed, the more rules a country has to regulate immigration, the more irregular immigration it will have (Heyman 1998; Castles and Miller 2003). For visa officers, the flip side of this principle is that individuals who have many opportunities to move and work abroad because they face relatively favourable global visa regimes have little incentive to risk engaging in fraud to circumvent the immigration rules of specific countries.

The other way that the macro-level context influences the choice to dig deeper stems from an officer's understanding of the relationship between socio-economic development and migration. Officers tend not to look for marriages of convenience when the sponsored spouse is from a wealthy country. Countries whose levels of socio-economic development resemble those of Canada are seen as having fewer push factors (see Boehmer and Peña 2012), so officers perceive their nationals as less in need of resorting to sham marriages as a way of getting into Canada. Referring to the spousal migration of Americans, a designated immigration officer stated,

> I only interview a small percentage of US citizens who marry a Canadian. I figure that if you are an American living in the US there is not much incentive for you to get involved in a marriage of convenience. You have a pretty good life ... and access to all kinds of services, so there is not that big a difference between the two countries. American-Canadian relationships are not really worth interviewing.[6]

Conversely, push factors are identified as stronger in countries whose socio-economic development is significantly lower than in Canada, which in turn results in more intensive investigations across the board in some offices. In an African office, a designated immigration officer explained, "We didn't used to interview everybody. Now we do. If the docs looked okay, you could waive the interview. Now, if a file comes in, with FC1 [spousal sponsorship] cases, we schedule an interview when the application comes in for five or six weeks away."[7]

The understandings of the link between socio-economic development and migration clearly result in a set of assumptions regarding which marriages are real and which are not. Moreover, nationals who can easily travel from country to country are further advantaged because they are assumed to have little reason to enter into a false relationship to get into Canada.

Client Behaviours: Fraud

The exercise of discretion also takes client behaviour into account (Lipsky 2010). Fraud is a significant form of behaviour that helps determine how officers approach certain kinds of applications. Of course, not all applicants commit fraud, but it is plentiful enough to affect the wider circle of applicants in particular application streams.

In several visa offices, and without any prompting from me, nearly every officer whom I interviewed immediately mentioned that "we have a lot of fraud here." Some was purely individual in nature: applicants may lie about their marital status, the existence of dependent children, or the biological parentage of children, or they may simply embellish certain aspects of their biography. Other types of fraud are organized and systematic, and they take various forms. Some arise from immigration lawyers and consultants who counsel their clients to invent stories about their relationship to satisfy the expectations of a visa officer. As one officer suggested, "In some cases, people have sold everything they own only to pay for a crooked agent, who cheats them out of their money by promising them something he cannot provide. People here often get cheated by agents."[8]

Fraud also ranges from the manufacture, sale, and submission of bogus documents to the staging of entire wedding ceremonies. A case that has become legendary in Canadian immigration circles was a 2008 "rent-a-guest" scheme in India where an entrepreneur organized sham weddings and receptions to convince Canadian visa officers that a real wedding had taken place (Keung 2008). In one office, a program assistant proudly showed me her "fake box," a large storage container full of dozens of fraudulent documents (bank statements, tax forms, educational certificates, and the like) that she had culled from previous applications and now used to train staff members in fraud detection.[9]

How an individual officer looks for fraud is complex and is tied to past experience. One Canada-based officer remarked, "I am not forgiving about fraud," and linked this to his experience at an early posting where, as he put it, fraud "was everywhere."[10] It is also connected to the understanding of trends and conditions in various countries, and certain specific traditions and patterns of fraud, but also to regional and visa category forms of fraud.

A deputy manager noted, "You develop a trend profile. You develop a trend in what to look for in fraud. You always rely on locals, local staff. That's where the expertise is. You need to develop local knowledge."[11] Overall socio-economic conditions also shape broad understandings of the likelihood of fraud: "There are instances of fraud here. People here are desperate to leave."[12] At the same time, the desperation to leave is not unique to just one country, so patterns and forms of fraud vary from country to country. As a Canada-based officer explained, "You have to adjust to the environment. There is more profiling in countries where there is a lot of fraud or misrepresentation."[13]

Visa officers are also alert to within-country variations. Fraud may be evident in some migration streams but not in others. As a Canada-based officer pointed out with respect to marriages of convenience at his posting, "We take a hand's off approach to marriage. Here it is okay to focus on fraud in educational documents, but not really with marriage. Here, they can fake some things, but not marriages."[14]

Though cautious about using the word "profiling" because of its relation to racism and policing in Canada (see Satzewich and Shaffir 2009), officers nonetheless relied on past experience and past patterns of fraud to apply extra scrutiny in some applications: "There are certain profiles you just know."[15] An officer explained,

> The profile of the individual applying is important. Which part of the country they are living. You get certain profiles for different regions. A profile, it's not a bias, but it is based on your experience. If you see a file from a certain place, you know what to expect. In family class, for example, you know that fraudulent marriages in south India are much lower than in the Punjab and Gujarat. So the profile helps to triage the files so you are not really approaching them like a blank.[16]

Past incidents of fraud, and the detection of certain patterns of fraud, inevitably influence how closely an officer examines an application. Having detected fraud makes him or her more sensitive to it. An officer admitted, "After you are burnt on a particular kind of case, I might go through a period where I am stricter with those kinds of applications. Then, over time, I might loosen up."[17]

Though referring to a different aspect of border control, a migration integrity officer highlighted the department's sensitivity to the word "profiling" while confirming that profiling played a key role in protecting the border:

> They tell us that we are not supposed to say that we use profiling, but we profile. They don't want us to use the term profiling. But in my first posting in Paris that's all I did. I profiled to stop people from getting on a plane. There's a guy in brand new shoes and new pants, and you can tell he's never worn shoes before. He's limping and walking funny because of the blisters. That's all I did was profile.[18]

It is important to point out that Canadian officers are not alone in their concerns about fraud in the visa application process. Dealing with fraud in its various manifestations is a chief preoccupation of the border control officials of many major in-migration countries. For example, the British immigration mission in Ghana reports that it has the highest visa refusal rate of all British missions and that it refers approximately 1,500 document fraud cases per year to the Ghana Immigration Service and Ghana police (Ghana Immigration Service 2011). In *Border Security,* the United States Government Accountability Office (2007, 1) noted that US consular officers at six of the eleven posts studied "reported that widespread use of fake documents, such as birth certificates, marriage certificates, and passports, presented challenges when verifying the identities of applicants and dependants," particularly among "Diversity Visa" applicants. The report stated that posts where fraud was a major problem also had an active "visa industry" of crooked consultants who extorted sums in excess of $20,000 from applicants and coerced them into "sham marriages" (ibid., 16).

Overseas Legal Contexts

The decision to dig deeper into spousal and partner relationships also involves visa officer understandings of the structural constraints that applicants face in trying to satisfy Canadian legal requirements. In some cases, not digging deeper involves not asking certain questions, as a way of facilitating acceptance. This is particularly an issue with bigamy and polygamy, both of which are illegal in Canada. Thus, "previously married applicants must be legally divorced before they remarry. In addition to proving that their marriage is legal, they must first prove their divorce is legal" (Citizenship and Immigration Canada 2011c, 24).

Multiple marriages are a tricky processing issue in the Philippines. As everywhere else, marriages break down, but the country has no divorce law, and though annulments and legal separations are possible, the grounds are very narrow. Annulments and separations are also expensive to obtain and they take time (Alave 2008), so legally exiting a marriage is difficult in the Philippines.

Interviewees in the Manila office repeatedly spoke about the importance of interpreting Canadian law "in the spirit" in which it was written. By Canadian standards, Filipinos who remarry or enter into a common law relationship while the first marriage is still legally valid are committing bigamy. As a Canada-based officer indicated,

> Here, divorce is not legal, and so a lot of people have second families. It's not really bigamy, as we would define it in Canada. They get married again because they are trying to legitimate their family. Here, a legitimate child inherits differently than a not legitimate child, and so someone might get married again because they are trying to stay legal. They are trying to do things the right way. You have to be sensitive to that.

When I asked, "So how do you write this up in the case notes if that kind of issue comes up?" he replied, "You tread a fine line. I don't go looking for bigamy. If the applicant states it outright, then you might be able to process it as a common law relationship. You try to find a compromise between the law and the real world."[19]

In this case, officers appear to use discretion to humanize decision making and to recognize that Canadian law cannot fully capture the legal constraints that every applicant might encounter. To some extent in this situation, immigration laws are made "from the bottom up" (Palmer 2012), where the actual practices of officers become the informal policy.

However, this approach to spousal applications is not the norm in other offices. The notion of interpreting the "spirit of the law" played a much less prominent role in my interviews with officers elsewhere. Perhaps this discrepancy exists because the Philippines is a major source of permanent and temporary residents for Canada (Citizenship and Immigration Canada 2012c) and because Canadian employers tend to see Filipinos as industrious workers who speak English and are relatively tolerant of substandard conditions (see Bakan and Stasiulis 1995). Thus, though my interviewees did not say so, one could argue that employers, who are also a client group of Citizenship and Immigration, pressure the visa office to be more facilitative in assessing applications from Filipinos. This more facilitative approach may spill over into the processing of spousal cases.

Collectively, these macro-level understandings of fraud, global inequalities, and broader visa regimes of Canada and other countries shape how deeply visa officers dig into applications. However, they also operate in tandem with officers' perceptions of what a real marriage looks like.

Culture and Normality

Clearly, what is normal in a spousal or partner relationship varies historically and according to culture, religion, age, social class, and sexual preference. It also varies on the basis of the unique values that individuals bring to their relationship and the socio-economic and political-legal constraints that they and their families face. However, what also varies is the way in which states employ the concept of normal relationships in their efforts to root out fraudulent marriages. In some in-migration countries, the credibility of a relationship tends to be measured against Western understandings of love and family. In Norway, Helga Eggebø (2013a) shows that immigration authorities assess relationships in light of what Anthony Giddens (1992) describes as a "pure relationship," one characterized by mutual benefit, emotional involvement, power balance, and sexual equality.

In Canada, the approach is somewhat different (as it is in Britain, see Webber 2012) because immigration rules recognize various forms of courtship and partnerships, including common law and conjugal relationships, and same-sex, arranged, proxy, telephone, and tribal marriages. Accordingly, Canadian visa officers "are required to assess ... [the relationship] in the context of the cultural norms of the country" (Citizenship and Immigration Canada 2011c, 44).

Describing the difficulty of determining whether a relationship formed in another country or culture is genuine, one visa officer said,

> With FC1 [spousal sponsorship] processing, there is a calculus in every case between the actual way that people get married and how they fall in love. Everyone has a calculus in terms of who they want to marry and fall in love with, and so you have to get a sense of the norms of the local culture and what that calculus is. I remember I was taken to task by a consultant once. He was criticizing us for a decision that he was unhappy with and what he thought were inconsistencies in how we were making decisions. He said to me, "It's not rocket science." I said exactly, "It is harder than rocket science." There is no simple formula you can use to determine what is a genuine relationship. In each country, you have to learn what that calculus is.[20]

At the same time, however, visa officers also apply their understandings of normal Canadian relationships in determining whether those of foreign applicants are genuine. As a designated immigration officer in an African office noted, choosing which cultural standard to invoke is highly discretionary, as is the interpretation of deviations from a particular culturally defined script:

> There has to be a natural progression that a relationship takes. There are aspects of that progression that are typical to Canadian and West African relationships. There is a typical progression. How they meet, how often they visit one another. When aspects of that progression are missing, this makes me question the genuineness of the relationship. This is where I have to use my discretion. This is the part where discretion is used the most. Relationships and marriages in West Africa are similar in construct to that of Canada.[21]

Although officers are legally required to consider how cultural contexts shape relationships and their development, Forsyth (2010) contends that they nonetheless tend to judge relationships according to Canadian, or Western, standards. These may not necessarily trump other culturally defined understandings, but they undoubtedly play a significant role in an officer's assessment of whether a relationship is real. As a designated immigration officer explained,

> It helps to know the cultural practices of where people are coming from. But in general, West African relationships are not that far off of Canadian relationships. So, a lot of time, there is not much that is culturally different. Here, if a couple met and then someone proposed within a week, I would question that relationship.[22]

But the same officer added that some aspects of relationships were culturally and religiously distinctive, and that her decisions took them into account:

> But you have to be sensitive to differences. In some cases, I will ask a woman about what her husband does, and she might say, "What business is it of mine to ask my husband about his job?" Finances might be a barrier to travel, and this might explain a lack of visits. You have to find out why there is limited knowledge about a husband's job. There is less gender equality here, and you have to be cognizant of that here. Religion is also a big factor. There are Muslim weddings and there are Christian weddings. In Christian weddings, you would expect there to be more disclosure. If one of the applicants has been previously married, if they are in their second or third

> marriage, they might not have the information about why those previous marriages failed. A woman might say, "That is none of my business." But if there is no knowledge about previous spouses, I would weigh that information significantly. I would want to know why my new husband or wife's previous relationships ended the way they did.[23]

Margaret Walton-Roberts (2004) suggests that in India, applications from individuals in relationships that do not develop, or are not celebrated, according to culturally defined customs are "easily" refused (see also Wray 2006 for a similar argument in the British case). Confirming the argument that culture constitutes the basis for an easy refusal, a Canada-based officer admitted, "There is some truth in that."[24] A locally engaged staff member also explained that "culture has been used too much here as the basis for refusals, and we have been losing those cases on appeal." He added,

> It is okay to bring in an applicant for an interview. A red flag is living together in rural India. Putting cases to interview is fine. But you cannot use a one-size-fits-all approach. You have to use cultural arguments judiciously and sparingly. Had we used culture more judiciously and sparingly, we would have won more cases. So I never use those kinds of concerns in my refusals. I concentrate on specific points. I would not keep repeating the phrase "In your society you do things like this." I never say that in my refusals.[25]

It is, however, too simplistic to claim that deviations from culturally defined scripts *necessarily* result in refusals. In describing a case in the Punjab, a Canada-based officer outlined his understanding of what was normal in Punjabi relationships:

> In the Punjab divorce is so stigmatized that it would be unusual for a family to let their daughter marry a divorcé. People in the Punjab only get divorced for immigration purposes. Otherwise they stay together and live in unhappy marriages. Divorce is so shameful for the family that there is incredible pressure for the couple to stay together ... In the Punjab it is normal for a girl to get married at twenty-three. Since the applicant was twenty-seven, her age is outside of the normal range of marriage ... There is a seven-year difference in age between the couple, which was also somewhat outside of the normal range of age difference. The other concern is that the sponsor is a divorcé ... Finally, only five days elapsed between when the couple first met and the marriage. This is unusual because the family would want to

> investigate the reasons for the divorce. All of this feeds into "this is unusual" and is why it has been flagged for an interview.[26]

Clearly, the officer initially suspected that these deviations from the culturally defined script signalled a marriage of convenience, which prompted him to interview the applicant. But as Chapter 9 discusses in more detail, an interview is not necessarily a self-fulfilling prophecy in which an officer who suspects that a relationship is not genuine simply uses it to confirm this impression. In the Punjabi case, the applicant was able to address the officer's concerns, and he approved the visa.

Moreover, officers understand that culture is not deterministic: they know that individual members of particular religious, ethnic, or other communities may not necessarily observe all the traditions associated with courtship and marriage. They recognize that socio-economic and other externally driven circumstances might prompt individuals and families to selectively reject or modify certain rituals. As a Canada-based officer explained,

> Take for example the bridal bangles. Women are supposed to wear them for a certain period of time after they get married. If they submit photos showing that they have taken the bangles off, then that is going to raise concerns. But that is the case in rural Punjab. Over time, we are seeing increasing deviations from these norms. People are getting married in civil marriages. There is a growing middle class. We might have an applicant from Mumbai, a young woman, educated, a professional, who applies and she can't wear the bangles because they get in the way of her work. So there are increasing deviations. So we still look at the big picture. You have to see if it makes sense in small town, rural Punjab, or in a big city. It depends on the context ... If they did not follow some of the rituals, then it can be a sign that something else is going on. It gives us a reason to dig a bit deeper. Again with the case of a woman from Mumbai, who is educated, professional, and she does not perform all of the rituals, I am going to accept that application. It fits the profile.[27]

As this comment suggests, officers insist that they take deviations from rituals into account because local cultural and religious groups take them seriously. One Canada-based officer stated that conformity to certain rituals is important in Punjabi culture and implied that overlooking non-conformity, which might be a sign of a non-genuine relationship, would be irresponsible from a credibility assessment point of view:

> The rituals are really important here. They are based on deeply held meanings. They have a lot of symbolism. The community does value the rituals. There is a lot of superstition about them ... In rural Punjab, the rituals and ceremonies are important, they really are. Think about it. Even Indo-Canadians, kids born in Canada, are coming over to enter into arranged marriages. Clearly, that is an important part of Punjabi culture in Canada. And they respect that aspect of their culture. So they come here for an arranged marriage; it would not make sense that they would do that and not go through with the other rituals that are part of a marriage.[28]

In practice, then, officers draw simultaneously on three overlapping frameworks in their understanding of normality: what is typical of all relationships; what makes sense from a Canadian perspective; and what is normal in the region where they work. Although these lenses are theoretically distinct, the differences between them necessarily become blurred in practice.

Conceptions of Real Relationships

The varying normative frameworks used to understand relationships play themselves out in visa officer constructions of what typically happens in relationships. However, their definitions of normality are grounded in more than their personal views: they also arise from the organizational culture and division of labour in the visa office itself.

In most offices, credibility is worked up and assessed through a division of labour that involves interactions between visa officers and locally engaged program assistants and/or case analysts. Although Canada-based and designated immigration officers make the final decision to issue or deny a visa, a case analyst or program assistant normally processes a family class sponsorship application first. They ensure that the application is complete and that all the supporting documents are included, and they also make an initial judgment about the file (see also Alpes and Spire 2013). Indeed, one of their responsibilities is to bring local knowledge to bear on the genuineness of the relationship. This aspect of the division of labour is important because it frames how the officer will approach the file. Case analysts and program assistants earmark anything that seems unusual and that would probably raise concerns in the mind of the officer. They flag potentially fraudulent documents, marriage ceremonies that appear to be staged, and couples who do not seem to be "compatible." Flagging is usually informal and can simply take the form of a handwritten sticky note on the cover of the file. If documents are thought to be falsified, a case analyst can ask the anti-fraud migration integrity officer to investigate their authenticity.

Typifications of Migration History

The migration and marriage history of couples is used to assess the genuineness of their relationship. Generally, the out-of-the-ordinary applications that garner additional scrutiny are those in which the sponsor originally came to Canada as a sponsored spouse and where the overseas applicant previously lived in Canada or the United States.

Depending on the cultural context, previously divorced individuals can face questions about the credibility of their current application. As the following field note indicates, a case analyst usually begins by checking the migration history of sponsor and applicant:

> The case analyst indicates that the first thing he does is do a FOSS [database] check on the applicants to get a sense of their respective migration histories in Canada. He could see that the application for sponsorship was made in September 2011, which was seven months after the couple got married overseas. He could also see that the sponsor is divorced from his first wife, but the divorce came eleven years after the sponsor landed in Canada. He explains, "The first marriage does not look like a marriage of convenience because they stayed together for nearly ten years after landing in Canada. If they separate within six months of the applicant's landing in Canada, then Case Processing Centre Mississauga can start an investigation. They can file an A44 Report [which deals with suspected cases of fraud], but that takes time, and it would be too late to use to factor into a decision."[29]

The applicant's migration history is important because it is used to assess the current relationship. If, in the case discussed above, the first marriage had swiftly dissolved, the analyst might have concluded that it had been a sham and could have been inspired to dig deeper into the current relationship.

"Poison pen letters" can also enter into the assessment of applications. Family and neighbourhood tensions, and personal and professional rivalries, sometimes express themselves in visa offices. Officers receive both signed and anonymous letters informing them that an individual's application for a visa is in some way irregular. One Canada-based officer described the nature of the letters and how he responded to them:

> We call them poison pen letters. We can follow up and use the information in forming a decision about a case. There is a range of letters: They go from "this is a bad guy" to fairly detailed allegations against a certain person. If the letter is signed it carries more weight with me. It means the person is willing to stand by the accusations. So, you have to judge how much weight to give to the letters. Poison pen letters are tools that we can use to assess the credibility of an applicant. We can use them to help us formulate a question. And then, you have to form an assessment of who is more credible ... Sometimes, you get involved in family rivalries, and so you see that someone is writing the letter to get back at the person for something that happened years ago.[30]

As he mentioned, poison pen letters in family class cases tend to come from neighbours, acquaintances, and relatives, and they usually allege that the sponsored spouse is not in a genuine relationship. An officer noted that "poison pen letters are important here. In about 5 percent of cases, there are poison pen letters. If we get a poison pen letter, we will usually recommend bringing them in for an interview. Most times, the poison pen letters are correct."[31]

Sometimes, the letters give tips on fraud strategies. A Canada-based officer stated,

> We get poison pen letters, usually unsigned, that tell us that the going rate for a North American marriage partner is $50,000 US dollars ... The community is fully aware of what is going on. It basically works like this. A family here pays a family in Canada to marry their son or daughter. That gets the applicant, and then the parents and younger siblings into Canada. They in turn offer up their children for marriage to an Indian, and they in turn get the money from parents in the Punjab looking for a way to get out. So you have to look at whether they are really in communication with each other. Would a reasonable person, based on what has transpired today, believe that they are married? We have never been able to prove, through a site visit, that this kind of money has changed hands, but we know it goes on.[32]

Though their suspicions are difficult to verify, the fact that officers know that money can change hands in a marriage prompts them to look for more solid proof that the relationship is fraudulent.

An individual's travel and application history also comes into play in the assessment of credibility. Examining a South American application, a

Canada-based officer remarked, "This is positive. She does not have a history of trying to get out of Colombia."[33] Alternatively, applicants who have already lived in Canada (and the United States) are treated with greater suspicion because they are seen as having a stake in returning. Of course, it is entirely possible that they could have formed a genuine relationship with a Canadian while they were in the country. However, the presence of a removal order in their history begs the question of whether their relationship with a Canadian sponsor is little more than the key that turns the lock. A visa officer in the Caribbean explained that "removal cases are very important for this office. Many applicants have been to Canada previously, and at some point they have been ordered removed from the country. Sometimes, people get married before the removal order is effected and I think 'come on.' It is a challenge to make sense of cases where removal orders have been involved."[34]

In such instances, the officer's assumption was that applicants who had lived in Canada and subsequently been deported had enjoyed their taste of Canadian life and thus had an incentive to resort to the sham marriage as a way of returning.

Typifications of the Development of a Relationship

Visa officers expect that genuine relationships will follow a logical progression in which couples meet and either marry or choose to live common law. They recognize that this process is culturally conditioned, but they nonetheless have a general understanding of how relationships should develop.

To assess a relationship's progression, they establish its timeline. Discussing a Sikh wedding, a case analyst said, "There is no timeline as such. A couple can get married one day, or a couple of months after first meeting. But there should be some kind of gap between the first meeting and the marriage."[35] My field notes record that certain unusual aspects of an application raised concerns for this analyst:

> The case analyst starts to read through the story of the development of the relationship. As he reads through the file he sees that the couple was first introduced at the funeral of one of their relatives. The case analyst says, "This sounds strange. The contradictions are starting already. It says here that within forty minutes of meeting, they decided to get married. Even with an arranged marriage, this is unusual. Forty minutes ... The story is made up. For an uneducated woman from the Punjab, it would have been normal for her to ask about his divorce, why it occurred, and things like that."[36]

In this case, both the circumstances of the first meeting (who talks marriage at a funeral?) and the suddenness of the plunge into matrimony detracted from the believability of the application.

In making their decisions, officers also try to link the story of the relationship's development with other material that applicants submit. Photographs play a crucial role here. They typically show the courtship, the wedding, the reception, and sometimes "the wedding night." One visa officer said, "I ask myself whether they are taking pictures for immigration." When I inquired how she could tell, she replied,

> Good question. That's kind of hard to say. Are they making out in the pictures if it is the first time they actually met? Are they being too affectionate? The pictures taken in the bedroom on the wedding night – they are half naked. I am thinking, "Is this a natural position?" How many people take pictures in the bedroom on the wedding night? Sometimes you get too many wedding night pictures.[37]

An officer in a different office elaborated on photographs that are staged solely for immigration: "With pictures, you can tell they are all taken on the same day because they are wearing the same clothes. There are doctored pictures submitted sometimes. The head is changed, and it just doesn't look right." Echoing the previous officer's view of wedding night shots, he also wondered, "You have to ask, who is taking the photos when the couple is in the bedroom?"[38]

Photographs can also reveal the nature of the wedding and who attended it. My field notes chronicle the way in which officers pore over photos for telltale clues:

> The visa officer looks through wedding photos. She notes that the applicants were well dressed and that they spent money on the wedding. The pictures show a roasted pig and champagne glasses on a table. There are other photos of family members who attended, perhaps thirty in total. A group photo had someone else's young boys in it; the visa officer guesses that they were someone's nephews. Others are well dressed. "This is good to see. You don't like to see too many people in jeans and t-shirts." There are also photographs of the sponsor, the applicant and her daughter together.[39]

But again, cultural context is relevant. This wedding was attended by thirty people, a normal allotment in South America, where it occurred.

In a Punjabi ceremony, however, visa officers expect to see several hundred guests:

> At a wedding, the parents and siblings should always be there. People will delay their weddings to make sure that the close family members will be able to attend. They would arrange a date so that the parents and siblings could attend. In the narrative about the ceremony, they say that 374 to 400 attended, but from the photos it looks like maybe 200 attended.

In this case, as the analyst examined the two-hundred-odd photographs that the couple had submitted to document their relationship, he commented, "I would have expected to see more people at the ring ceremony." Eventually, he found a snapshot that showed a few more people at the ceremony. "With this one," he said, "I can give them the benefit of the doubt."

However, after further inspection of the pictures, he changed his mind:

> The case analyst keeps looking through the photographs of the couple and of the participants. He explains that "nobody in the photos is smiling. They have done the ceremony. It's a Sikh temple, so it's a serious occasion, but nobody is smiling. Nobody seems happy. This is a concern." He looks over some more photos and can see one of the reception. "People are dancing, but still, nobody is smiling. There are no photos of private moments between the couple."[40]

In this particular case, an initially favourable impression was undercut by a closer examination of the evidence. Ultimately, the analyst recommended that the sponsored spouse be brought in for an interview.

Typifications of Compatibility

Visa officers generally believe that normal couples are "compatible." Like other typifications of normality, this one is culturally relative and can involve physical appearance, age, and religion. Here, too, photographs play an important role. Officers typically examine physical characteristics in assessing credibility, but they employ both Canadian standards and those of other cultures. As she looked at a photograph of a couple, one officer implied that compatibility equated with appearance: "They look good, there is a good physical match here."[41] An officer who applied a Canadian view in assessing physical suitability revealed that she used a code language to flag anomalies:

> You can't say certain things in the notes. You have to phrase things more carefully. For example, I am looking at a family class spousal sponsorship case. If the woman who is a sponsor is really ugly, and the guy is a good looking man. He has all the right assets. The woman travels to the Caribbean and marries the pool guy. I can't say she is ugly and he is too good looking for her. I will say something like they do not appear to be physically compatible, or something like that.[42]

Officers also refer to the culture of the region in which they work, asserting that in some cultures, couples whose appearance is dissimilar are seen as compatible, which is what they focus on in their assessment. A designated immigration officer and an interpreter explained, "Compatibility is important in the Punjab, and the family's concern is that the couple looks good together. Usually the woman has to be better looking than the man."[43]

In other contexts, the assessment concentrates on age, as significant age differences may reveal a non-genuine relationship. After reviewing an application, a case analyst summarized his concerns: "There is an age difference. The applicants are not compatible in age or marital status. It is very unusual in Punjabi culture for an unmarried girl to opt to marry a divorcé older than her by nineteen years."[44] In one instance, the age difference between the Canadian sponsor and her husband, greater than ten years, was seen as atypical. In his region, as the officer pointed out, "It is very unusual for a younger man to marry an older woman with a child."[45]

Typifications of Communication

Visa officers believe that genuine couples communicate with each other. As a result, the frequency, type, quality, and content of their contact is part of the assessment of credibility. Both too little and too much of it can be seen as strange and can undermine believability.

To support their claims of regular communication, applicants submit chat logs, telephone records, and emails. Taken on their own, such records rarely establish that a relationship is genuine, but an officer can use them to confirm a concern. In a Caribbean office, an officer commented that "love letters are out of this world. They know that we are reading them, so they write them for us."[46] An officer and an interpreter who were interviewed together in an Asian country said, "Correspondence is not such a big issue here. Telephone bills could be fabricated. Lots of things can be fabricated here."[47] Phone records can easily be dismissed: as he showed me a pile of calling cards that had been submitted as proof of communication, an officer asked rhetorically, "Calling cards are proof of communication? She could have picked them up off the street."[48]

An officer in another office noted that the couple's telephone calls lasted only a minute or two and asked, "How much can you say in a minute? I know that when I phone my brother or sister abroad, I talk for hours. But in this case they only talk for a minute or two at a time."[49]

Communication records are important because the expectation is that if the couple were in regular contact, they should know a considerable amount about each other:

> I look at the content of emails ... I read the emails. I read the things: "I love you, I miss you"? Really? What else? I look at money receipts. If someone other than the sponsor is sending them money, I want to know why. How often do you communicate? They say every day. Really? I focus on the length of the calls. Then I ask knowledge questions. "What do they know about past relationships?" Often they don't know. So I ask, "Why don't you know?" I look at the content of the communication. They have to show me that they have combined their affairs. Things like property, trips, plans.[50]

As this excerpt reveals, many applicants say that they contact their partner every day, either by phone, email, or another form of electronic communication. For those who claim that contact is frequent, expectations regarding familiarity with a spouse correspondingly increase.

Letters, birthday cards, and anniversary cards all form part of the picture of the relationship. If an applicant submits letters, offices will check whether the paper has been folded to fit into an envelope and may ask to see the envelopes themselves to determine whether the postage stamps have been franked. Like other evidence of communication, these types of documents seem to be accorded relatively little weight.

Mapping Credibility

Visa officers must map applications for spousal visas in terms of relationships that are credible and non-credible. Their understandings of how broad macro-level and structural forces pressure people to migrate prompt them to dig deeper into some applications and not others to determine whether a relationship is genuine. They also use various typifications of normality to assess applications as credible or non-credible.

But assessing credibility, and deciding to issue a visa, is not necessarily a linear process that can be reduced to adding up the checkmarks in predefined boxes. This is why Michael Lipsky's (2010) metaphor of applicant mapping is particularly useful. Road maps show many ways of reaching destinations. They do not necessarily indicate the correct route because, in a sense, there is no correct route. How drivers choose their path will depend on numerous factors: some dislike busy roads and will opt for a quiet country lane; owners of clunkers may nervously steer clear of high-speed expressways; some drivers may avoid construction along certain roads; and others might select the most scenic route. How visa officers arrive at their "destination" – approving or refusing a visa – hinges in part on whether they are facilitative or enforcement-minded, but it also depends on larger contextual factors. They are required to reach their destination quickly, so they must put their time to its best possible use. Their perceptions of the normal will guide their decision whether to probe more deeply into an application. But this choice is also conditioned by the organizational culture and macro-level contexts in which they work. Making decisions in spousal sponsorship cases is inherently ambiguous, in part because relationships take many different forms. Though economic class visa categories appear to be based on more objective selection criteria, officers must nonetheless make discretionary decisions for them as well, and as for spousal sponsorship cases, their decisions are structured by a variety of organizational and contextual factors. The next chapter considers how these factors shape decision making in the selection of federal skilled workers, the largest component of Canada's immigration program.

7

Federal Skilled Workers

Discretion is everywhere. It permeates what we do. Even if there are rules for what we do, we still have discretion. (Field notes, December 13, 2011)

Officials in many countries see Canada's skilled worker selection system, which is based in part on the points system, as the gold standard for managing international migration flows for the purposes of economic development (Marshall 2011). Canada introduced a points system for immigrant selection in 1967, and other countries have since followed suit. After monitoring the Canadian experience for several years, Australia created its own points-based selection process in 1979 (Freda Hawkins 1989, 142). The United Kingdom and Denmark developed their versions in 2008, explicitly drawing on both the Canadian and Australian models. Several US commentators have praised Canada, Australia, and the United Kingdom for their "value added" approach to immigration and their emphasis on the selection of skilled immigrants, and have lamented that a similar system does not exist in their own country (Marshall 2011; Borjas 1999).

Though widely admired, Canada's system is far from perfect. Too many people who are admitted under the system face barriers and challenges in convincing Canadian employers and licensing bodies to recognize their educational credentials and experience (Biles, Burstein, and

Frideres 2008). Also, the application stream has historically been oversubscribed, resulting in inefficiencies in matching immigrants to the labour market.

This chapter begins with a short history of the points system and reviews some of the controversies about the racial and other biases that were said to creep into its early versions. It then explains some of the ways in which the selection of federal skilled workers changed with the introduction of the Immigration and Refugee Protection Act. Though the system is lauded as purely objective and transparent, there are still places where visa officers are explicitly allowed to exercise a discretionary judgment about whether a federal skilled worker visa should be issued. Commentators suggest that this creates a space for biased decisions and thus determines who gets in. The bulk of the chapter then continues the ethnographic analysis of how officers match the immigration rules to cases, how discretion plays a role in the selection of federal skilled workers, and how it is fashioned by the organizational culture in which officers work.

A Brief History of the Points System

When the points system was introduced in 1967, its stated purpose was to enable the fair, non-discriminatory, and transparent selection of immigrants and to supply the needs of the Canadian labour market to enhance economic development (Freda Hawkins 1988). Before that time, Canada's selection system was both highly discretionary and unambiguously racist. Until 1962, it was guided by a strong policy preference for white immigrants from Europe and the United States (Satzewich 1991). An overarching assumption of immigrant recruitment and selection was that white applicants would assimilate and integrate more easily than their non-white counterparts, so there was a marked organizational and operational bias in their favour. Within this preferential framework, overseas immigration officers had considerable leeway in selecting permanent residents. Their interviews with applicants focused on their drive, motivation, and likelihood of successfully establishing themselves in Canada. According to a retired visa officer who worked overseas during the 1950s, officers assessed "successful establishment" on the basis of an applicant's age, education, and on-the-job experience: young workers with some education and experience were seen as more likely to fit into the labour market and make positive economic contributions to Canada.[1] As a result, approving or refusing permanent resident visas was based largely on the officer's subjective judgment about whether an applicant could make it in Canadian society.

The points system was initially acclaimed for ushering in a new era in which fairness and transparency would guide immigrant selection (Kelly and Trebilcock 1998, 360). It was expected to provide explicit, unbiased, and universally applicable criteria that officers would use to select applicants from around the world, regardless of their nationality, ethnicity, or race. The rationale behind the new system was that successful economic establishment in Canada was strongly conditioned by the demographic and human capital attributes that immigrants brought with them, by their intended province of destination, by the demand in Canada for their particular occupation, and by the existence of relatives who were already in the country (ibid., 359). In that light, the system emphasized factors such as age, education, fluency in English and French, occupational skill, and whether the applicant had arranged employment in Canada. The selection grid specified the maximum number of points for each criterion, and visa officers were required to assess applicants along every category in the grid (Freda Hawkins 1988). Immigration authorities set a pass mark, and applicants who achieved it thus became eligible for admission, barring the discovery of adverse security or medical considerations.

At the same time, attaining the pass mark did not necessarily guarantee admission, and failing to achieve it did not necessarily preclude it. With the concurrence of a superior, immigration officers had the discretion to refuse a visa to someone who had reached the pass mark and to issue a visa to someone who had not (Kelly and Trebilcock 1998, 360). These "substituted evaluations" were meant to enable officers to override the points system in cases where they judged that the points did not accurately reflect an individual's settlement prospects in Canada.

The points system has been revised several times since 1967. Pass marks have been raised and lowered, criteria have been added and subtracted, and the weights assigned to certain criteria have occasionally been adjusted (Li 2003; DeVoretz 2003; O'Shea 2009). A full accounting of all these changes is not possible here, but for our purposes, two features of the points system are particularly relevant to the issue of bias in the immigrant selection system: how points are assigned for fluency in French and English and for "personal suitability" for life in Canada.

Depending on which version of the points system was in place between 1967 and 2002, visa officers could assign a maximum of between ten and twenty-four points for an applicant's proficiency in English and/or French

(DeVoretz 2003). Before 2002, language proficiency was not measured via a standardized test. Instead, applicants rated themselves on their spoken and written language abilities, and visa officers were responsible for confirming whether those self-assessments were accurate. Almost all applicants for a permanent resident visa in what was then called the "independent category" were required to attend an interview, which officers used to determine whether their language skills matched what they had stated on their application. The language assessments tended to be done informally. Officers usually gauged applicants' verbal abilities first (Citizenship and Immigration Canada 1998, 20). Those who spoke English or French well, whose accent was easy to understand, or who could be interviewed "in a reasonable manner without an interpreter" (ibid.) tended to be assigned the maximum number of points based on their conversational skills alone. Because they spoke good English, their other competencies were assumed to be strong as well. Conversely, if their verbal skills seemed less strong than their application indicated, or if they spoke with a heavy accent, officers probed deeper and asked them to read a paragraph or two from an English or French newspaper, magazine, or other document at hand, and/or had them write out a brief dictation. Since the assignment of points was not standardized, individual officers could vary in their definition of proficiency, which was measured in terms of the ability to speak, read, and understand English and/or French "with difficulty," "well," or "fluently." Given this, one officer could assess a particular applicant's proficiency as "with difficulty," whereas another might rate the same person's skill as "well," which resulted in differing assignments of points (Simmons 2010, 99).

In addition, prior to the 2002 introduction of the Immigration and Refugee Protection Act, the selection grid included an explicitly discretionary criterion called "personal suitability." The stated rationale for this category was that the grid should leave room for officers to exercise their professional judgment about an applicant. It was believed that certain intangible factors, such as "adaptability, motivation, initiative and resourcefulness" (Citizenship and Immigration Canada 1998, 40), played a role in whether applicants could "successfully establish" in Canada. Thus, officers should be able to add their own subjective assessment of these intangible characteristics to the grid (Kelly and Trebilcock 1998, 360). Between 1967 and 2002, the maximum number of personal suitability discretionary points ranged from ten to seventeen (DeVoretz 2003).

Like the assessment of language skills, the assignment of personal suitability points was inherently subjective (Citizenship and Immigration Canada

1998). By design or default, the immigration department never defined the values on the personal suitability scale: thus, what differentiated a score of three from five, seven, or ten was essentially left up to the officer. As with language skills, two officers in the same office could assess the same applicant in very different ways based on their own views of what made him or her personally suitable for Canada.

Perhaps a fictional example, that of a Chinese man who applies for a skilled worker visa, would be useful here: Let us assume that he has an engineering degree and has spent his entire career at a steel plant in China. He has extensively researched his job prospects in Canada, learned about the licensing requirements for his profession, and hopes to move to Toronto in January. One visa officer could see his job-related research as a sign that he is well prepared and motivated to succeed in Canada and thus has strong settlement prospects. As a result, the applicant could score seven or eight points on the personal suitability scale. Another officer might think that holding just one job, originally assigned by the Chinese authorities, translates to zero experience of actually looking for work. This officer could suspect that the applicant has little knowledge of Canada and that his expectation of securing an engineering position is unrealistic. The officer might also question the wisdom of relocating to Toronto during the winter. Therefore, the applicant might score only two or three personal suitability points.

Despite its reluctance to officially set the numerical values for personal suitability, the immigration department's own internal research showed that in the 1980s and early 1990s, the number of personal suitability points had a strong correlation with "successful establishment" in Canada (Citizenship and Immigration Canada 1998). Skilled workers who achieved the most points had the highest employment earnings and the lowest incidence of unemployment (ibid., 40). The research also showed, however, that by the mid-1990s the points were losing their effectiveness as predictors of economic success. The research also found that the allocation of points had become more generous over time. In the latter half of the 1980s, only about a quarter of applicants scored eight or higher, but by the early 1990s half had reached this top tier (ibid.).

During the 1980s, the personal suitability points became a focus for accusations of racialized bias in the decision-making process. Many Canadian scholars and NGOs who were involved with immigrant advocacy argued that personal suitability allowed officer prejudices to inform decisions. In particular, they claimed that earning personal suitability points was easier for white applicants than for non-white ones, and that the category was enabling racism to infiltrate the skilled worker selection system. As Alan Anderson and James Frideres (1980, 227) explain, "Depending on the selection officer's bias (or views about racial groups), the applicant can receive zero points in this category, thus lessening the applicant's chance of entering Canada. As the saying goes 'If you're White, you're right; if you're Brown, stick around and if you're Black, stand back'" (see also Jakubowski 1997, 21). To my knowledge, the claim that race-based bias guided the assignment of personal suitability points was never supported by systematic research or empirical evidence and seems to have been based on a mix of suspicion and anecdote.

The introduction of the Immigration and Refugee Protection Act (2001) was the first major overhaul of immigration legislation since 1978. The act brought a number of changes to the immigration program. With respect to skilled workers, a main intent of the changes was to ensure that economic immigrants continued to "provide significant economic benefit to Canada" (Citizenship and Immigration Canada 2001, 4507). However, another stated objective of the new act was to improve transparency and consistency in the decision-making process for issuing visas (ibid., 4509). This concern was certainly evident in the reformulation of the selection criteria for federal skilled workers, which occurred shortly after the act took effect. Although the points system was retained, the selection grid was modified in two important ways: personal suitability was removed, and visa officers no longer made judgments about the language skills of applicants. In part, these two measures were meant to reduce the discretionary aspects of the selection process. According to the "Regulatory Impact Analysis Statement" (ibid.), which justified the introduction of the new selection procedures, "Many of the current selection factors rely on subjective assessments by visa officers ... [and] this leads, in practice, to considerable inconsistency in how applications are assessed at different offices and by individual officers."

Three interrelated dynamics were probably responsible for the department's decision to reduce officer discretion in the skilled worker selection grid. First, senior immigration officials were no doubt aware of the allegations regarding bias, but like many policy-makers who seek to reform a public service, they faced a dilemma – how to find "the correct balance between compassion and flexibility on the one hand, and impartiality and rigid rule–application on the other" (Lipsky 2010, 16). They may not have accepted the claims of racialized bias, but they did recognize the unfairness of grounding a meaningful portion of the selection process in subjective judgments. Senior bureaucrats who had started out as front-line officers and worked their way into upper management positions found the situation particularly troubling.[2] Their own experience had shown them that the points were assigned inconsistently, both within and between visa offices, and at least some of them were increasingly uncomfortable with a selection system that was supposed to be fair and transparent but that essentially permitted the opinions of visa officers to make or break applications, particularly in cases that hovered near the pass mark (Citizenship and Immigration Canada 2010d).

At the same time, two resource-based factors – efficiency and litigation – may also have accounted for the reduction in officer discretion. As public service resources atrophied and caseloads burgeoned, senior officials recognized that interviewing applicants was one of the most time-consuming aspects of visa processing. Before the Immigration and Refugee Protection Act was introduced, nearly all applicants for a permanent resident visa were interviewed by an officer, no matter how strong or weak their paperwork. Interviews for "good cases" might last just a few minutes, but those for refusal cases could consume an hour or two. In the early 2000s, hoping to improve efficiency, the department began to encourage officers to make more decisions solely on the basis of the paper application: strong ones could be accepted without an interview, and certain categories of weak ones could be rejected without an interview, on the grounds that nothing significant would be learned by talking to the individual (Citizenship and Immigration Canada 2001, 4514). Today, interviews are no longer expected or required, so an officer has little opportunity to form personal judgments about applicants.

Like the drive for efficiency, litigation probably contributed to the demise of the personal suitability rating (Citizenship and Immigration Canada 1998, 40; 2010d). Applicants who were refused because they did not attain a pass mark on the selection grid and were granted only a few points (or none) for personal suitability or language skills could appeal their case to the Federal Court. During the 1990s, the Appeal Division of the Federal Court was clogged with cases that turned on personal suitability and language points. They tended to claim that the points had been awarded incorrectly, so visa officers had to explain to the court why they had assigned the scores. Though they were required to record their decision-making process in the office database (and still are), appeals could be heard many months, if not years, afterward, and officers sometimes had difficulty in articulating why an applicant had received so few points. Interestingly, Citizenship and Immigration Canada (1998) also cited the prospect of litigation as a possible reason for the progressive inflation of personal suitability points during the 1990s. As the report noted, "The 1990s have been a time of intense scrutiny and threat of litigation. This may have been translated into the reluctance of visa officers to fail applicants who were short only a few points. The shortfall may have been made up by awarding slightly higher personal suitability points, thereby pushing total scores into the low 70s" (ibid., 40).

Regardless of whether appeals were won or lost at the Federal Court, they were costly for the department (and, of course, also for applicants). Defending an officer's refusal decision cost the department legal fees, but it also cost time. Officers whose decision was subject to appeal had to prepare an affidavit that clarified their thought processes and might have to testify before the court (usually via telephone if they were still working overseas). From the department's perspective, the time spent dealing with the appeal of a case that had been processed a year or two earlier was time that could be better applied to processing the growing backlog of new applications. In an increasingly litigious world, narrowing officer discretion was probably seen as a way to reduce the grounds for an appeal, and for the department to conserve progressively scarce resources.

Nonetheless, the Immigration and Refugee Protection Act did leave some scope for a visa officer's subjective judgment through "substituted evaluations." These had been allowed under the earlier skilled worker selection system, and they were retained in the act. A substituted evaluation is a mechanism that enables an officer to override the points system for federal skilled workers on the grounds that the points assigned do not accurately reflect an applicant's ability to "successfully establish in Canada." This discretion can work either in favour of or against an applicant. A positive substituted evaluation can be made if an applicant does not achieve a pass mark but the officer believes that some aspect of the case, though not captured by the grid, nonetheless makes the individual a good bet for Canadian society. Conversely, when a pass mark is attained, an officer can make a negative substituted evaluation on the grounds that the applicant is unlikely to successfully establish in Canada (Citizenship and Immigration Canada 2001, 4516).

Despite these changes, the federal skilled worker selection system was a target of continuing reform when Jason Kenney became immigration minister in 2008. Prior to his appointment, the Federal Skilled Worker Program was highly oversubscribed: every year, the number of applications far exceeded the department's target levels of admission and were far more than it could process during that year. The department did provide an online "self assessment" grid that enabled would-be applicants to find out for themselves whether they could achieve a pass mark, but in the end, anyone could apply for a federal skilled worker visa. Once the application was accepted (with the fee of nearly $1,000), Citizenship and Immigration was legally obligated to process it. But significant challenges resulted from this situation. The case inventory became badly backlogged, and many applications remained in the queue for a long time; eventually, thousands waited in the queue, often for six or seven years. When they finally did reach the processing stage, much of their information was "stale," and visa officers had to expend additional resources in contacting applicants and obtaining current data. As a result, turnaround times dragged even further.

Hoping to correct this dysfunctional procedure, Jason Kenney introduced a number of reforms to the skilled worker application process. In 2008, Bill C-50 accorded him the authority to introduce "instructions" to the department about how applications were to be processed, accepted, and prioritized. Since these Ministerial Instructions could be issued without parliamentary debate or public consultation, critics argued that Bill C-50 permitted the minister to "make up the rules" as he went along (Canadian Council for Refugees 2008). As noted in Chapter 3, twelve sets of Ministerial Instructions have been issued since 2008, most of which set new processing priorities and selection and admission criteria for federal skilled workers. Intended to clear the backlog in federal skilled worker applications, the Ministerial Instructions inevitably created their own mini-backlogs. By 2010, overseas visa offices were trying to process federal skilled worker applications from three streams: those submitted before the introduction of Bill C-50 (called the pre-C-50 inventory), those submitted under Ministerial Instruction 1 (MI 1), and those submitted under Ministerial Instruction 2 (MI 2). The processing targets for federal skilled workers were filled by applications from all three streams. Thus, offices juggled files from the various streams, pulling applications from all three to reach their yearly target. As an Economic Class Unit manager explained,

> One challenge we face is managing the different kinds of cases. We have pre-MI cases. The processing standard for MI 1 and MI 2 cases are six to twelve months, but the reality here is that we are only processing MI 2 cases. There is not a large backlog of pre-MI cases. But it is a delicate balancing act. There is one target for all federal skilled workers, but we are not working at all on pre-MI cases. We are not even touching the pre-MI cases, so one of the challenges is juggling priorities and the inventory.[3]

Depending on the date of submission and the rules and Ministerial Instructions that were in place at the time, federal skilled worker applications are evaluated in slightly different ways.

Missing Personal Suitability?

When I began this research, I expected that officers who had worked overseas in 2002, when the personal suitability points were removed from the selection grid, saw the change as an insult. Since it explicitly narrowed their discretionary authority, I thought they would interpret it as an indirect attack on their ability to make a professional judgment about who should receive a visa. In reality, many of my interviewees were not working as visa officers in 2002, and few remembered any dissent over the change, although some did recall lunch- and coffee-room grumbling at the time. Only a few, perhaps two or three, reported that they missed the opportunity to assign points for personal suitability. A long-serving Canada-based officer had little trouble describing the kinds of cases where, under the previous rules, he could exercise his discretion and professional judgment to favour an applicant. Speaking somewhat longingly of the old regime, he said,

> I remember I had a case in Pakistan. The applicant was a doctor, and his wife was not well educated. The kids were a bit older. They did not have enough points, but they came in for an interview and I could see that the kids had just graduated from school, and they were going to make it. At the end of the interview I told the kids to leave the room and I said to the applicant, you don't have enough points on paper, you do not meet the criteria, but I am going to approve your application because of your kids. I kind of miss that. I want to use my judgment.[4]

In this instance, the officer seems to have made a substituted evaluation rather than assigning extra points for personal suitability, but his comment nonetheless demonstrates that some officers lament the current operational environment's reduced scope for discretionary decision making.

Though she had not worked under the previous system, another officer was well aware that it had once included broader scope for discretion. Asserting that the current selection system was too mechanical, she rather pointedly remarked, "It's a bit of a puzzle to figure some things out, but really today, the job is more boring; you could train a monkey to do it."[5]

Other officers who worked under various iterations of the pre-2002 system were glad to see the back of personal suitability. Like the officials who drafted the change, some may have felt that transparency and consistency were poorly served by subjectively assigning points for personal suitability. Others, however, were evidently relieved by the change because they lacked confidence in their own abilities or their capacity to justify and stand by their decisions. A long-serving Canada-based officer who had worked at several postings when the pass mark was seventy points recalled a case where a visa officer could have used his discretion to give more points for personal suitability but instead asked his program manager to essentially make a substituted evaluation:

> For some, the change was welcomed. A lot of people did not want to use their judgment. Under the old system, some officers were afraid to use the discretion that they had. I remember a guy; he gave the applicant four points for personal suitability, and when he tallied the points, the applicant came to sixty-six points. He then went to the program manager to recommend that he use his discretion to approve the application. The program manager said, "Well why don't you just give more points on personal suitability?" But the guy was afraid to do that.[6]

Thus, though some officers felt nostalgic for the old system, it seems to have expired without arousing significant uproar in their occupational subculture.

Although official procedures were revised as long ago as 2002, some long-serving officers reportedly still employ the old mindset in processing skilled worker applications. Expressing some frustration on the topic, an Economic Class Unit manager explained,

> With regard to discretion, before 2002, maybe there was more discretion. Visa officers are different now. Older officers, pre-IRPA [Immigration and Refugee Protection Act] officers, they process cases differently. The pre-IRPA approach is still a way of thinking. They want to do everything they can to find a way to get an applicant in. They talk about suitability. They use terms like "on balance." But in the new act, it is more black and white. With new officers there is a different way of thinking. The act, the way it is written now, does not talk about personal suitability. If we use discretion, it's not something that is expected. You can see it in the CAIPS [database] notes that the old and new officers write. Even if I don't know the officers, they still use the old language. They talk about issues that are no longer

appropriate. They use terms like "on balance," "appears to." I don't say that. The person meets the points, and that's it. There is no room for "on balance."[7]

In this case, the unit manager's disdain for phrases such as "on balance" reflected her concern that visa officers were still trying to subjectively weigh whether an applicant would be good for Canada and implied that discretion applied only when a substituted evaluation might be in play. This view is rather narrow and it is important to recall that discretion applies to numerous aspects of skilled worker and economic class applications – it is not confined solely to the substituted evaluation. An immigration program manager made this clear:

Even for something like the Skilled Worker Program, where there are rules, there are discretion issues, and so your interest in the thought process of visa officers is very interesting. For a visa officer, it ranges from what weight to give to a document on file, whether to verify a document, or whether to call someone in for an interview. These are all calls that need to be made before we formally exercise our discretion within the points system. In every line of business that we do, it is like this.[8]

The Social Constitution of Digging Deeper

As with family class spousal processing, visa officers must use their judgment in deciding whether or not to subject skilled worker files to deeper scrutiny. One officer noted that productivity expectations helped determine how much time was spent on files:

Another part where judgment plays a role is in what to do with a file. We have time constraints. Sometimes you have to base a decision on your judgment rather than the facts. When you open a file, what is your gut feeling? Does the story make sense? If there are no apparent concerns, I do not have time to dig to try to find something.[9]

As is the case in family class, officers who process skilled worker applications employ informal profiling to ration their time:

We are always told not to profile, but we need a framework to make sense of what we see. Judgment plays a big role in what we do. Knowledge of the country is fundamental to processing. We have the Immigration and

> Refugee Protection Act, but we process files made up of documents. We need to know how the country functions to understand how documents are produced.[10]

This designated immigration officer added,

> A big part of the job is that you have to pick and choose what you want to spend more time and energy on, or what to focus on in the file. There is no such thing as a perfect application. The rules say you need "x," "y" and "z" doc, but often those documents are not included. So when I look at a file, it is not one file in particular, but the whole of immigration processing comes into play.[11]

Time constraints and client behaviour in the form of fraud are also part of the broader organizational context in which officers decide to dig deeper into applications. One Canada-based officer said,

> I also work with statistics and data to see where the fraud is. With files that I have no concerns with, I can move faster with them. If the office data shows that students from Beijing pose no problems, there is no need to invest further energy digging into that file. You have to pick your battles as they say. Even after document verification comes in, you might have inconsistent results. You need balance. You have to pick your battles. You can't sit on a file for weeks because you can't verify a document, or you can't get a site visit to some location. So I have to ask myself whether it makes sense to delay a file further. You have to ask yourself what is in the best interests of the program. Our priority is immigration processing times. We have to deliver results.[12]

Fraud forms a significant part of the context within which economic class applications are processed and decisions are made. Fraud and misrepresentation take various forms in skilled worker and broader economic class applications, but much of the concern focuses on the documents that applicants submit and whether they tell the true story of their background, ability, and experience. One officer said, "Fraud is significant here. The easiest thing to get away with in fraud here is in the supporting documents. It's easy to get fraudulent documents here. You can get your friend or pay someone to write you a letter to say that you worked for so and so company for this long."[13]

The Economic Class Unit manager in the same office also commented on the ease with which false documents could be acquired: "In the embassy area around here, you can walk around and see cell phone numbers written on the sidewalk saying that 'we can provide certificates for anything you like.'"[14]

Even seemingly objective third-party language tests raise concerns about fraud. A unit manager described the high-tech trickery in his country of operation, which posed challenges for assessing the language skills of applicants:

> There are companies that do photo blending. They combine the photos of imposters and applicants. They will bring the combined photo to the test, and the imposter will write the test. Now, the way they do it is that they bring photos at the same time that they write the test. But there can be a thousand people writing the test at the same time and it gets hard to screen for all the blended photographs ... Companies who do this have "gunners." Companies have lists of students who are good in English; they have a database of these students and they run through the photographs that the applicants supply to see if they can come up with a close enough match. We had one of our assistants call a consultant one day to pretend they needed a "gunner." They basically said that if they cannot match the applicant with a gunner, they will not accept the money because they don't want to draw attention to themselves ... If the applicant gets caught, the applicant receives a lifetime ban from writing the International English Language Testing System exam. But the impostor goes free. They go free because nobody knows who the impostor really is. So there is some pretty high-tech fraud here.[15]

Officers are also concerned about "source of funds" issues for applicants who wish to move to Canada under the investor category. These individuals must demonstrate that their earnings and/or funds have been acquired legally. Depending on their circumstances, some may find this a challenge; conversely, proving that money is ill-gotten can be equally challenging for visa officers. In one office, some investor applications were stalled in the processing queue for ten years due to suspicions about the way in which the individuals had originally come by their money. The unit manager noted,

> Processing business applications takes a long time. There are fraud issues, and there are source of funds issues. Here, the problem is with seed businesses.

> They might be operating legally now, but the question is about where they got the money to begin with. You have to sometimes interview to understand the source of funds. You have to determine whether it makes sense; is it reasonable that they accumulated their initial wealth that way. Usually we will ask for docs, and if there is suspected fraud involved, we will express our concerns.[16]

Refusal letters for would-be investors are couched in careful language, with an eye to the likelihood of an appeal. The unit manager explained, "With investors, it is tricky. I can refuse an application by saying that 'I am not satisfied that you are not inadmissible.' I don't have any proof of criminal activity, but I don't have proof of legitimate activity, and that can be a ground for refusal."[17]

The Substituted Evaluation

Although discretion is exercised all along the processing path, the substituted evaluation is still one place in the skilled worker selection system that is explicitly discretionary. Nearly every officer who processed skilled worker applications responded in virtually the same way when I asked how often they used a substituted evaluation to override the points system: they seemed both puzzled and slightly surprised by the question. Though they knew that they could recommend a substituted evaluation, most said that they had done so infrequently. Most longer-serving officers claimed that they could count on one hand the number of times they had used this mechanism, either in a positive or a negative way. Some new officers who had been working overseas for a year or two said that they had never used it.

Those who did recall using a substituted evaluation usually referred to instances in which it was positive, not negative. A unit manager who appeared to be more enforcement-minded than facilitative said,

> I have recommended a substituted evaluation once in three years in this unit. It is more narrow than people think. People think that it is like humanitarian and compassionate [considerations] but that is not correct. The case I had was an applicant who had two university degrees, and so they got twenty-two points for that, but they still didn't meet the sixty-seven point mark. The degrees were in medical fields. The applicant was really employable in Canada. In that case, I did give her points that did not reflect her experiences. Substituted evaluations should be rare. I have never used a negative substituted evaluation. As a visa officer, we should not bring our personal

feelings into a decision. There should be no opinion when we assign points. With negative substituted evaluations, personal biases come into play. "I don't want to admit someone because –." That is not for us to judge.[18]

A Canada-based officer remarked,

Well, if there is something in the file that a person is not awarded points for, then I will include it. But if an applicant has already been awarded points for it, I don't see any reasons to double count it. For example, I remember one case, an applicant had one year of computer training, but then he took a whole bunch of short courses to build his skills. These courses were relevant for his career, but he could not really receive credit for them in the grid. Clearly he was working toward his career goal and building his skills, and so I recommended it in that case.[19]

A visa officer in another office also recalled that he had made one negative and two positive substituted evaluations during the past four years. Although he could not recall the details of one positive case, the other two were quite fresh in his memory:

That positive case was a tool and die maker in Pakistan. He had forty points I think, but I brought him in for an interview and during the interview I asked him to make me a tool. So in an hour, he drew me a tool. It was amazing. We did some further verification of his workplace, and sure enough, he could do that job and do it very well. I thought that this guy would have no problem getting a job in Canada as a tool and die maker, so I recommended it to my supervisor.[20]

This officer also had little difficulty in remembering the negative case, partly due to the applicant's candour and demeanour during the interview:

The negative case was a judge in [country deleted]. He made a lot of money, and he came in with his wife. He basically told me in the interview that he had no intention of settling in Canada. He has a good life in [his country] ... has a good job and makes lots of money and that the only reason he was applying was for his kids ... so that his kids could move to Canada. He sat there and told me that. After I explained to him that I was refusing his application because he had no intention of settling in Canada, he said, "See you in court." He did take it to judicial review, and he lost.[21]

In this instance, both the likelihood of an appeal and the perceived arrogance of the applicant factored into the officer's decision to exercise his negative discretion.

Recalling a negative substituted evaluation, another officer said,

> I had a middle-aged man. He was working on his third PhD. But the only work experience he had over the past ten years was as a teaching assistant. He also said that he worked as an editor, helping students write their papers in English. He submitted as part of his application a copy of the advertisement he used to market himself, and it was full of English mistakes. So I thought, "What kind of service could he offer?" Also, it did not seem like any university would hire him. He had all these degrees and all he seemed to be able to get were kind of teaching assistant positions. So I interviewed him and he just seemed kind of [long pause] crazy [under her breath]. And so I made a negative recommendation.[22]

This officer recalled a situation in which she had intended to make a negative substituted evaluation but changed her mind after interviewing the applicant:

> A woman was working at a bank. She had a lengthy history of working for a bank, but her career seemed to be full of demotions. She was moving down rather than up. So I called her in for an interview, and she explained that some of those positions had only been acting appointments, and they were not really demotions, and so I accepted that explanation and decided to not make a negative recommendation.[23]

Another Canada-based officer vividly recalled one of his few negative substituted evaluations:

> I do exercise negative discretion on occasion when the points just don't make sense. Someone applies as a Bangladeshi social worker. Under the old rules, they have points for experience and education, but it turns out they know nothing about Canada, they don't do any preparation. You show them a map of Canada and they can't pick out a single place. And when you probe further you find out that their main experience as a social worker was counselling villagers in Bangladesh to not eliminate their body waste in the water supply. This really isn't a transferable skill.[24]

The relatively uncommon use of substituted evaluations is confirmed in two immigration department publications: Citizenship and Immigration Canada's (2001, 4516) regulatory impact statement regarding the Immigration and Refugee Protection Act indicates that "in the past five years, discretion, whether positive or negative, has been used to make immigration decisions in only 2.3 percent of cases ... [and] positive discretion has historically been used 16 times more often than negative discretion." It adds that "there is no public policy or operational reasons why this is so," perhaps revealing some puzzlement over the infrequency of use. Citizenship and Immigration Canada's (2010d, 22) evaluation of the Federal Skilled Worker Program also notes that "positive substituted evaluation is rarely used, and negative substituted evaluation is almost never used." The 2010 evaluation report also states that immigration consultants and lawyers feel that visa officers do not make effective use of this aspect of their authority. It suggests that they regard the substituted evaluation as one of the least successful aspects in the processing of skilled worker visas. This is not surprising, in part because consultants and lawyers tend automatically to counsel their clients to ask for a substituted evaluation, regardless of the actual details of their case. The supporting letters often include boilerplate requests for the evaluation. As a unit manager indicated,

> Consultants ask us to make substituted evaluations, but that is just by habit. They always request a positive substituted evaluation [her eyes roll]. We always consider it, but it is given in such rare circumstances. The consultants just make a blanket request; they don't make it specific to their case. If they edited their requests more, it would be better for their clients.[25]

Why are visa officers reluctant to exercise their discretion via the substituted evaluation? Citizenship and Immigration Canada's (2010d, 53) report on the Federal Skilled Worker Program offers a reason: "The drop in the number of substituted evaluations (less than 1% of all applicants are accepted on positive substituted evaluation) reflects the increased confidence of management and other visa office staff in the objectivity of the selection process and the reliability of the points system in selecting skilled workers." Indeed, an Economic Unit program manager expressed this confidence: "The points system is pretty accurate in gauging whether someone is going to successfully establish."[26]

Although visa officers and unit managers may feel that the points system can accurately predict the successful establishment of immigrants, here, too, a complex of organizational and contextual factors explain their reluctance to use their discretionary authority. This includes their own micro-level views of the immigration system per se and the meso and macro levels of organizational culture, processing targets, and subsequent bureaucratic trajectory of their decisions.

In some instances, personal orientation seems to shape officers' unwillingness to use their discretion in skilled worker cases. Some feel that the bar in the points system has already been set too low and that individuals who score below it do not really "deserve" their discretion. The skilled worker processing queue is full of applications, and finding cases that unambiguously meet the selection criteria and pass over the bar is not difficult. As a result, officers are less inclined to use their discretion, even if an applicant is only one or two points short:

> Originally the pass mark was seventy-five when I started working. Now the pass mark is sixty-seven. Sixty-seven is not that hard to reach. Because the points are set at a reasonable level under the current system, there is a continuous supply of people who pass. There is no shortage of people who pass. Most people who apply know they are close, and so we don't see many applications that only get fifty points. I want to bring in strong cases. I think we already admit enough people who are really borderline cases. There are lots of borderline cases that we say "yes" to. So, in some ways, it kind of feels good to say "no" to someone. Canada already takes in plenty of people in other categories where there is really no judgment about whether they are going to be good for Canada.[27]

In this case, the officer seems to prioritize "Canadian society" as a client of the Federal Skilled Worker Program. Serving her country's interests by accepting the strongest applicants entails refraining from the exercise of discretion.

Office cultures also play a role in the use of substituted evaluations. Since officers must obtain the agreement of either their unit manager or their immigration program manager if they wish to make a substituted evaluation, the wider office culture and the tone set by managers influence their willingness to employ this mechanism. Some offices encourage the use of substituted evaluations, whereas others do not. In an office that discouraged it, a newly minted officer who had just completed the Foreign Service Development Program (FSDP) said, "I have not used one in one year in this unit ... I get my guidance from [the unit manager]. We were instructed in this in the training with the FSDP and in the on-the-job training. It is an iterative process of talking and checking with others."[28] Her unit manager, who leaned toward enforcement, saw little room for a visa officer's judgment in federal skilled worker cases and made it clear to staff that she would entertain substituted evaluations only in highly exceptional circumstances.

Other offices were more amenable. One officer attributed her frequent use of substituted evaluations to her good relationship with her program manager, who took a facilitative approach:

> In Bucharest I used positive discretion a lot. I accepted a lot of applicants on the basis of a substituted evaluation. I would do six or eight interviews a day, and I would say that about 5 to 10 percent of the acceptances were on the basis of positive discretion. And, you know what, those cases have turned out really well. The program manager there trusted me. I understand that you have to make the selection process as transparent as you can, but if you leave out the human element, you don't always get the best decision. Some officers are risk management averse. Some don't trust their own judgment. They want to be led, they want it to be easy, they want a grid for everything. But you have to develop a sense of risk management. FSDPs – that is the hardest thing for a new officer. They want a template for everything.[29]

As with spousal sponsorship cases, the organizational demand for efficiency and productivity constrains the exercise of discretionary authority. The push for efficiency limits opportunities to dig deeper for details that might augment the information in an applicant's file. Officers are expected (and urged) to make their decisions on the basis of a paper application only, and hence this structural impediment discourages them from assessing the intangible factors associated with successful establishment in Canada. As applicants have no face-to-face interaction with officers, there is little chance for new information to come to light that might boost marginal applicants above or below the pass mark.

The demand for productivity spills over into the demand to reach the processing target. Officers must also process applications quickly, and making a substituted evaluation takes more time and work than reaching a decision solely on the basis of the paperwork. When I asked a Canada-based officer why substituted evaluations were so uncommon, he replied,

> With the Immigration and Refugee Protection Act, there is everything on file that I need to make a decision. And there are enough applications in the stream in order for me to meet the targets. With substituted evaluations,

they take extra work, both if you do a positive or a negative. You know that you will have cases in order to meet your target. The way that the legislation is written is that you need to have the concurrence of another person to support your decision, and it takes work to do that.[30]

As Citizenship and Immigration Canada (2010d, 57) recognized, in "normal" cases where there is no substituted evaluation, "refusals may be more resource intensive to process than approvals." As already noted, this tends to produce a structural bias in favour of accepting applicants. A Canada-based officer complained that targets hampered discretion:

I'm sure it's not something that other officers will be willing to talk to you about. But targets do fetter discretion. You get to December and there is pressure on you to push the button and issue a visa. The immigration program managers put the pressure on you. How can you reach an impartial decision when you are pushed to reach a target? I'm sorry, I think I am a good officer, I have worked at the port of entry, and I have interviewed people at the border who have committed atrocities, who are terrorists. They are "t" for terrorists. They are unapologetic about what they have done, and I don't want to let those kind of people in. I've worked in [country deleted], and you get people involved in terrorist activities, and you want to dig further, but sometimes you are not allowed. You have to make a decision. The environment fetters discretion, supervisors fetter discretion.[31]

Time constraints also come into play when an officer contemplates making a case for an applicant who might be a good immigrant but has not achieved a pass mark on the selection grid. Potentially deserving applicants suffer because officers are unwilling to put in the necessary time to make the case for a positive substituted evaluation. An officer's goal of selecting "good" immigrants for Canada is limited by the demand for productivity. A long-serving officer explained,

Yeah, there are substituted evaluations, but you have to request it. And here, it sounds like I am shitting on my government, but the problem is that I have to work a lot harder to make a case for a positive substituted evaluation than I do for a refusal. It might take me an hour to do a refusal, but it could take me an hour and a half or more to make a positive substituted evaluation. If I do this, then I am going to miss my target.[32]

Time and target constraints, and the prospect of an appeal, seem to end up benefitting marginal, potentially undeserving applicants. Just as officers must work harder to say "yes" to a potentially good immigrant, they must also work harder to say "no" to an applicant who otherwise meets the minimum points threshold but who might not be of much benefit to Canada:

> The fact is that you have to work harder to do a negative evaluation. You might have to work for two or three hours on a file to say "no" to someone who has enough points, but then I can see some officers who might think, what's the point? It will probably be appealed, and they could win. And you would really have to justify your recommendation, and that all takes time. So I could see that happening.[33]

Overlaid onto time constraints is the likelihood of an applicant's appeal, particularly in negative substituted evaluations. Refused applicants can appeal to the Federal Court, and many people use lawyers or consultants to help them through the process, so officers may see the time spent on crafting a negative substituted evaluation as time wasted. Refusing a visa to someone who scores a pass mark on the selection grid must be grounded in a very strong conviction that the points do not accurately reflect the applicant's chances of successfully establishing in Canada. Officers know that if their decision were challenged in the Federal Court, they would be asked to explain their reasons for refusal: "With negative substituted evaluations, you have to be satisfied that the applicant is not going to establish economically in Canada. You have to have rock solid evidence to refuse them. I have never used a negative. It would have to be something that was really serious otherwise you would lose in Federal Court."[34] Another officer in a different office voiced similar sentiments: "Substituted evaluations could have value, but the system is set up to make it easier for an officer to say yes than it is to say no. The problem with substituted evaluations, the negative ones, is there are few cases that can be supported when they get to the courts. I would reserve 'no' for really extreme cases."[35]

Thus, a theme that came up repeatedly when officers explained their disinclination to employ this mechanism was "What is the point?" Given that the courts will probably overturn their decision anyway, using discretion seems a futile exercise:

> It takes a lot of officer time to support a negative recommendation. I could dig, dig, and dig. I could spend three hours digging into a file, doing an

> interview, and then have the decision overturned by the courts. So I wonder what's the point? In extreme cases, they have a place, but in borderline cases, it's not worth the effort.[36]

Discretion as Both Narrow and Broad

Though it is narrowly defined under the Immigration Regulations and in the form of the substituted evaluation, discretion in the skilled worker selection system is exercised fairly broadly. It comes into play all along the processing chain, not solely when points are tallied to determine whether an applicant has attained a pass mark. Officers can choose to investigate the authenticity of documents, the experience and education of applicants, the incongruous elements in their stories, and the way in which they made their money.

All discretionary decisions exist within a complex mix of variables at the micro, meso, and macro levels. At the micro level, personal attitudes may influence the willingness to exercise discretion, and some officers seem more enforcement-minded than others. This variability may also be linked to career stage and whether an officer worked under the pre-2002 rules in which he or she could assign points for personal suitability. Moreover, newer officers with less experience, and perhaps less confidence in their judgment, may be more risk averse, and so may be reluctant to use discretion. At the meso level, office cultures play a role as well. In a world of time constraints and processing targets, officers must work to exercise their discretion and may even refrain from doing so because their decisions can be upset in court.

Visitor visa processing, which is the subject of the next chapter, is also characterized by a significant amount of discretion. Although a refusal decision in visitor visa cases cannot be appealed, many of the micro-, meso-, and macro-level variables that guide permanent resident processing also come into play.

8

Visitor Visas

> *I can process about sixty files per day. But sometimes I get stuck with ugly files, and they take more time. I have been [here] for two and one half years now. The processing here is very good. It is challenging work. And the good thing about here is that you don't have people who scream at you ... In other offices, the job is a bit harder. In Kyiv, there was a different clientele. They would argue with you. They would say I was discriminating against them!* (Field notes, April 25, 2011)

Canadians love to travel. In 2012, we made over 32 million overnight trips abroad. Nearly 23 million of these were to the United States, but that still leaves over 9 million overnight excursions to more distant places. Though we are not known as great tippers, we nonetheless spent about $30 billion abroad in 2012 (Canadian Tourism Commission 2012). Our country, on the other hand, does not rank particularly highly as a destination for international travellers. Ukraine, which does not immediately come to mind as a tourist hotspot, had 21 million overnight visitors in 2012 and ranked fourteenth in the World Bank's list of top travel destinations (World Bank 2014). In that same year, Canada had 16 million overnight visitors and ranked sixteenth. According to the Canadian Tourism Commission (2012, 1), the overnight visitors to Canada spent an estimated $12.3 billion, which means that our international travel account deficit was about $17.7 billion.

There are two ways of bridging this deficit: We could spend more of our travel dollars at home, or we could encourage more tourists to come to Canada. But unless they hail from a visa exempt country, they must obtain a visa before they arrive. Because of this, most tourists (along with other people who are classed as temporary residents) will confront the Canadian immigration bureaucracy. Though Canada's immigration program is not normally seen as encompassing foreign nationals who visit for the purposes of commerce or tourism, one of its major goals is to facilitate their entry (Immigration and Refugee Protection Act 2001). Thus, overseas immigration offices devote significant time and energy to evaluating applications from, and issuing visas to, people who hope to visit Canada. Though the movements of short-term visitors are often conceived as distinct from those of people who wish to secure permanent resident status, Canadian immigration authorities see a *potential* connection between them. It arises because some visitors want to do more than just visit – they may intend to work illegally or to claim refugee status once they arrive. Thus, in addition to screening individuals who apply for permanent resident status, Citizenship and Immigration also screens people who say they want to enter Canada only temporarily.

There are a number of temporary resident visas, including those for students, temporary foreign workers, business people who wish to explore opportunities in Canada, and people who require a temporary residence permit. This chapter focuses on the narrower category of the tourist, or visitor, visa. In processing them, officers must differentiate between genuine and non-genuine visitors, and must evaluate credibility and risk. And, as with other categories of visa processing, caseload volumes and time constraints determine how deeply they inspect an application and how they allot their time. But with visitor visa applications, the assessment of credibility and risk also involves elements of prediction. Officers must try to predict whether applicants will leave Canada before their visa expires, work without official authorization, or make a refugee claim after they arrive. Predicting individual-level behaviour is exceedingly imprecise, and so their decisions about visitor visas are also inherently discretionary. As in other categories of visa processing, discretion here is socially constituted in important ways. At the same time, however, most refusals cannot be appealed, so the prospect of an appeal generally does not factor into the decision-making calculus (Alpes and Spire 2013).

The Politics of Visitor Visas

In an age of globalization, having to secure a visa simply to visit another country to see friends and relatives or take in the sights seems like an oxymoron. Globalization, with its attendant improvements in communication and transportation technologies, involves the accelerated movement of goods, services, ideas, and people around the world (Sassen 2006). It has supposedly made borders more porous and less relevant. The inconvenience and annoyance of having to secure a visa to visit another country slows the process of movement. It also imposes additional financial and time costs on those who wish simply to visit another country.

Canada takes visitor visa issuance very seriously. Unlike some countries (Jamaican High Commission in the United Kingdom 2014), it does not issue visitor visas at the border: travellers must apply for a visa well in advance of their arrival date. However, Canada does not impose visitor visa requirements on all countries. Perhaps not unexpectedly, the list of visa exempt countries, about 50 in total, includes the United States, Australia, the United Kingdom, and most of Europe. It also encompasses Japan, South Korea, Singapore, and the Special Administrative Region of Hong Kong. Citizens of British-dependent territories such as Bermuda, the Cayman Islands, and Gibraltar do not need a visa; nor do passport-holders from some Commonwealth Caribbean countries such as Antigua and Barbuda, Barbados, and the Bahamas. The rest of the world, about 140 countries, is not so lucky. Passport-holders from all countries in Central and South America and Africa require a visa if they wish to visit Canada, as do most passport-holders from Asia, with the exception of the countries noted above. Passport-holders from several central and eastern European countries must also obtain a visa, including Ukraine, Russia, Romania, Serbia, Montenegro, and most recently the Czech Republic (Citizenship and Immigration Canada 2014f).

Various factors determine a country's visitor visa requirements, including levels of socio-economic development, historical ties and physical proximity to other countries, security or health concerns, travel and business volumes, trade and common market arrangements, and political conflicts (Boehmer and Peña 2012). In many cases, visitor visa regimes between countries are symmetrical. For example, Ghana does not require visitor visas from neighbouring Mali, Togo, Nigeria, and Sierra Leone, and they in turn do not impose visitor visa requirements on Ghanaians. These countries belong to the Economic Community of West African States, part of whose mandate is to promote the free movement of goods and people between member states (Economic Community of West African States 2014). Canada, the United States, and Mexico all participate in the North American Free Trade Agreement, but only the United States and Canada exempt each other's citizens and legally settled permanent residents from a visitor visa requirement. This mutual exemption also exists because the volume of travel is so large that visitor visa processing would be a bureaucratic nightmare. Due to their historical ties, and also because their levels of socio-economic development are broadly similar, British and Canadian passport-holders do not require a visa to visit each other's country. Generally speaking, the logic behind this type of symmetrical arrangement is that individuals already enjoy safe and comfortable lives in their home country and therefore have little incentive to work illegally elsewhere. Reciprocal visa requirements are also based on understandings of risk: some countries believe that nationals of certain other countries pose little risk to their health, security, and economic well-being. Symmetries also work in the negative. For instance, Ghanaians must obtain a visa to visit Canada, and Canadians need a visa to visit Ghana. In the case of these negative symmetries, national pride and prestige are probably at work. If "they" impose a visa on "us," we will almost certainly respond in kind.

There are also asymmetries in visa requirements. In 2005, the Ukraine government issued a decree that Canadian visitors no longer needed a visa to visit, which was taken as a sign that Ukraine wished to encourage Canadians of Ukrainian descent to help build the country in the aftermath of the Soviet Union's collapse. However, Canada did not reciprocate. Ukrainians still need a visa to enter Canada, a decision that undoubtedly rubs many Ukrainians, and Ukrainian authorities, the wrong way.

At times, visitor visa requirements are part of the collateral damage when governments quarrel over other matters. In 2010, Canada and the United Arab Emirates were embroiled in a dispute over landing rights for Emirates Airlines and Etihad Airways at Canadian airports; the Emirates government disallowed the Canadian military from using its facilities as a staging base for the war in Afghanistan, and it also imposed a new visa requirement, which cost $250, on all Canadians who sought to visit the country for thirty days or less. A six-month multiple-entry visa cost Canadians a rather hefty $1,000. Tensions between the two governments have since eased, but the visa requirement is still in place, though its cost is expected to drop by a third in the future (Clark 2012).

In Canada, visitor visa requirements are also intimately connected to domestic politics, particularly those surrounding the refugee determination system. When federal ministers are appointed to their positions, they are given "mandate letters" that outline the prime minister's expectations and policy goals for their respective departments. Mandate letters are generally not made public, but a key part of Immigration Minister Jason Kenney's mandate was reportedly to "clean up" the refugee determination system and to reform the skilled worker selection system.[1] At the time, refugee processing in Canada was severely backlogged, and many members of the Conservative government thought that the refugee determination system simply encouraged people who landed in Canada as visitors, students, or other temporary residents to claim refugee status as a way of staying permanently. Kenney implemented reforms in 2010, but before that time the in-Canada (or inland) refugee determination system was slow, and expensive, for everyone involved. An average of nineteen months elapsed before claimants had a hearing for their case. Because the appeal process was so cumbersome, claimants whose appeals had failed could linger in Canada for an average of four and a half years before they were finally removed. During that time, they were permitted to work and had access to social assistance and health care benefits. The federal government estimated that refugee claims cost Canadian taxpayers about $50,000 per applicant, a sum that did not include legal aid (Citizenship and Immigration Canada 2010a). Though advocacy organizations such as the Canadian Council for Refugees (2010) disputed Ottawa's mathematics, it is clear that the refugee determination system came at a financial cost to Canadian society and that the government was determined to address the problem.

Though the reforms were mainly about refugees, the refugee determination system is inherently connected with visitor visa requirements. Part of the government cost-management strategy entailed screening out visitors who intended to make a refugee claim once they reached Canada. The connection was clearly evident when Ottawa imposed a visa requirement on visitors from Mexico and the Czech Republic in 2009. The government's rationale for taking this step was that visitors from these two countries formed a disproportionate number of refugee claimants. Unimpeded by the need for a visa, they could simply board a plane and identify themselves as refugees as soon as they touched down in Canada. By imposing its visa requirement, the government sought to protect the country from what it regarded as the unfounded refugee claims of Mexican and Czech visitors.

This move generated considerable tension. Both Mexico and the Czech Republic were angry, and for a time, the Czech government contemplated imposing a reciprocal requirement on Canadian tourists. But this retaliation never materialized. Equally dissatisfied, Mexico never publicly floated the idea of imposing a visa requirement on visiting Canadians, no doubt because it realized that it relied more heavily on Canadian tourist dollars than Canada relied on the pesos of Mexican tourists (CBC News 2009). Further, Canadians could choose between a number of winter vacation getaways, and a visa requirement might easily tip their decision to holiday elsewhere. Plainly, Mexico was not in a strong bargaining position, so the asymmetry in visa requirements still exists.

As the spat between Canada, Mexico, and the Czech Republic shows, the politics and economics of visa requirements are complex. Generally speaking, countries like Canada impose visitor visa requirements as a layer of protection against unwanted and non-genuine visitors. The requirements enable them to push their borders beyond their physical ports of entry. Visitor visa regimes represent the virtual borders of a state, a checkpoint to deflect those whose stated purpose for travel is pleasure but whose true intent is to become permanent residents or to work without authorization. How risks are constructed and defined is a matter for both macro and micro levels of analysis. How and why visas are imposed on some countries and not others is important to understand, as are the micro-level decisions by the officers who have the authority to issue or deny them.

Visa Application Centres and the Visitor Visa Process

Overseas visa offices are normally divided into a Temporary Resident Unit and a Permanent Resident Unit. The former processes visitor, student, temporary foreign worker, and temporary resident permit applications. Depending on the caseload, officers either specialize in processing one type of temporary resident visa or they handle the full range of applications that the unit receives. Offices normally have a number of locally engaged program assistants who do the initial screening of applications to ensure that they are complete and to flag potential concerns. Smaller offices may have only one or two Canada-based officers and/or non-immigrant officers, but high-volume offices may have as many as four or five. Applications for visitor visas significantly increase in advance of Canada's summer tourist season. In many offices, processing permanent resident applications is temporarily suspended or slowed during the spring and summer, and visitor visa processing takes priority.

In pursuit of the immigration department's current modernization goals, International Region and office managers are constantly searching for ways to rationalize the visitor visa application process and to streamline the flow of decision making so that it consumes fewer organizational resources. As already noted, high caseloads demand efficiency in decision making, and one consequence of this is reduced contact with applicants. In the case of visitor visas, officers can potentially interact with applicants at three points: when an application is submitted; if it arouses concerns; and when passports, visas, and other documents are sent to applicants. To conserve resources, the general principle at all three junctures is that direct contact with applicants should be minimized.

As noted in Chapter 4, Citizenship and Immigration has recently entered into an agreement with a third-party private-sector company, VFS Global Group, to establish a network of Visa Application Centres that work in conjunction with visa offices. The department expects that 130 Visa Application Centres will be operating in more than ninety countries by the end of 2014 (Citizenship and Immigration Canada 2014i). When I was conducting the fieldwork for this project, several visa offices allowed applications to be dropped off in person, but as the use of the Visa Application Centre has expanded considerably in 2013 and 2014, most no longer do so.[2]

Clearly, the role of the Visa Application Centre is to eliminate office contact with applicants at both the front and back ends of the application process. The centres are responsible for ensuring that applications are complete, that supporting documents are included, that the relevant fees are paid, and that passports (with a visa placed inside) and other documents are returned. However, "they play no role in the decision-making process and are expressly forbidden to provide any visa related advice to applicants" (Citizenship and Immigration Canada 2012a).

The manager of a Temporary Resident Unit explained what the centres do:

> The staff at the Visa Application Centre go through the checklist with the applicant to make sure they have filled out the application accurately. The purpose of the visit [to Canada] is there, whether it is for business, to visit family or friends, as tourists, or as students or workers. The applicants sit with the intake officer. The intake officer sees if the docs are provided. They will also counsel the applicant whether they should submit the application if they don't have all of their documents ready. Once the application is submitted, we take their money, so if the application is not complete, or they do not have all of the docs, they will just be wasting their money.[3]

Though they are not involved in decision making, the centres help conserve visa office resources because "they take away a lot of the back-and-forth between us and the applicants."[4] As a Temporary Resident Unit manager explained in more detail,

> The centre does a good job for us. They are a good front line. We have outsourced the initial screening, and this saves us a lot of time. We started that in 2008. With the centre we have better client service. We get complete applications. We don't have to ask for docs. Cost recovery is easier. They fill in the forms with the applicant. They make sure that the applicant's name is correctly entered, the name that appears on their passport, and not some other name that might appear on some other document. Like they say, if you have good data coming in, you have good decisions coming out.[5]

Visa Application Centres are not part of the physical infrastructure of the embassy or consulate. Most are located in the same city as the visa office, but some are in other cities in the country or region. When an application is complete, the centre delivers it to the visa office for processing, usually in a day or two. Depending on its location, a large-volume office can receive dozens of heavy mailbags or boxes from its Visa Application Centres each morning for processing that day. In a busy large-volume office, a Temporary Resident Unit manager remarked that "the centres collect 99 percent of our caseload from all over [the country]. This is a godsend. The files come overnight from all over ... and what we get in the morning is our intake for the day."[6]

The application requirements for a visitor visa are explained in detail on the Citizenship and Immigration website and those of individual visa offices (Citizenship and Immigration Canada 2014b, 2014c). In addition, the department has published an online guide titled "Applying for Visitor Visa" (ibid., 2), thirty-two pages of rather complex instructions on how to apply for a visa. The guide is intended to make the visa issuance process more transparent, but its purpose is also to reduce the need for people to contact a visa office or Visa Application Centre with questions about how to fill out the form. The complexity of the visitor visa application process is certainly not lost on officers: as the head of a Temporary Resident Unit lamented, "I pity applicants. The whole process can seem so complicated."[7] No doubt, many applicants concur.

Astute individuals can read between the lines of the department's instruction guide to figure out how visa officers think about processing their documentation. When I was conducting my fieldwork, some offices sent further signals about what they were looking for by explicitly outlining *how* applications would be assessed. For example, in a webpage that has since been discontinued, the Manila office revealed,

> In reaching a decision whether the applicant is a genuine temporary resident, the visa officer considers several factors, which include:
>
> - the applicant's travel and identity documents;
> - the reason for travel to Canada and the applicant's contacts there;
> - the applicant's financial means for the trip;
> - the applicant's ties to his or her country of residence, including immigration status, employment and family ties;
> - whether the applicant would be likely to leave Canada at the end of the authorized stay;
> - the applicant's health condition.
>
> Officers make decisions on a case-by-case basis. The onus is on applicants to show that their intentions are genuine. (Citizenship and Immigration Canada 2013d)

Not all offices provided this additional information, which was arguably a reflection of whether they were more facilitative or enforcement-minded. Now, however, processing information for applicants is confined to the generic online guide, which may indicate the department's general reluctance to tip its hand regarding what it wants to see in an applicant.

As with permanent resident visas, offices attempt to manage expectations by informing applicants of their "average" processing time (measured by how long it takes to process 80 percent of applications). As of May 2014, the turnaround time for an average visitor visa ranged from five working days in Kyiv and Warsaw to fifty-two days in Moscow and sixty-two days in Ankara, which had the longest time of any office (Citizenship and Immigration Canada 2014o, see also 2014p). This wide variation reflects differences in the operating environment of each office and perhaps staffing levels as well. Offices with longer times are debatably those where "risk," defined in its various forms, is higher and/or where applicant credibility concerns are of greater significance. Some offices subject all visitor visa applications to an extra layer of security screening, whereas others do so only for files that raise specific concerns. Each office has its own informal standards for turnaround, and whether those match average processing speeds depends, in part, on the philosophy of the immigration program manager.

As a Temporary Resident Unit manager explained, "The service standard is five days, but [the immigration program manager] likes us to make it one. He says if you can't make a decision in one day, you won't be able to make that decision two days later."[8]

Time Pressures

As with permanent resident processing, officers are under pressure to make swift decisions about visitor visas. Once a file is opened, the expectation is that they will approve or refuse the application within a few minutes. Specific workloads vary by office and officer, but the trend seems to be that Canada-based and non-immigrant officers are pushed to work ever more quickly. In a busy Asian office, an officer who dealt exclusively with visitor visas said that she was expected to make seventy-five decisions a day, which translated to about three minutes per file, not including the time she devoted to writing up her notes in the database.[9] In the same office, another officer who handled temporary foreign workers said, "I spend about five to seven minutes per file" and added trenchantly, "This office is ridiculous."[10] In another Asian office, a Canada-based officer said that she made about 100 decisions a week on all types of temporary resident files but was being pressured to increase that to 75 a day. She noted that a locally engaged non-immigrant officer in her office made over 14,000 decisions in 2011 alone, compared to her own 4,400.[11] As elsewhere in the system, time and productivity pressures provided the overarching context for decision making. A Canada-based officer remarked, "There's so much pressure. They want the numbers. They don't want waiting times ... It's always about the numbers."[12]

When an officer has concerns about a visitor visa application, office culture and the program manager's approach seem to determine whether the applicant will be interviewed. In several high-volume offices, there are no interviews at all. If the supplied information is ambiguous or incomplete, or if an officer has concerns, the application is simply refused. Due to time constraints, credibility is assessed very swiftly, and a refusal can arise from just one or two aspects of a file. Such is the case with "self-serving" letters, as a non-immigrant officer in an Asian office explained: "If applicants have self-serving letters of employment, I have to look at that. Say an applicant is the owner of a small business and he writes a letter saying that he has permission from his employer to be gone for three weeks ... This is a self-serving letter."[13] In this instance, refusal turned on a single factor. Moreover, applicants who submit ambiguous or incomplete information tend not to be given the benefit of the doubt:

> Applicants are supposed to provide translated docs when they apply, but it is fifty-fifty whether they actually do that or not. I can read [the local language] so it is not a big deal for me. In this case, I can see that they own a business, but it is small. I don't know what their income is. They haven't provided me with that information. In this case, I can take a risk if I want, but I don't want to take a risk, so I am going to refuse their application. I am under no obligation to ask for more documents.

Citing the endemic nature of fraud in the country, this officer felt that requesting more documentation was pointless, because "if you ask, they can provide."[14]

Other offices appear to be more facilitative because they permit applicant interviews. In a Caribbean office, for example, a mother and her two children were interviewed because the officer had noticed discrepancies in the photographs of one child. The application photograph appeared to show a birthmark on the child's forehead, but the passport photo did not. At the interview, the mother explained that the "birthmark" was a painted bindi, and since she had brought the child with her, the officer could see it and thus approved the application. In other cases, the interview addresses ambiguities in an individual's personal history. In one office, a man applied for a visitor visa so that he could sit a nursing exam in Canada. His paperwork revealed that he was in a same-sex relationship with someone in the United States and that his young daughter lived there. He himself had lived in the States for several years, but it was unclear whether he had worked there. His application did not provide any indication that he had worked as a nurse since returning to his country of origin. The officer felt that "the overall story did not add up," so she interviewed the applicant to assess his credibility. After concluding the interview, the officer decided to refuse the visa.

All Temporary Resident Unit officers work under considerable pressure, but some find this more stressful than others. How they manage stress may reflect personal coping skills and attitudes toward their work, but it is also connected to the client base at their particular office and their perception of the harm associated with making an incorrect decision. As a group, applicants from certain countries are not seen as posing a threat to the safety, security, and well-being of Canada, so erroneously approving one of them tends not to evoke fears about harm to Canadian society. Many officers feel that the consequences of making a mistake are largely focused on the individual involved. Legitimate visitors who are refused a visa will certainly be inconvenienced, but far less so than the genuine skilled worker or family class applicants who are denied a permanent resident visa. For refused visitors, life will go on, and they can always reapply if they wish. Indeed, for all these reasons, some officers prefer working in a Temporary Resident Unit because, despite its pressures, they can walk away from the job at the end of the day.

For others, the fast pace, the heightened sensitivity to risk, and the desire to protect Canada from non-genuine visitors means that working in a Temporary Resident Unit can take its toll after a while. A unit manager confirmed this: "Everyone says that a Temporary Resident Unit is the worst place to be, and that my position is the worst one to have ... I have been doing this for a bit more than a year, and I will do this for a while longer, but I could not do this for four or five years in a row. I couldn't do it."[15]

This rather enforcement-minded individual tended to concentrate on the negative repercussions for Canada of making a wrong decision. In his view, visitors who launched spurious refugee claims in Canada, overstayed their visa, worked illegally, or endangered health, safety, or security all constituted a harm to Canadian society, so the weight of a wrong decision was a constant reminder of his role as gatekeeper.

Jumpers and Genuine and Non-Genuine Visitors

Visitor visa requirements function as an aspect of border control and are intended to prevent non-genuine visitors from landing on Canadian soil. Non-genuine visitors come in many forms: some plan to work in Canada without proper authorization; some will make a refugee claim once they arrive; some have committed serious crimes and/or hope to harm the safety and security of the country; and some intend to seek medical treatment under the pretense of being a Canadian citizen or permanent resident. Though visa officers vary on the facilitation-enforcement continuum, the acute sensitivity toward screening out non-genuine visitors is embedded in their broader occupational subculture. Every occupational subculture has its own values, symbols, and language, which serve to distinguish insiders from outsiders, to reinforce group norms, and to facilitate communication (Hughes 1958; Prus 1997). During my discussions with Temporary Resident Unit officers, they very commonly referred to "jumpers," which is short for "queue jumpers." The word has both a general and a specific meaning. According to one program manager, it applies generically to visa overstayers, "working in your uncle's shop without permission," studying in non-accredited programs, and claiming refugee status after being admitted as a visitor.[16] In other words, a jumper is anyone who bypasses regular channels by using a temporary resident visa to gain permanent resident status or some other benefit in Canada to which he or she is not entitled.

In its narrower definition, "jumper" refers specifically to people who make a refugee claim after reaching Canada. Though the system tries to protect Canada from visa overstayers and those who want to work illegally, officers cannot know whether granting a visa to any given individual was the wrong decision unless that person is caught and charged by police or immigration authorities in Canada and there is some type of follow up. At her current posting, a Temporary Resident Unit manager said, "There are not a high number of jumpers here. They probably overstay their visas and end up working illegally, but then we don't really know what happens to those cases."[17] Refugee claimants, on the other hand, publicly "out" themselves, and in their case the officer's wrong decision can be an issue, at least at Citizenship and Immigration. People who make a refugee claim after landing in Canada must come forward and assert that they are refugees; in so doing, they essentially admit that they were not truthful when they applied for their initial visa. For International Region, this raises the question of whether a visa officer *ought* to have made a different decision, or whether something in the file should have alerted the officer that the applicant was not a genuine visitor. As a result, officers tend to be most concerned about this form of jumper, and the ones whom I interviewed tended to see jumpers in this more narrow sense.

Though it is not illegal to make a refugee claim inside of Canada, visa officer and wider departmental concerns about screening out potential claimants arguably indicate a general belief that most are not genuine. The federal Conservative government certainly reinforces this view, which is reflected in several of the changes, noted earlier, to the processing of inland refugee claims. As Josiah Heyman (2001a, 136) observes about US immigration officials, "Officers are not necessarily opposed to immigration, but see themselves as maintaining the proper ways to obtain it." Canadian officers are no exception to this. In their view, travelling to Canada as a visitor (or a student or temporary foreign worker) and then claiming to be a refugee is not a proper way of acquiring permanent residence status. Indeed, as several officers stated, their desire to maintain the integrity of the immigration system and to protect Canadian taxpayers from unnecessary costs motivated them to screen out jumpers. Though he could not name an exact figure, one officer asserted that "jumpers cost the Canadian government a lot of money; they cost taxpayers."[18] A Temporary Resident Unit manager in another office expressed a similar sentiment, and he did quote a specific figure, albeit estimated: "Every officer puts it on their shoulders to not have a jumper. To have a jumper is like a failure for all of us. We know how much it costs the taxpayer when we have a jumper. I don't know the exact figure, but it is something like $65,000 for the first few months in Canada."[19] Though his estimate may be somewhat high, he clearly felt that, as one of the main clients of the immigration system, Canadian taxpayers should be protected.

The point at which a person chooses to jump has significance in the subculture of visa offices. Visitors who make a refugee claim shortly after landing in Canada are viewed differently from those who launch their claim after spending several months or even years there. Professional pride is at stake, as a Canada-based officer suggested:

> If a student jumps and they do it a couple of months after I approve the application, then I kind of take it personally. On the other hand, if I admit a student, and they go to school in Canada for a year or two, and then they jump, if they jump in the long term, then I don't take it personally.[20]

Jumping after living in Canada for a year or two lets officers off the hook and absolves them of responsibility for having made the wrong decision. In a sense, they can explain away the choice to jump by noting that any number of things can happen to visitors during their stay in Canada, that their safety and security circumstances back home might have changed, or that they may have met someone in Canada who counselled them to claim refugee status as a way of circumventing normal immigration channels. However, even when people jump shortly after arrival, officers still mitigate responsibility by asserting that they cannot possibly control everyone that applicants meet in Canada, or what kind of advice or encouragement they receive from friends, relatives, or consultants to make a refugee claim. As an officer noted, "Things can change between the time you grant an applicant admission and when they actually arrive in Canada. They could have sold their house and business, who knows?"[21]

In both formal and informal ways, visa office culture reinforces the idea that officers must protect Canada from jumpers. Formally, when an individual jumps, International Region asks the office that processed the file to forward it to Ottawa to prepare for the refugee adjudication process. However, before the file is transferred, the program or unit manager usually informs the relevant officer that the person has jumped. If this occurred soon after arrival, the officer reviews the file, checking for anything that should have prompted a refusal decision. Often, nothing in the file suggests that the applicant intended to jump. A Temporary Resident Unit manager pointed out, "It is okay for an officer to make a mistake. When we get a jumper you let the officer know. But sometimes, there is nothing you could have done differently. We have had UN workers, well paid, who are jumpers."[22] In this case, working with the UN was defined as a good, stable job, and a sign of good character, so there was little reason to suspect that a refugee claim would be made in Canada.

In other instances, re-examining the file may bring something to light that should have resulted in a refusal. Of course, the decision cannot be changed, but officers can learn from their errors and keep them in mind for future reference.

Both officers and offices regard jumpers as a fact of life, so it is expected that an officer's name will be attached to jumper files at some point during his or her career. Inadvertently letting the occasional jumper slide through the net does not seem to result in any formal sanctions for an officer. However, the consequences are more significant when the jumper turns out to be inadmissible to Canada due to medical, security, or criminality reasons. As a deputy program manager put it, "The only kind of case where you could get your hand slapped is if you admit someone who is inadmissible."[23]

Except for inadmissibility cases, informal teasing within offices and inter-office comparisons help to reinforce the occupational expectation that jumpers must be deflected. When I asked if having a jumper on one's record had any negative consequences, a long-serving officer replied, "Not really, not from the department's point of view. It is more like mocking from colleagues ... It is more about your colleagues bugging you. I have never seen an office where an officer has a mess of jumpers."[24] As a Temporary Resident Unit manager explained, inter-office comparisons in jumper rates are regularly distributed by International Region:

> In the Temporary Resident Unit, we are always under pressure to not miss anything. But we don't have the time, we have to make decisions quickly, ten or fifteen minutes. With refugees, they can interview, take their time. But also the pressure is on yourself. Because we see every month the worldwide jumpers from every mission. We get sent that information about the number of jumpers from each mission.[25]

A program manager mentioned that his busy, large-volume office normally had about forty jumpers every month and added that his colleagues in other offices sometimes wondered "what is going on" at his office.[26]

However, if individual officers or offices as a whole fail to detect telltale patterns regarding who jumps, or if the numbers are seen as too high, informal processes seem to be mobilized to correct the problem. Neither program managers nor the immigration department takes the issue of jumpers lightly. One program manager noted, "I don't like it because we are missing something."[27] As a Temporary Resident Unit manager made clear, the concern about jumpers extends beyond individual program managers:

> With the rate of jumpers we have now, we are fine. If, on the other hand, we have 10 percent jumpers, headquarters wants to know what is wrong with the quality of decision making. In an overall sense, [the program manager] ... would be responsible to headquarters for accounting for that kind of rate. As for individual officers, there is variation in the proportion of jumpers they have. The more productive officers tend to have few cases of jumpers, the less productive officers have more cases. In each case of a jumper I will get a note from headquarters saying that a person had jumped. If I see a pattern, I will bring the officer in and we will develop a remedial plan. I will say, "You seem to have a problem with a certain kind of file." Often they will say, "I know. I have been worrying about these kinds of cases for a while" – for example applications from businessmen, who then jump. I will tell them that if they are thinking about approving the application, then send the docs for verification. Assessing applications is not rocket science ... We have a set of criteria. It doesn't take too much thought to figure out if a person is going to jump. If they are from a small company, you should be able to figure out if they are from some random small operation, whether the operation is genuine.[28]

Though there are no set limits when it comes to the number of jumpers that officers must have on their record before they are informally sanctioned, program and unit managers are expected to step in if the number is too high. This is particularly true for newly minted officers, whose failure to detect jumpers may reflect a gap in training: "There is no consequence. But if it is a new officer and they have a high percentage of jumpers, it could be a training issue."[29] However, even for longer-serving officers, high numbers of jumpers can prompt informal corrective action. A Temporary Resident Unit manager told me, "If an officer has say 20 percent jumpers, you would have to talk to them to see what they are missing. You would have to coach or mentor them to see what they are not properly looking at."[30]

At the same time, however, program and unit managers must tread a fine line when they mentor officers, taking care not to be overly directive or fettering their decision making. A long-time Canada-based officer explained the negative consequences when managers take a too-heavy-handed approach with officers who let more than the occasional jumper slip through: "I have had only, maybe two immediate jumpers, maybe six long-term jumpers. Some program managers try to micro-manage this, and keep too close an eye. This is a problem because it freezes you up. It is hard to make a decision if the program manager is always looking over your shoulder."[31]

He added that he had "never heard of any kind of penalties for jumpers, although when people put in for postings in different locations, program managers might talk between themselves, 'I don't really want this person.'"[32] This highlights the role that informal sanctions and relationships play in ensuring on-the-job conformity.

From a wider organizational point of view, having too few jumpers is as undesirable as having too many. Though none of my interviewees had a sense of what the correct jumper-to-approval ratio should be, senior management interpreted too few as indicative of flawed decision making. A Temporary Resident Unit manager clarified the department's thinking:

> We get about ten per month. I think zero is best, but for Citizenship and Immigration, if it is zero, it's a problem. Maybe you are being too strict, and refusing people who should be admitted. I can see that makes sense from the department's point of view, but as individuals, and as a mission, we don't want them. But with jumpers, it is the ratio that is important. Sure, we might have two hundred jumpers, but we have fifteen thousand applications.[33]

In another office, a designated immigration officer said, "You don't want jumpers, but on the other hand, we are encouraged to take risks."[34] Other officers confirmed that having no jumpers on one's record could also be taken as problematic by a program manager. One Canada-based officer said, "We had very few jumpers but that was because we had very few approvals. The program manager once said to us, maybe loosen up on your risk management a bit. Let some people in."[35]

Another officer pointed to the problem of striking a balance between having too many and too few jumpers on one's record, and the ways that organizational and external pressures can determine how officers think about jumpers.

She remarked, "If there is a pattern to my decisions, then they will say I'm being too soft. But if I keep refusing, MPs complain that I am being too hard."[36]

Though deterring jumpers is a cornerstone of Canada's temporary resident visa enforcement regime, the system is not airtight, and non-genuine visitors do manage to slide through the cracks.

Distinguishing between Genuine and Non-Genuine Visitors

A main task in visitor visa processing is divining the intentions of individuals who wish to come to Canada. As a designated immigration officer put it, "Our job is basically all about prediction."[37] A program manager elaborated: "The basic question [officers] have to ask themselves ... is 'will they comply with their conditions of entry and return. Are they bona fide? Will the person leave after authorized to stay in Canada, and do they have a reason to come back?' It's not black and white."[38]

As social scientists know, predicting individual behaviour is extraordinarily difficult. They can describe and explain broad patterns of behaviour for social groups, along with various social trends and tendencies, but foreseeing how a member of a particular group or social category will behave is fraught with uncertainty. How do visa officers try to predict whether visitors are genuine? How do they gauge whether someone is likely to jump? As with all other visa application categories, they repeatedly emphasized that the information in a file must "add up." The immigration department certainly recognizes that no two officers will apply the selection criteria for temporary resident applications in the same way. A long-serving non-immigrant officer stated, "We have Immigration and Refugee Protection Act guides, but the fact is that each officer applies the criteria differently."[39] What adds up for one officer might not compute for another. At the same time, however, certain patterns and regularities come into play when visa officers assess whether a file adds up.

Officers in Temporary Resident Units commonly distinguish between "easy" and "hard" files. In the former, the information in an application adds up quickly, and approval is swift. But "easy" also applies to files that clearly fail to add up and that are quickly refused. One Canada-based officer noted that in her office, "70 to 80 percent of the cases are easy approvals or refusals."[40] As I spent a full morning with a Canada-based officer who reached decisions on fifteen visitor visas, I wrote the following field note, which details the steps in an easy approval:

> A male is applying to visit Canada for six months. All of his children live in Canada. His daughter works at a university in Canada, and his son is a

> nurse. The visa officer explains, "I don't have any concerns about funds to support him while in Canada. I have no concerns. He is an old guy. He is not going to work in Canada. But because he is applying to stay for six months, I need to issue meds [which means he has to undergo a medical exam]. Unless his children in Canada receive social assistance, which is virtually unheard of for [people from their country], this might be a harder case. But this is an easy case. The majority are easy cases, and I will approve."[41]

In this instance, the officer invoked the applicant's age and the socio-economic status of his children to clarify why acceptance was easy. Since the applicant was elderly, she did not expect him to work illegally in Canada. Moreover, his children had respectable, middle-class jobs and thus could support him while he visited them. The officer's views of people from his country – that they are hard workers who tend not to rely on social assistance – also helped slot this case into the "easy approval" category. The officer's sole concern was health and duration of stay, so she asked the applicant for evidence regarding his medical state. If the medical history were to contain adverse information, she would revisit her provisional approval. Notably, age is a factor in easy acceptances at other offices. As a non-immigrant officer in an Asian office stated, "Elderly people don't jump. There are language barriers, the weather. They just go to visit and then come back."[42]

Easy cases are also easy refusals, files that do not add up. Asked to describe an easy refusal, a non-immigrant officer in an Asian office replied in concrete terms:

> When the application does not make any sense. For example, a person works as a clerk, they only make ... [$350] per month, and they want to go on a three-week trip to Canada. I ask myself, how can they afford it? I look at their bank passbooks to show me how much money they are carrying in their account every month. If there are relatively recent deposits into their account, I don't give those a lot of weight.[43]

The Canada-based officer mentioned above, who had approved the elderly visitor, discussed an easy refusal – an applicant whose ties to her country of residence were weak:

> This lady, this is going to be interesting. She wants to visit her two brothers in Canada. She is a farmer. She has worked in Bahrain. She has been employed abroad and does not have strong ties to [her country]. All of her siblings are in Canada or the US. She has no leisure travel. She visited her

> father in Saudi. The applicant says that her brother is going to pay for her ticket and her support while in Canada. While this shows he has funds, it shows she does not. She has no proof of her income, but chances are that it is low. She is single, no dependants, all siblings are in Canada. She has weak ties to [her country]. This case is more high risk because of previous employment abroad.[44]

Here, a number of macro-level considerations informed the officer's decision. The applicant's socio-economic status, as a farmer with few financial resources, and her history of working outside her country suggested that she might take up unauthorized employment in Canada. The fact that she had no family in her home country also fed into the officer's perception that the case carried a high risk. Due to this bundle of considerations, she concluded that the woman was likely to overstay her visa or to work illegally in Canada, so she refused the application.

Officers often confront cases that they define as hard, in part because they take up extra time, but trying to avoid them is not considered acceptable. As a non-immigrant officer explained, "We work on an honour system here. We don't cherry pick. Sometimes I might want to put a file back so that someone else is stuck with it, but you just don't do that."[45]

Often cited as "hard" were cases in which applicants wished to attend funerals or visit sick or dying relatives in Canada. In addition to taking up more time, they are difficult because they play on the emotions of officers (Eggebø 2013b). In her analysis of Norwegian public servants at the Directorate of Immigration, Helga Eggebø (ibid.) notes that emotions have an ambiguous status in this type of work. Though visa officers are expected to make decisions on the basis of objective criteria and to bracket their personal feelings, they are also ethical human beings who must manage their emotions as they work. In most instances, they succeed in separating their feelings from individual files, but death and sickness cases pose special challenges. A Canada-based officer said,

> For me, one of the most difficult decisions are death cases. They want to go to Canada for a funeral. I have to be cautious with those because there is fraud even in those cases. There will be fraudulent letters from funeral homes, fraudulent relationships. It really bothers me because ... [one of my children died at a young age], and I know how heart wrenching that is. If he died in another country, and I was not given a visa to go to his funeral, I know how devastating that would be. I've been there. It's tough. Last

> week, our office approved a death case, and he jumped. Sometimes, you are struggling with a decision like that and you say, "Screw it, if they jump, they jump."[46]

These cases are also hard because, from the department's point of view, they are potentially explosive. Refusals that are associated with sickness and death often attract media attention in Canada and can spark public outrage. In such instances, officers and the department for which they work are portrayed as cold and heartless martinets whose thought processes are both unreasonable and incomprehensible. Sometimes, even those who work in the system can see a refusal as unfathomable. A program manager mentioned an episode of a few years earlier, in which the parents of a young woman who had died while attending school in Canada were denied a visa. When they reapplied, they were refused again. The program manager stated, "This case blew up in the press. My response was 'what the hell is going on there?' This is a problem with management because the problematic aspect of it should have been caught by the manager."[47] In this point of view, the "problematic aspect" of the situation was the failure to anticipate the ultimate trajectory of the refusals – that closing the door on the grieving parents of a dead daughter would achieve little beyond tarring the image of the department.

Sickness and death cases are also hard because they require officers to strike a balance between their identity as ethical beings, their role as upholders of Canada's immigration rules and procedures, and their motivation to protect the reputation of Citizenship and Immigration. In some cases, officers are virtually certain that a would-be visitor plans to jump but feel powerless to deny the visa, given the negative attention that a refusal can attract in Canada:

> Sometimes you will have life and death cases. They are also seen by the immigration program manager. I can see that in some cases, there is nothing there. I had a case, her son was an inland refugee claimant, and her son had a child in Canada. And the child was dying. I will discuss the case with the program manager, and I will use humanitarian and compassionate grounds to look at the file again. Sometimes I will see the same applicant a couple of different times. I refused this applicant a couple of times. I had refused her two or three times before. But now her child was employed in Canada. I still had concerns about her ties to [her country]. But I asked for medicals, and I was glad to know that there were no meds, and Canada will not be on the

> hook for that. But I came into the office on Saturday to issue her visa this time around. She will probably jump. If Canadians knew more about how people use the system, they would be horrified.[48]

As this person mentioned, officers can refer a file to their Temporary Resident Unit supervisor or program manager if an applicant does not meet eligibility requirements but where humanitarian and compassionate factors, such as death and illness, could potentially override a refusal. My field notes record the complexity and implications of pushing the decision up to a higher level of authority:

> A woman is applying to visit Canada for eight months where she wants to visit her father and her sister. She also has a daughter in Canada. Her father has been diagnosed with lung cancer. The visa officer explains, "So, her parents are in Canada, her daughter is a live-in caregiver in Canada, and she has a sister in Canada. Her father is sick, and the chances are her father is not going to live for a long time. She has a low level of savings, not even Cdn$1,000." [The officer] ... checks the case analyst notes, which are on a small piece of paper clipped to the folder of the application. The notes indicate that the applicant was refused a visa in 2006. "She was born in 1965, so she is definitely of working age. She says she is a businesswoman, but she has not submitted any docs. She has no travel history. I will forward this to the unit manager. She does not meet the entry requirements, but out of compassion she might be given a temporary resident permit. The unit manager has [the] delegated authority to make the decision on humanitarian and compassionate grounds. There are high-profile controversial cases, or there are cases where there is a compelling reason to travel to Canada. In this case, I know he is going to say no, the man is not dying. So I have to ask myself do I want to put my name to this file?"[49]

As this case highlights, officers can sometimes let themselves off the hook by recommending to a superior that he or she accept a hard case on humanitarian and compassionate grounds. Although the officer knew that her unit manager was unlikely to do this, at least the file would be off her desk. If the manager rejected her recommendation, she could nonetheless take some comfort in the fact that she tried. On the other hand, if he complied, she would be absolved of responsibility should the applicant choose to jump.

Adding Up

Reaching decisions in visitor visa cases is an iterative process in which officers weigh the pros and cons of every application. It is akin to creating a balance sheet of credibility, with various credits and debits. However, there is no specific formula for how that balance sheet is to be summed up. Though several variables go into its creation, how they are invoked and weighed to determine credibility is discretionary. But, as with other types of visa processing, discretion is constituted socially and contextually, so certain patterns in the decision-making process can be identified.

The following field note illustrates the iterative nature of the visitor visa decision-making process. It documents the morning-long session, mentioned earlier, during which I watched a Canada-based officer work through her caseload. In the eleventh case of the morning,

> A woman is applying to visit her husband in Canada. From the program assistant notes, the officer sees that a previous application to Canada was refused in 2002. "Right away I am concerned. I am going to have to check into this one." The officer starts going through the file and she can see that the applicant's husband is in Vancouver on a job-training course on a temporary resident visa. "A visitor wanting to visit a visitor, that is not good. But, I can see that the husband is a Telus employee. That spins it a different way. We don't usually have problems with Telus training. My concerns have dropped. She is a bank manager and her income is very good. This is good. They just got married, in July 2010. This isn't good. But Telus is a reputable company. They go, they come back. She wants to stay for two weeks. That's plausible. The issues are what will bring her back ... and what ties she has to Canada."[50]

As noted above, the credibility of a visitor visa application is assessed by weighing the ties that applicants have to both Canada and their current place of residence. Ties are defined broadly as both familial and economic. Too many ties to Canada and too few to the home country are taken as a flag or indicator that a visitor is not genuine and perhaps might jump. Unemployed or marginally employed individuals who are single and who have few family members in their home country are generally seen as risky cases because they are thought to have little incentive to return home. Conversely, though applicants for a visitor visa must have a letter of invitation from someone who lives in Canada, possessing too many ties to relatives there can count against them because it raises concerns that they will not go home when their visa expires. As a result, officers tend to search for their reasons to go back.

Although *individuals* apply for a visa to visit Canada, whether they actually receive one can be based on factors that lie beyond their control, including if they apply to come as part of a larger group. The track record of the person and/or organization in Canada that issued the invitation also comes into play. A non-immigrant officer in an Asian office noted, "This is a business delegation. With business delegations, we do a queue count. We look at the inviter's record, to see the number of applicants they have invited, the number of refusals and the number of jumpers." After showing me a handwritten note in which a program assistant had recorded information about the inviter, the officer said, "I have to ask myself whether it makes sense for the inviter and the applicant to match. We get a lot of fraud in business delegation applications. But it is hard because they might have a gotten a referral from the commercial section [of the embassy]."[51]

This case also reveals how external pressures from embassy staff are brought to bear on decision making. The officer added that the credibility and past performance of the tour operators that organize trips to Canada are also taken into account: "With tour operators, we also keep track of the number of invitations they have extended, the numbers of refusals and the number of jumpers."[52]

The application history of relatives is also considered germane. In some cases, the "sins" of family can be enough to scuttle an application, particularly if a family member is defined as a jumper. From the perspective of prediction, the underlying logic is understandable, if not entirely fair. People who are perceived as having abused the system are seen as predisposed to encourage an invitee to follow suit: "I will look to see whether there is anything adverse in FOSS [the database], whether the inviter violated immigration laws."[53] During our conversation, in which an officer thought aloud about how he assessed files, he examined the application of a woman who wished to visit her son and daughter in Canada. She had nearly US$100,000 in the bank and was planning to bring her young third child with her. Her healthy bank balance and good letters of invitation counted in her favour. However, as the officer delved deeper into the file, he discovered that it gave no information about the immigration history of the son and daughter. He remarked, "If they complied with the law and followed the rules to get in, that will be good. But if they got in by trying to cheat the system, then I will probably refuse." He had his program assistant check the database for their application history. It revealed that the son and daughter had reached Canada through normal channels. "That's good," the officer said, adding, "If they wanted to they could sponsor this lady and she would probably get it. So, I am thinking if they really wanted her to stay in Canada, that would be the route that would make sense. So my sense is that she really is going just for a visit, so I am going to approve this one."[54]

As noted above, claiming refugee status in Canada is not illegal, but visa officers commonly see it as a mechanism to jump the queue for permanent residency. Referring to those who successfully claimed refugee status from within Canada, one officer said, "The problem is that even those people who are accepted by the system, they say the system worked for me, and so the system can work for their relatives. It can be discouraging. You see so much more, more variety. If a child made a refugee claim, then I am going to look at the case more carefully."[55] Though parental visits to their children in Canada are considered normal, in this case how the son or daughter ended up living in Canada can be taken as a strike against the parent who wants to visit.

The socio-economic standing of one's inviting relatives is also a consideration in the assessment of credibility. Visa officers use published low income cut-off data to check the financial status of Canadian inviters. The data reveal whether they can afford to support the visitor during his or her time in Canada. Officers look at the size of inviters' families, the number of dependants, and the family income to determine whether they have the resources to pay for an individual's visit, particularly if it is expected to last for more than a few weeks.

Finally, an applicant's own track record can determine whether a visa is granted or denied. If the departmental database reveals that someone has previously applied for a visa, officers will take this fact into account as they assess the file. However, if the previous application was refused, they must overcome the original officer's concerns: "If there is a previous refusal on record, we have to give it to another officer for review. If I approve the application, I basically have to overcome the previous officer's concerns. I don't like those files. They take more work."[56]

A program assistant explained how a track record once played a starring role in determining the fate of an application: When a woman dropped off her paperwork at the embassy, the receptionist noticed that she was pregnant and recorded it on the cover of the file. A subsequent check of the departmental database disclosed that the woman had previously applied for a visitor visa, which had been granted. During her trip to Canada, she gave birth to a child. Sensing that history was in danger of repeating itself, the officer refused the application.[57]

Travel history is also taken into account when credibility is assessed. The analysis of travel history turns on three points: destination, duration of stay, and country of origin. Applicants who have the resources and networks to visit Western countries tend to have more credibility than those who lack a travel history or have never visited a Western country. For example, some officers accord regional travel within Africa less significance than travel to the United States, Britain, or Continental Europe. The underlying logic here is that applicants who have visited a Western country have already had their opportunity to jump the queue. The fact that they did not is taken as a sign that they are genuine visitors to Canada.

However, as the following example from my field notes indicates, travel to a developed country can sometimes generate a refusal. The applicant wanted

> to visit her sister and the son of her sister's employer. Her sister is a caregiver in Burnaby, BC. On her application she also says she wants to visit Niagara Falls. [The officer] raises her eyebrows and says, "That's a long way from Burnaby." She explains that the applicant has visited the US. She works as an accountant, but there is no indication of her salary. "The good thing is that she has been to the US. The bad thing is that she has been to the US, but stayed for a long time. She has a valid US visa, and she stayed in the US for six months. But she does not list family members there, so who was she staying with? There is no invitation letter from her sister. Her sister is a permanent resident. It does concern me that she has been to the US for such a long time with no family members there. She is an accountant here. I am going to refuse. It is probably an indication that she worked illegally in the US for six months."[58]

In one case, an applicant's story about wanting to help establish a business during his stay in Canada did not add up. The officer recalled,

> From his passport something did not seem right. The applicant had too many stamps from known people-smuggling hubs and his occupation did not seem to correspond with so much international travel. When I called him in for an interview, he had gold rings and chains around his neck, and came with a local lawyer to try to intimidate me into a positive decision. I could tell by his body language, and the whole package, that he was not simply involved in trying to set up a business in Canada. I refused the application.[59]

Visa officers can place differing weights on previous travel history, especially in connection with the applicant's country of origin. A Canada-based officer noted,

> How I think about a file depends on the post. In India and Jamaica, in those places, if there is a good international travel history, then that is a good. But here I am tougher. If the documentation isn't there ... if they don't provide tax documents, I ask why. I want to see three months' worth of tax documents, not just one.[60]

In this case, the source of funds, and in particular whether the funds were legally acquired, trumped travel history.

Some officers are reluctant to rely on travel history as a sign of credibility because of uncertainties about what it actually means. Some also know that a double standard may be at play when certain kinds of past travel are seen as more genuine than others. Recognizing the difficulty of differentiating between a good travel history and a suspicious, non-genuine one, a Canada-based officer posted in Africa admitted,

> I don't like previous travel that much. I've had emails from applicants complaining that [they] have been to Benin, to Botswana, Tanzania, and [they] have been refused for lack of previous travel. But it is not previous travel to a developed country. It is travel, but it is not outside of Africa. And then again, they might have visas for Schengen countries, and have lots of back-and-forth travel to Europe. But you never know what happened with them there. They might have claimed refugee status and been returned, so even that is not a reliable measure. With travel history, some officers put a lot of weight on that; they put a great deal of reliability onto that criterion. But for me, it is more about the funds, the reason for travel, do they have a reason for return, do they have children in Canada?[61]

In this instance, the officer tended to place less weight on travel history because of ambiguities in what it actually meant.

The Temporary Resident Unit Is the Real Front Line

Visitor visa processing differs somewhat from permanent resident visa processing. Though both assess credibility, risk, and the facts in the file, prediction is more salient in the former than in the latter. In a sense, officers who handle permanent resident applications generally do not "care" about how applicants fare once they reach Canada, because their job is simply to assess eligibility. Whether a federal skilled worker lands the perfect job in Canada or fails to find employment is an abstract question for them, and though they are aware that immigrants sometimes have difficulty in getting Canadian employers and/or licensing authorities to recognize their credentials, they generally have no way of knowing what happens to them after they arrive in Canada. Thus, the in-Canada life of migrants, with its attendant difficulties and triumphs, is largely beyond their purview. Such is not the case for visitor visa processing, however, because officers are vitally concerned with the in-Canada future of applicants. They must try to predict whether someone will jump or overstay the visa. And if a visitor makes a refugee claim in Canada, they will be informed of it. Though there may be certain profiles and indicators of whether an applicant will jump, they are not deterministic. Every applicant presents a unique biography and set of circumstances, so several considerations, such as financial status and history, ties to Canada, and country of residence, are weighed during the decision-making process. Which factors an officer invokes is a matter of discretion. Though more individual-level discretion may be exercised in visitor processing than in permanent resident processing, discretion is socially constituted there as well. Productivity expectations limit how much time officers spend on a file. And their understandings of the broader macro-level forces that shape migration are also invoked to prevent jumpers from reaching Canada. Though visitor visa decisions cannot be formally appealed, officers are aware that public opinion and media coverage can sometimes function as an ad hoc court of appeal, particularly in emotionally sensitive cases where illness or death are involved.

Much of the decision making in visitor visa processing, as well as skilled worker and family class spousal applications, does not entail face-to-face interaction between applicants and officers. However, interviews do occur when an officer requires additional information to evaluate eligibility, credibility, and risk. And everyone who applies as a government-assisted or privately sponsored refugee is interviewed to help establish identity, credibility, and settlement prospects in Canada. The next chapter examines officer interviews for spousal, federal skilled worker, and visitor visa applications. Further, the chapter shows how, under pre-2013 procedures, simply submitting an application in person could stimulate an officer to dig deeper.

9

The Interview

> *Our office is so strapped that you have to make a system. You lose time; you lose momentum if you start to make exceptions. You really can't make exceptions. People often think their cases are exceptional, but when you look at it, there is nothing special in their case. But sometimes you have to. I had a lady, in tears. She needed a travel document. Her father was ill. She had lost her permanent resident card. She was confused about the details of what happened. And then at some point when I was talking to her I thought, "What has happened to me in my life where I have lost my humanity?" I thought, "If I was in that situation, I might not be able to remember all the details of what happened." But generally, you can't give anyone special treatment.* (Field notes, December 13, 2010)

Since the introduction of the Immigration and Refugee Protection Act (2001) in 2002, overseas visa offices have moved to inoculate their employees from direct contact with applicants. As applications for most categories of permanent residence status are first sent to a processing centre in Canada, overseas offices have virtually no direct contact with applicants at that initial stage. Due to the new subcontracting arrangements with Visa Application Centres, the same is true for temporary resident applicants.

Citizenship and Immigration is also reducing contact between officers and applicants at the selection stage of processing. International Region expects officers to base most of their decisions solely on the information provided in the application. Many high-volume offices, as a rule, do not interview applicants for any form of temporary resident visa and require that officers make their decision on the basis of the application. Similarly, International Region expects them to approve or refuse most applications for permanent resident status without resorting to an interview. The effort to create a firewall between applicants and decision-makers is driven largely by resource limitations and the demand for efficiency; interviews take up scarce organizational resources and slow the decision-making process. As one program manager rather starkly put it, "We can either process applications or we can answer questions. We can't do both."[1] However, in isolating themselves from applicants, offices may be foregoing opportunities to assess credibility and risk.

Reinforcing the Client Status of Applicants

Sociologists who study how discretionary decisions are made in the context of micro-level interactions between street-level bureaucrats and clients recognize that broader structural processes set the context for how discretion is exercised and how decisions are made (Frohmann 1991; Gilboy 1991). Furthermore, though all interactions between bureaucrats and clients are unique, they are characterized by certain rituals. In and of themselves, these rituals do not produce specific outcomes, but they do set the tone and direction of the decision-making process.

Visa applicants can be described as "non-voluntary clients" (Lipsky 2010, 54). That is, if they want a visa, they have no choice but to deal with the Citizenship and Immigration bureaucracy because it holds a monopoly on a "benefit" that they cannot get elsewhere. Though every applicant is a unique individual with a particular background, personality, and set of life experiences, bureaucracies must inevitably transform individuals into categories and standardized units that can be processed under pre-existing rules and procedures. As Michael Lipsky (ibid., 59, emphasis added) notes, "The processing of *people* into *clients,* [and] assigning them to categories, is a social process." In Canada's case, slotting applicants into categories occurs anonymously, and there is virtually no interaction with a street-level bureaucrat. Unaided, or perhaps with the help of a lawyer or consultant, applicants must figure out what type of visa they need. To discover how and where they should submit their application, they must refer to the Citizenship and Immigration website (or a lawyer or consultant). In most circumstances, they never interact with anyone at the department and must simply wait while an anonymous officer makes a decision.

However, interaction does sometimes occur, and whether it is virtual or face-to-face, it will be grounded in an unequal power relationship. As Max Weber (1964, 152) defines it, power is the "probability that one actor within a social relationship will be in a position to carry out his own will despite resistance, regardless of the basis on which this probability rests." At the most basic level, visa officers impose their will on clients by either approving or refusing their application. They control a highly significant public benefit – the legally acquired visa, which permits its holder to visit, study, work, or take up permanent residence in Canada. Though refusals for permanent resident visas can be appealed, applicants are generally in a subordinate position where officers are concerned. To put it plainly, their lives can be made miserable by officers who ask for more documents, drag their feet, and ultimately deny them a visa. For their part, applicants are rarely in a position to return the favour, though as I will argue, there are ways of lashing out after a refusal decision has been made.

In the visa office, interaction is generally routinized to reinforce the client status and subordination of applicants. As non-voluntary clients who are relatively powerless, applicants are forced to conform to the structures and processes that have been created by both the department and individual offices: they are told how to submit their paperwork, how to interact with offices, and how and where they will be interviewed. In this, they are constantly reminded of their unequal status and repeatedly taught to play the client role. They are instructed to refrain from contacting offices if the processing of their application falls within the expected time. Depending on which visa they have requested, they can electronically track their application through the processing stages, and this, too, is intended to diminish their contact with offices and officers. Offices do not publish the names or contact information of individual officers, which reinforces the idea that efficient processing overrides an individual's need to inform an officer of the unique nature of his or her case. It also helps ensure that clients cannot complain about particular officers or discipline them for taking too long to process a file. As a result, waiting for a visa, or for word from an office, is a constant reaffirmation that an applicant is both a subordinate and a client.

If an officer has concerns about a permanent resident application, applicants are normally first asked to provide written documentation to clear up those concerns. They are given a deadline for compliance and are warned that their application can be refused if they fail to meet it. If the additional information does not materialize, or the concerns remain unresolved, applicants can be "invited" to come in for an interview. Since they have normally already received a concerns letter that details the specific issues the visa officer wants them to address, they will no doubt realize that something about their application is problematic. They also know that the officer is the bureaucratic agent who stands between themselves and their visa, so there is a structural incentive for them to adopt a deferential manner.

Applications that prompt concerns take longer to process, so people who receive a call, email, or letter that invites them to attend an interview have every reason for accepting the suggested date and time. Although they are asked about their availability, and there may be some negotiation of the particulars, they are more than likely to agree to the interview slot offered to them. Depending on the office and type of application, interviews can be scheduled a few days, or a few weeks, in advance. Applicants must arrange their schedules, gather their documentation, and prepare themselves to address the officer's concerns lest they lose their opportunity to make their case and their interview is scheduled for an even later date.

On interview day, the client status of applicants is further emphasized, but now they are also defined as potential threats to safety and security. Those who are interviewed at a Canadian embassy or consulate must undergo a security check that involves passing through a metal detector and having their bags, purses, and briefcases searched. They will leave their cell phones at a security desk or in a locker and will not retrieve them until they vacate the premises. In some offices, the locally engaged security guards who check their possessions will be armed. In one instance, a Canada-based officer who was giving me a tour of the operations was surprised to discover that the guards who regulated physical access to the high-rise tower where the embassy was located carried loaded side arms.[2]

After passing through the initial layer of security, applicants are directed to office reception where they inform a locally engaged receptionist of the reason for their visit. Receptionists are usually told in advance whom to expect on particular days, and after checking in, applicants are normally instructed to remain in the reception area until called. Waiting rooms are usually simply furnished with rows of institutional-style chairs. Some have posters of typical Canadian sites and scenes, historical immigration promotion posters, or posters advertising the presence of a Canadian production in town, such as an upcoming Cirque du Soleil performance.

Interviews commonly begin after the scheduled time, and this, too, strengthens the power position of the visa officer. Though there was no indication that officers deliberately made people wait as a way of exerting dominance, the fact that they did wait tacitly affirmed their client status. In regions where employee safety is a concern, some waiting rooms have paid security staff who keep an eye on clients. In those cases, a security guard escorts applicants to the interview booth when their names are called. If safety is not an issue, the receptionist simply directs them to a particular booth, or the officer summons them over the intercom. Even though International Region expects that interviews will take place in the booths, some officers may choose to conduct them in their private offices because they are less "cold" than the booths.

Interview booths are generally quite Spartan and small, no more than a few square metres. On the applicants' side, they often contain only a chair or two. Sometimes, there is no chair, and applicants must stand for the duration of the interview. They are separated from officers by a bulletproof glass divider, and communication occurs via a telephone connection between the two booths or by talking through a small screened opening in the glass. The ledge that supports the bulletproof glass is usually fitted with a sliding panel, so that documents can be slipped between officer and applicant. On the officer's side, booths have a chair or two, a desk, and a networked computer. Officers type their notes into the computer, and during the interview they will use it to check information on the departmental database.

The micro-level ritual that unfolds in the interview booth also tends to reinforce the unequal status of applicants and involves more lessons in their role as clients. Interviews are typically dominated by officers, who assert their control in a number of ways. Depending on the location of the office and the associated safety and security concerns, officers may introduce themselves by their full name, their first name only, their last name only, or generically as "the visa officer who is responsible for your case." Sometimes, interpreters are brought in to facilitate communication. Depending on office location, they are either paid outsiders or locally engaged staff who add this task to their other duties. After ensuring that applicants understand what is being said, officers start the interview by explaining that its purpose is to address certain concerns or to clarify issues.

At the beginning of the interview, officers normally counsel applicants to "only answer the questions that I ask" and to stay on point, which further solidifies the understanding of who has the upper hand in the exchange. As a Canada-based officer explained, interviews commonly turn on a power struggle:

> The interviews are often about a struggle for control. The applicant wants to control the information they give out about themselves, and only wants me to know the information they want me to have. Sometimes they give non sequiturs as a way of not giving up control. I have to go back to the original question to keep them on track and to not give up control. For example, I had a case where the employment letter of an applicant was fraudulent. The applicant took the approach of trying to be my friend, my buddy. He started kidding around with me at the beginning of the interview. Later, when I confronted him with the false document, he said, "Would it make a difference if I had a million dollars?" Afterwards, one of my colleagues jokingly said that I should have said, "It would make a difference if I had a million dollars!"[3]

The officer added that applicants can also lose control of an interview by supplying too much information about themselves. Sometimes, they divulge so much that they talk themselves out of a visa:

> In other cases, you will have a student, and when you ask them why they want to study in Canada all they talk about is how hard life is as a Chaldean in Iraq. Or, an applicant wants to go into the theatre, but all they talk about is their hard life as a child. These people just made their refugee claim in front of me, so I'm not going to let them in.[4]

A general air of distrust frames the face-to-face encounter in the interview booth. A Canada-based officer described his job, only half-jokingly, as "separating good liars from bad liars. The bad liars we catch, the good liars get into Canada."[5] The point of the interview is to address concerns about an application, so it is inevitably premised on some degree of suspicion about an applicant's biography, identity, relationships, and/or credentials: in other words, something doesn't add up. Interviewees perceive this as well, so caution and doubt hang over both sides of the interaction. In the interview, officers are looking for information that confirms their doubts, but they must also be open-minded enough to allow for new information that addresses their concerns.

For applicants, the climate of disbelief underscores their subordination and forces them to adopt a cooperative or compliant stance. Compliance, or the simulation of compliance, is an essential aspect of their efforts to put their best foot forward. At the interview, they must appear to accept the legitimacy of both the officer's authority and the decision itself. They must be acquiescent and deferential. At the same time, because they know that their application has aroused suspicion, they must exhibit the relaxed confidence of someone who is telling the truth, has nothing to hide, and is deserving of a visa. But confidence must never veer into abrasiveness and must be tempered with natural befuddlement and surprise that they are being interviewed in the first place.

Compliance also entails keeping a firm hold on emotions, even if the interview seems to be going badly. As the interview progresses, officers engage in procedural fairness by detailing which concerns remain unresolved, providing applicants with another chance to address them. Though it may not necessarily affect the outcome of their case, applicants probably feel that directing an emotional outburst at an officer could potentially torpedo it. Thus, controlling their emotions is critical, even when an officer essentially tells them to their face that they are not being truthful. Since they are non-voluntary clients, they have no choice but to appear compliant in the hope that they can satisfy the officer's doubts, and venting indignation is obviously incompatible with deference. The end of the interview can be fraught with tension, and officers are legally mandated to use a certain code language when they reject applicants. That code language essentially involves articulating the words "I am not satisfied that –." Even at this stage, applicants generally seem to understand that deviance from the script is undesirable. Those who lose their temper, or express frustration or aggravation, fail to accept their role as subordinates.

Compliance with the applicant role also needs to extend beyond the interview. As they wait for a decision on their visa, applicants must be careful to maintain the impression that they are legitimate visitors to Canada lest their words or demeanour be taken as proof that they are not. As he explained how understanding local culture could play a critical role in decision making, a Canada-based officer referred to the Middle Eastern idea of *wasta*, which roughly translates to "clout" or "who you know," and recounted an episode in which it destroyed an applicant's credibility, even after the interview:

> I had a case where an applicant for a visitor visa works as a locally engaged person for the United States. He had a good letter from his supervisor, and based on his employment, his letter, I told him I was willing to give him a

> visa [if his security check came through]. A day after, I got an email from his supervisor, the one who wrote him the letter of reference, saying that this guy was going around the office saying that he was going to stay [permanently] in Canada. His supervisor wrote the email to me because he didn't want his name attached to this case if the guy was going to stay in Canada illegally. He didn't want his letter on file. So he called.[6]

When I asked the officer what he could do with this new information, given that the interview had already occurred and he had provisionally approved the visa, he replied,

> His wife came to apply the next day, and on the basis of that letter I didn't issue her a visa. When the mandatory fifteen-day waiting period expires [for a security check to go through], I'll reopen the case, and won't approve. I could also cancel the visa so when I enter that into our FOSS database, Border Services will not let him in.[7]

When Does the Interview Begin?

When I conducted my fieldwork, many visa offices still allowed individuals to drop off their temporary resident applications in person. This changed in 2013, however, and now most of these applications go to the Visa Application Centre. This measure may have conserved departmental resources, but it also came at a cost for the assessment of credibility. In shifting the task to Visa Application Centres, Citizenship and Immigration sacrificed the opportunity to assess credibility and risk as people submitted their applications. Before 2013, when paperwork was dropped off in person, locally engaged staff, typically a program assistant or receptionist, ensured that the application was complete and that the necessary supporting documentation was present. If this were not the case, staff encouraged people not to submit their application, because they knew that a visa officer was unlikely to approve it. Thus, applicants would have paid the non-refundable visa-processing fee for nothing. In counselling individuals to hold back their applications, staff saw themselves as doing them a favour.

Program assistants and receptionists also played a key role in triaging applications. They assessed whether the cases were relatively simple and straightforward or whether the officers in the Temporary Resident Unit were likely to have concerns. An example from my field notes (with some of the details changed to protect the identities of applicant and officer) shows how receptionists triaged files. It also shows how applicants were subject to the disciplinary regime of the visa office and how unwillingness to play the compliant role did not pay any dividends:

> A man from Bolivia who is in Canada on a visitor's visa that is valid until the end of the next month comes into the office with a Canadian woman. They have travelled to the visa office in the US from eastern Ontario. When his number is called he presents himself to the locally engaged program assistant and explains that the woman with him is his common law spouse and that they want to extend his visitor visa. Together, the couple explains to the program assistant that the man needs to go back to Bolivia to visit his sick mother and then wants to come back to Canada, but by that time his original visitor visa will have expired. The program assistant explains to them that since he already has a valid visa, the office cannot issue him another one and that he must reapply to enter Canada when he is back in Bolivia. The assistant tries to discourage the applicant from submitting the application by explaining that the "immigration officer will say the same thing," and that if she accepts the application, they will have to pay the $150 non-refundable fee to process it. Despite this seemingly sensible advice, the Canadian spouse continues to demand to see a visa officer. She argues with the assistant, who puts the application into a red folder, which is the office's code to indicate that this is a "problematic" file.
>
> The program assistant comes to the backstage of the office steaming mad. She explains to the visa officer that she has a "difficult case." She explains that the two came to the office without any forms or documentation, demanding that they be allowed to apply for another entry visa for the man. The assistant also reports to the visa officer that the woman is becoming quite belligerent, and is demanding "to talk to a Canadian."
>
> The non-immigrant officer takes the file and starts looking through the application. She then quickly checks the database regarding the man's previous visas. She notes that the man had a previous visa for Canada issued a few years earlier. She can see that on both previous applications the applicant indicated that the reason for his coming to Canada was to study. The officer begins to wonder about "where the common law wife has come from?" She sees that there is no mention of his being in a common law relationship with a Canadian in his most recent visa application, "and now suddenly he has a wife?" I can see that the officer is getting more agitated as she is going through the database and thinking things through. In the meantime, the whole office now seems aware of the case, and that the wife

is a troublemaker. After a few minutes, the visa officer goes into the interview booth and calls the applicant in over the intercom, but clearly says, twice, "applicant only." The visa officer makes a point of leaving the door to her side of the interview room open slightly because the assistant wants to listen in.

The visa officer expects that the wife will want to come into the interview booth. She accompanies the man to the door of the booth expecting to enter. As she looks in, she can see from the visa officer's face that she expects her to wait outside of the booth. She does not argue and steps back. The visa officer asks the applicant if he understands English. The applicant looks slightly confused and indicates that he understands English "a little." The visa officer asks the applicant, in a number of different ways, why he is coming to the office for another visa. The applicant explains in halting English that he is in a common law relationship with the woman, needs to leave Canada to visit his mother, and then wants to return to Canada. The visa officer listens closely to what the man says, but quickly determines that there is no point in continuing the interview because his English-language skills are too poor. The visa officer informs the applicant that he needs to come back to the office with a third-party interpreter on another day in order for the interview to continue. The officer hands back the application and a printout with information about how he can go about hiring a local interpreter. The man looks completely confused, and the visa officer abruptly leaves the interview booth.

The officer expects the Canadian wife to come back to the program assistant's window to start arguing again. I can see through another window that the man and woman are reading the information sheet the officer gave to the man. Everyone in the back room of the office is now aware of what is going on and expects her to come storming back to the reception desk. In the end, she doesn't, and they both leave.

The officer and I go back to her office and she explains why she did not want the wife to come into the booth and interpret for her husband. "It is the man's application and he needs to explain the situation himself." She also explained that if an applicant needs an interpreter, the interpreter has to be "at arm's length." It is inappropriate to allow applicants to use family members as interpreters because they are not at arm's length. The officer explains that she also speaks Latvian and remembers a case where a Latvian applicant brought in a family member to interpret. In the interview, the interpreter said things to the family member like "don't say that" and "tell them this." As a result, they strictly enforce rules about third-party interpreters.[8]

Triage at the application submission stage also involved assessing demeanour. As they walked down the street to the embassy or entered the reception area to hand in their paperwork, most people probably had no idea that their mannerisms, behaviour, and body language were being scrutinized for anomalies that could reroute their application to the "problematic" folder. For example, if they were a "little bit too friendly," receptionists might intuit that they had something to hide and could alert the visa officer to this potential concern. Even the subcontracted security guards who regulated access to the office could play their part in triage. In one case, an embassy guard noticed that two young men embraced and kissed as they left the office after dropping off their applications. The intimacy of their embrace led him to conclude that they might be gay, and he reported his observation to the receptionist. She had noticed that the men were "sitting too close together," thought she saw them "holding hands" in the waiting room, and felt that "they might be in a relationship." She relayed the guard's observation and her own suspicions to the Canada-based officer who was processing the applications. As the officer later explained, "The receptionist is supposed to note impressions of the applicant when they hand the file in ... So, what they [the two men] will probably do is study in Canada, and then at the end of their course, they will make a refugee claim. It will be interesting to see what the Temporary Resident Unit supervisor will do."[9] Though the outcome of this particular case is unknown, it does reflect the importance of locally engaged staff in triaging applications, as well as the role that stereotypes and prejudices could play in raising concerns about an application.

Family Class Interviews

Visa officers can approve a family class spousal and partner application without conducting an interview. By the same token, they can also refuse it without an interview, but they generally schedule one when they have concerns. If the sponsor lives in Canada and the spouse does not, only the latter attends the interview. If, however, the sponsor is available overseas, both sponsor and spouse can be interviewed.

Depending on the officer's preferences, interviewing couples can vary. Sometimes, the pair is seen together and then separately. In other cases, the spouse is interviewed first, the sponsor second, and then both together. Interviews that I observed lasted between one and two hours, and usually began with simple, factual questions that were easy to answer and would not have alarmed the applicant. A designated immigration officer described this as setting the baseline:

> In the first twenty minutes you ask questions about how they came here. I ask them about their relationship. I look at body language, eye contact, their demeanour, if they are fidgety, if they are looking at the wall. There is a baseline. For example, this morning, I could have picked at the fact that the guy was not wearing a ring. Some other officer might have focused on that, "Why aren't you wearing a ring?" But to me, devotion to the child is part of the bigger picture, so I wouldn't bother with the ring. You can be trained in this type of thing, but you develop your own style.[10]

When I asked the officer what she meant by "baseline," she replied, "It's like on a lie detector test. I ask questions about things they shouldn't be lying about. I start by asking factual questions to set a baseline to see what the person is like. Then I ask questions about the relationship. If they need to look at their papers to answer the questions, then that's a problem."[11]

Many officers claim that they know within a few minutes after an interview begins whether a spousal relationship is real. One remarked, "In family class, within the first thirty minutes you can tell if a relationship is genuine."[12] After I observed an interview, the designated immigration officer said, "I knew he was lying after about ten minutes."[13] In forming their impressions, officers focus on demeanour, body language, and even how applicants enter the room, and they claim to develop a "gut feeling" about how people with nothing to hide step into a room and answer questions.

Although a distinct impression of credibility is formed early, the interview process eventually turns to more personal, private matters in the couple's relationship:

> Sometimes you end up asking rude questions. Sometimes I ask a question just to see the type of response I will get. That helps to understand the person. I can sense him getting tense. You have to ask pointed questions ... But being upfront is the way to go. Sometimes you ask a question just to see what the response is. Sometimes I might say to the client that "I am going to have to ask you some personal questions." This helps to make clear the direction of the questions. But it can be hard. It's not easy to ask some questions. But the patterns of response can be used to detect misrepresentation. If there are contradictions in what the client is saying to you, I will suggest

to the client that "you haven't been truthful," or "you haven't been forthright." There are different ways of saying it.[14]

Notably, some Canada-based officers disliked working in the Family Class Unit precisely because the investigation was so intrusive. One admitted,

> I hate family class. I hate asking those questions about whether their relationship is genuine. You have to hear these intimate stories about how they met, how they consummated the marriage. In [one posting], I had a lesbian couple explain to me how she had sex with her partner the first time ... My interpreter was horrified, and so was I, so I quickly ended that line of questioning.[15]

Since applicants are usually familiar with the officer's concerns before the interview begins, they sometimes prepare by getting coaching from friends, relatives, or people who have gone through the process. Visa officers claim that they can tell when someone has been coached: "Applicants are very well informed about immigration. They come so well prepared for the interview because they are coached. They are so well coached that when they start answering questions, we know something is not right. There are websites that list the questions that have been asked in previous interviews."[16]

Though somewhat lengthy and characterized by a kind of bullying that did not occur in the other spousal interviews I observed, the following field note gives the flavour of the micro dynamics in a spousal interview where the officer suspected that the couple had entered into a marriage of convenience. Several details have been altered to conceal the identities of everyone involved. The interaction between applicant and officer displays themes that have already been mentioned, namely, the unevenness of the power relationship and the reinforcement of the applicant's client status:

> Tom [the Canada-based officer] comes into the program manager's office and says, "I am ready for my 10:00 a.m. interview" and asks if I would like to join him. The three of us walk downstairs to one of the four interview booths. I sit down at the back of the booth and Tom quietly goes through his last-minute preparations for the interview. He has some handwritten notes about the file and it takes him five to ten minutes to check them over and go through the questions he plans to ask ... After Tom refamiliarizes himself with the case, he describes the broad outlines of it to me. This is an FC1 (spousal sponsorship) case. The applicant came to Canada as a student, studied at a high school in Calgary and after he graduated he made a refugee

claim. His claim was refused by the Immigration and Refugee Board and he was eventually removed from Canada. He married a Canadian woman before his removal to Poland and she is now sponsoring him ...

Tom has to go to the reception desk about twenty feet from the interview booth to ask the receptionist to call the applicant in ... The applicant comes in with a folder full of papers. He sits down and smiles broadly at Tom and me. Tom introduces himself with his first name only, and explains that he is the officer responsible for making the decision in this case. Tom introduces me by my first name and explains that I am a university professor from Canada who is studying visa officers. He asks the applicant if he has any objections to my sitting in. Tom goes on to explain that my presence will have no bearing on the decision that he will be making. The applicant smiles and agrees. Tom begins by asking questions about whether the applicant is comfortable conducting the interview in English ... The applicant indicates "yes."

Tom then asks, "Did you sleep well last night?" "Do you feel tired?" ... The applicant answers that he is tired because he was up late last night talking to his wife in Canada. Tom jumps on this answer and rather aggressively says, "Just tell me if you are tired or not. If you are too tired, we do not have to conduct the interview today." I am taken aback by the aggressiveness of Tom's approach; he is clearly not interested in setting "a baseline" ... Tom's style of questioning seems meant to put the applicant on edge, and I can see that this is going to be a rather different interview from the ones I have observed already. I wonder about Tom's question about whether the applicant is "tired." I conclude that this must be one way of undercutting the applicant's ability to say later in the interview that he did not answer a question properly because he was tired for not having slept well the night before. Tom must have heard this before in interviews, and so he wants to be able to take that potential reason off the table if the interviewee starts to give inconsistent answers to his questions.

Tom then asks about where the applicant learned English. He says he learnt English when he attended high school in Canada and reaches into his folder to pull out his high school diploma. He tries handing the diploma to Tom through the slider underneath the glass partition, and Tom says, "Just give me everything you have. Give me the whole folder. Just pass the whole folder through." The applicant continues to try to give Tom just the diploma but Tom continues to demand that the whole folder be handed over. The applicant hesitates, and I can see he never expected this to happen. He decides to comply. Tom then asks the applicant to leave the booth for a few minutes so that he can review the documents in the folder ... I have never seen an interview where an applicant was required to hand over the entire contents of their folder and wonder to myself whether this is fair to the applicant.

The applicant leaves the interview room and closes the door. Tom does not say a word and proceeds to go through all of the papers that are in the folder. He looks at everything, which includes a copy of the application, what look like bank transfer receipts, plane tickets and a package of photographs and other items I cannot identify. After a few minutes ... Tom comes across two handwritten pages. Tom turns to me and says, "This is what you would call a cheat sheet." He shows me the two pieces of paper with writing in pencil. I can see that the sheets are a series of questions and answers about the couple's relationship. "When did you get married? How many people were at the wedding? Who attended the wedding?" I can also see that there is a sentence about "my husband's things were in my closet," or something to that effect. I ask Tom, "Is it fair game to ask for the folder?" Tom says, "Yes, he brought it to the interview, so it is." He puts the sheet aside for a moment and continues to look through the papers. After another minute or so, he pulls out two letters from two banks in Canada. He does not show them to me but I can see that they appear to be on official bank letterhead. He puts those two letters aside, finishes going through the folder, and then goes back to look at what he called "the cheat sheet." After a minute or so, he says to me, "This looks like his wife's cheat sheet."

Tom calls the applicant back in and resumes the interview. Tom puts the "cheat sheet" out of sight and returns to his list of questions. He begins asking about how the relationship developed. The applicant answers that they first met in high school. "When did you start dating?" "What did you do on the first date?" The applicant said they went out to a movie and then had a "snow fight," and then smiles to at least appear to think back fondly on their first date. Tom says, "Snow fight?" and the applicant says yes, "a snow fight." Tom realizes he is talking about a snowball fight. The applicant starts to talk further about the relationship and how much he loves and misses his wife, but Tom cuts the applicant off: "Please keep your answers short, don't deviate too much. Just answer my questions." The applicant stops talking immediately.

Tom then focuses attention on the applicant's knowledge of his wife's family. He asks about the name of his wife's mother and father, what her father does for a living, the names of her two sisters and her brother, where they live, the names of their children, their ages, etc. The applicant seems to have good knowledge of these details ...

Tom then asks questions about when the applicant proposed, how they got married, and who attended the wedding. The applicant explains that they got married in a civil service, and only one other couple attended as witnesses. He gave their names ... Tom then asks why [the wife's] parents, and her sisters and brother, did not attend their wedding. The applicant explains that her two sisters live outside of Canada and her brother lives in Halifax and could not travel to attend the wedding. He further explains that his wife's mother and father were on vacation in Mexico at the time, and that was why they were not present. Tom asks how long were her parents in Mexico. The applicant says they left in November and were coming back in March; "They don't like the cold." Tom asks, "So you got married at the end of February, why didn't you wait a month for them to get back?" The applicant says that he does not really know. He explains that his wife ... wanted to get married right away. Tom continues to press the point. "How does your wife get along with her parents?" The applicant says, "Good, they have a good relationship." For Tom, this raises even more of a concern. The applicant can see that this is an issue for Tom and says they were young, his wife was twenty when they married, and she did not think it was important for them to be there. Tom ... continues to probe why her parents were not present. I can see that the applicant is increasingly frustrated by this line of questioning, and he eventually says, "I don't know why my wife did not want them there. It is none of my business." The applicant begins to become argumentative and begins to question Tom's authority: "Why are you focusing on this issue so much?" ... All Tom says in response is "This just does not make sense."

Tom then turns to questions about whether his wife has ever visited him in Poland. He says "no" ... Tom asks, "Why?" The applicant says that she started a new job last March and her employer has not given her any time off ... Tom says to the applicant, "That's not true. In Canada employers have to give their employees holidays after one year of employment. She should have been eligible for some holidays so that she could visit you" ...

The applicant is getting increasingly agitated and more argumentative. The applicant once again tries to engage Tom in a debate about why he is asking certain kinds of questions. Tom does not respond and makes no move to elaborate on his interview strategy. Instead, Tom enters into the case notes that the applicant is "being argumentative."

Tom then pulls out the cheat sheet and shows it to the applicant. He puts the two sheets up against the glass and asks, "What are these?" The applicant hesitates a moment, and then says that he and his wife used it to fill out the application together, "just so they made sure they got their facts straight." Tom says, "But the things that are on the sheet are not questions we ask on the form, so why would you need to write them down?" The applicant does not give an answer and just sits there. Tom types into his notes "no response."

Tom asks about the removal order that made him return to Poland. He asks about why he did not leave Canada after his refugee application was denied and his original removal order was issued. The applicant said that he did not leave because he was appealing the decision and was exploring all of his options to appeal. He said he left when he exhausted all of his appeal options ...

Tom then closes off the interview and asks the applicant to leave so that he can review his notes and consider the documents. Tom turns to his computer and starts writing out his "concerns." I can see that he is getting ready to refuse the application. He writes out his three concerns: 1) absence of his wife's mother and father at the wedding; 2) no visits from wife; 3) the existence of the cheat sheet. As he is writing, he notices the bank statements that he put aside earlier and realizes that he has forgotten to ask about them. He calls the applicant back in to ask about the bank statements.

"Do you have any joint bank statements?" The applicant points to the letters, saying he has opened joint accounts, but that the banks forgot to put his wife's name on the two letters. He did not submit any actual bank statements, just letters indicating that the accounts had been opened, but only in his name. Tom asks why his wife's name does not appear on the letters. The applicant says that this was a mistake made by the bank. He begs Tom to call the two banks in Canada to confirm that they are joint accounts ... I can see that he has no intention of calling.

At this point, Tom outlines what are now four concerns, and gives the applicant a chance to respond to each. The applicant responds, but provides no new information. He repeats what he has already told Tom ... Tom eventually says, "I have heard enough. I am refusing your application because I do not believe that your marriage is genuine." Tom starts to give the folder of papers back to the applicant. The applicant is talking to Tom while he is pushing the papers through the glass. He says that he does not harbour bad feelings for Tom but I can see he is very angry and frustrated. He says that he is going to appeal the decision. Tom says, "Go ahead, that is your right under Canadian law." The applicant walks out.[17]

Clearly, the interview situation is charged with inequalities in power. Instructing someone to "just answer the question" and "get to the point" is all about control. Tom did have discretionary choices along the way: He could have contacted the banks, but the ten-hour difference between the office and the bank branches in Canada meant that verifying the joint statements would take time. A program assistant would have to call the banks during the next few days; if they confirmed the joint account, Tom would go back to the file, add the new information, and perhaps rethink his decision. Whether a bank would disclose this confidential information to a voice on the telephone is doubtful, so Tom's refusal, though seemingly hard-hearted, was not unreasonable in the wider context of the bureaucratic culture in which he worked. Revisiting the file a few days or weeks later was not really an option, because he had thirty other files sitting on his desk, all waiting to be processed. As in this case, officers are at liberty to examine the contents of folders or envelopes that applicants carry with them. Everything that is brought into the booth is fair game when it comes to assessing the development of the relationship. In a different office, I observed an interview where the applicant also carried a folder. When the officer asked what was in it, the applicant told her that it contained original documents, copies of which had already been submitted. She chose to accept this response at face value and did not pursue it further. I could see that she was forming an opinion to approve the application. In not pressing to see the contents of the folder, perhaps she was avoiding opening a door that might have disrupted her evolving understanding that the relationship was genuine.

Safety, Security, and Bureaucrat Bashing

Public servants generally do not like to admit that they work for the federal government (Carroll and Siegel 1999, 183). Often perceived as both overpaid and underworked, they bear the brunt of public frustration regarding the government's failings of the moment. Bureaucrat bashing is a popular sport, although Barbara Carroll and David Siegel (ibid., 197) argue that the most hurtful and damaging criticisms come from elected politicians and the government in power. Carroll and Siegel (ibid.) also note that bureaucrats' reluctance to reveal what they do for a living has a negative impact on their social life. In seeking to avoid situations where they must listen as people rant about what is wrong with government, or the particular branch for which they work, many public servants retreat into a world where their main social interactions are with colleagues. Others are deliberately vague in social situations when someone inevitably asks, "So, what do you do?"

Decisions in which deserving applicants receive a visa virtually never excite public praise. Moreover, few people complain when the application of a friend, relative, colleague, or client is approved. It is a different matter when an officer refuses an application, and here bureaucrat bashing can take a number of forms. Immigration is a fairly visible field of Canadian public policy, and refusals are often subject to public criticism and condemnation. In certain kinds of permanent resident applications, refusals can be appealed to the Federal Court or the Immigration and Refugee Board, so there are legal mechanisms to review the original decision. Appeal channels are more limited for temporary resident visas, and refused applicants generally cannot launch a court appeal; they must reapply and hope that a different officer will reach a different decision.

Citizenship and Immigration is certainly sensitive to public perceptions of its activities. Part of this seems to stem from its concern that criticism could undermine public confidence and trust in the system and support for the wider immigration program. Thus, it attempts to manage and monitor public criticisms of its decision making and of its operations more broadly. Headquarters in Ottawa distributes an electronic newsletter called the *Daily Wrap* to its overseas offices. Based on a scan of the Canadian media, the *Daily Wrap* is a compendium of press reports on immigration matters. Every day, all employees in International Region receive the *Daily Wrap,* or what one designated immigration officer satirically christened the *Daily Crap.* Most officers report that they pay attention to the *Daily Wrap,* if only to ensure that their name has not been splashed across the front page of a newspaper or that a controversial case making headlines in Canada has not been attached to them. The department now also reportedly distributes the *Evening Wrap,* its daily scan of social media.

Individual officers can often find themselves in the crosshairs of the public, the media, lawyers, consultants, and elected politicians. They make difficult decisions, and a refusal can have serious consequences for the people involved. An officer who believes that a spousal relationship is not genuine will withhold a visa. Though the decision can be appealed, the couple will probably endure months if not years of further separation, and will incur significant legal costs, before their case is heard. An applicant who wishes to travel to Canada for a business meeting but who has a criminal record due to a drunk-driving offence a couple of years earlier may not be issued a visa. His failure to attend the meeting might scupper a lucrative deal and could even jeopardize his career.

Applicants can fret about the slow pace of processing and are naturally disappointed if they are refused. Sometimes, they complain to the program manager about their treatment. Several program managers reported that they regularly receive letters and emails from disgruntled applicants who claimed that the officer was "rude," "unprofessional," "wrong," "biased," and/or "racist."

Perhaps not surprisingly in an age where everything from hotels, restaurants, airlines, and hospitals, and anyone from physicians, university professors, mechanics, and plumbers, is ranked and rated by clients, customers, and students, visa applicants have also resorted to the Internet to voice their opinions. Though not exactly a "rate my visa officer" website, there are a number of Internet chat rooms and forums in which applicants exchange information about officers, processing, and how to interpret the department's bureaucratese. They often concentrate on the quality of service and/or the nature of the decision. As they are relatively powerless and lack any other form of recourse, one of the few costs they can impose on officers is to publicly question their reputation. Occasionally, officers are mentioned by name, and they become objects of criticism, ridicule, and abuse. As the following two examples show, the tone can be nasty, to say the least:

> I am just grateful he had a good IO [immigration officer], and not that crazy [name deleted] in [office deleted]. (CanadaVisa.com 2010)

> The same BITCH ... refused our application. Wait till I show my husband this post. We have SO much contempt for this person I can't even tell you. (Canada Immigration Forum 2005)

An officer explained that she is the object of repeated disparagement because she deals mainly with family class applications, which for applicants, tend to involve more emotional investment than other types of visa applications. Unhappy sponsors and spouses whom she refuses complain over the Internet about her decisions. She said, "I have been called a Nazi, racist, not educated. People have complained that I am biased against them because they are black."[18]

These criticisms can affect both visa officers and their families. As I arrived to begin our interview, one designated immigration officer greeted me with,

> You might have already heard about me. There have been lots of things in the press about [this office]. I have to identify myself in my refusal letters. People write about me, and mention me by name on the Internet. My

> daughter came to me crying once, saying that she googled my name on the Internet and people were saying terrible things about me, about my decisions.[19]

Such attacks are no doubt hurtful, though like most professionals whose decisions are subject to public scrutiny, officers develop ways to discount, minimize, and neutralize them.

During an interview, officers who decide to deny a visa can defuse conflict by not announcing their decision. Though, as noted above, applicants are forced to adopt a deferential, respectful stance, they are sometimes unable to maintain it, particularly if the interview ends with the revelation that they will not be receiving a visa. In an understandable desire to forestall unpleasantness, some officers conclude the interview by thanking applicants for "answering my questions" and saying that they need more time to review the information that has just been provided. This ensures that they retain control and that applicants, who are unaware of their true status and can thus hope for a positive outcome, remain deferential. Even those who fear that the interview did not go well will probably refrain from bad behaviour. In effect, employing this tactic amounts to what Erving Goffman (1952) describes as "cooling out the mark." On the other hand, some officers choose to reveal their refusal decision at the end of the interview, and a few even seem to relish the task. In such cases, deference can crumble as applicants argue, shout, or resort to verbal abuse.

Verbal abuse sometimes crosses the line into more menacing encounters, intimidation, and threats of physical violence. Though they are rarely publicized and are far from an everyday occurrence, most long-serving officers can recount incidents in which they felt uncomfortable, and even threatened, after they refused an application. Several officers told their own stories of being threatened by disaffected applicants, and even more could recall incidents in which colleagues were threatened. One officer who had worked in an eastern European office narrated an episode involving an applicant for a visitor visa. Suspecting that the man had connections to organized crime, he called him in for an interview. By the end of their talk, the officer was even more convinced that the applicant had "mafia" connections, so he said that he would not approve the visa. Upon hearing this, the applicant stared him down through the bulletproof glass of the interview booth, and not saying a word, slid his index finger across his throat. Probably not unreasonably, the officer interpreted this as a threat to his life, and for the next few weeks, he looked over his shoulder whenever he walked down the street.[20]

An officer in an Asian office reported being followed and harassed by a resentful applicant and his father as she went home at the end of the day. Another officer recounted the harrowing experience of a colleague:

> An officer was driving down the ramp leaving the building with his wife in the passenger seat. He had rolled his window down already but she was adjusting something and hadn't rolled hers down yet. A guy that the officer refused was waiting at the bottom of the ramp for his car, and when he drove by, the guy threw battery acid at the passenger window. It's lucky his wife didn't roll her window down yet.[21]

This officer also recalled a number of instances where she herself felt threatened:

> I was doing interviews in a hotel room, a small conference room all by myself. I was sitting across the table from this guy, a big guy. When I refused him, he stood up and leaned over the table towards me and said, "I'm going to get to Canada regardless of what you say." A few weeks later he did – I learned he was apprehended at the airport! [laughs]. I was threatened in [offices in Africa and eastern Europe]. That kind of thing happens more in face-to-face interviews. Now, I tend not to give verbal decisions.[22]

Recalling one posting, another officer commented, "I got the feeling that if you said 'no' to someone, they could slit your throat and not even think about it."[23]

Visa officers attempt to manage potential threats of physical harm, and the broader bureaucrat bashing that arises when they refuse an application, by concealing their identity and controlling the information they release about themselves. As mentioned above, depending on the perceived security and safety risks in their region, some do not give their names when they interview applicants; instead, they protect their privacy by introducing themselves as "the visa officer who is responsible for your case." Although they are required to sign their refusal letters, some sign with an illegible scribble that is hard to decipher. In cases where threats are of heightened concern, program managers seem able to modify procedure. Speaking about security considerations, one Canada-based officer explained,

> When I was in [a Central American office], this was an issue. There, it was decided that anyone who conducted a face-to-face interview with an

> applicant did not have final decision-making authority. We did not want applicants to connect the decision to a specific person. A locally engaged staff member would conduct an interview and then explain to the applicant that an immigration officer would make the decision. The file was then passed to a Canadian for the official decision.[24]

Other identity protection mechanisms include not admitting to working for Citizenship and Immigration, or for "Canadian immigration," even to friends and family in overseas postings. Most officers whom I interviewed said that they did not tell neighbours or new friends at their postings what they did for a living and did not disclose it in casual social settings. In one case, a locally engaged staff member concealed the specific nature of her job from her husband, hoping to spare him worry. Part of her work involved determining whether visa applicants had committed war crimes, a situation in which refusals could potentially trigger retaliation.

In social settings, Canada-based officers commonly say that they work for the "trade section" or some other branch of the Canadian embassy. Their business cards often feature neutral job titles such as "first secretary," "second secretary," "minister-counsellor," or "consul," rather than "visa officer." Depending on the context, the cards do not refer to the immigration section of the Canadian embassy or high commission.

Though this reticence is intended to protect personal safety, it also enables officers to avoid awkward or compromising encounters in which individuals buttonhole them about a current or prospective application. This concern also extends to locally engaged staff, one of whom remarked,

> I live here, and sometimes I am at the airport or at the mall and someone comes up to me and says, you refused my visa application. I can't even remember them, and there is not much I can say. But that kind of thing led me to take my name out of the phone book. It is not listed any more.[25]

Some locally engaged staff are careful about disclosing where they work and know that helping someone circumvent procedure could result in an accusation of malfeasance. One staff member said,

> My close family knows that I work at the embassy for immigration. My mother, my father, sister-in-law, and my three closest uncles. One or two of my close friends do. If they let it slip that I work at the embassy, I tell them

> to say that I am in the trade section, or the communication section. But I have to tell them that they must never tell what I do here, because if they do, it will put my job at risk. I could lose my job. Even my brothers, they are high up, I tell them if you want a visa, just submit your application downstairs. Don't ask me to do anything to help you.[26]

The need to conceal the truth of their employment poses certain barriers to forming friendships in the countries where officers work. Though some do make friends, they are cautious about letting local people into their lives. All officers explained that concern over personal safety did not affect their decision making at work, but as one lamented, "The sad part of it is that it affects how you make friends here. I have a few personal friends here, but not many."[27]

Conclusion

In July 2013, on his last day as minister of citizenship and immigration, Jason Kenney issued a farewell message to the employees of his department. In it, he listed a number of reforms to the immigration system that had been accomplished under his watch. He also expressed his gratitude for having been permitted to oversee a department that had such an important "human dimension":

> One reason why working at [Citizenship and Immigration] is such a privilege is, of course, the human dimension of what we do. While dealing with complex systems, endless acronyms (I am still learning new ones!) and the sometimes Kafkaesque rigidities of government, many of us still have the ennobling opportunity to meet some of the wonderful people who we welcome to Canada, their new home. I often meet hugely successful immigrants who remember, with great fondness, the name of the visa officer who interviewed and took a chance on them decades ago; and I know retired visa officers who, years later, run into the people they selected, who have gone on to live fulfilling lives in this land of dreams come true (Kenney 2013b).

Ironically, his references to immigrants who fondly remember officers from decades ago and retired officers who re-encounter immigrants they had admitted to Canada years before conjure a world that by and large no longer exists. Prior to the 2002 introduction of the Immigration and Refugee Protection Act, most applicants for permanent resident visas were interviewed by an officer. Though the trend to waive interviews in relatively "straightforward" cases arose during the late 1990s, before Kenney was appointed minister, under his guidance officers were progressively cut off from the immigrants (and visitors) whom they selected. Their face-to-face interactions with applicants became increasingly rare, with the result that most now see only a small handful of the thousands of people whose files they will process during their careers. Although some may recall a few names and perhaps distinctive aspects of an application, it is hard to imagine that decades from now, perhaps while shopping at the mall or taking their grandchildren to a Blue Jays game, they might run into an immigrant whom they had admitted years before. Moreover, since interviews today occur only when an officer has concerns about an application and are thus tinged by suspicion and distrust, it is unlikely that immigrants recall them with fondness. Their memories are probably quite different from those of people who were processed before 2002, when most applicants were interviewed and when officers had the time to talk to them and could also offer advice and words of both encouragement and caution about the difficult transition to life in Canada.

At the same time, one should not be too nostalgic about the past. A little over fifty years ago, Canada's immigration system was unabashedly racist. Officers had a wide range of discretionary authority that empowered them to select white immigrants, who were seen as better nation-building material than non-whites (Satzewich 1991). Moreover, a bureaucracy that does not change the way it does things and does not keep up with the times would be truly remarkable and subject to considerable public ridicule. Front-line bureaucracies, including Citizenship and Immigration, must confront certain externally imposed realities that lie beyond their control. In times of fiscal austerity, budgets shrink and all branches of government and the public service are constantly challenged to do more with less. Innovation, or "modernization" in the case of Citizenship and Immigration, is driven by the need to conserve scarce resources and is the watchword of the day for both public- and private-sector managers. Interaction with applicants and clients eats up time and resources, so it is perhaps inevitable that the push to economize has entailed its diminishment. Organizations, both public and private, are obsessed with the efficiency of their workforce and develop increasingly sophisticated mechanisms to ensure that employees produce. Setting quotas and publishing service standards help hold a bureaucracy's feet to the fire and ensure that the work gets done. In the age of the Internet and new communication technologies, many of the public's interactions with front-line bureaucrats occur indirectly, either through email, some type of web-based interface, or robotic telephone systems where one presses endless buttons in the hope of actually speaking to a real person.

In a litigious world, it is perhaps inevitable that Citizenship and Immigration is concerned about the transparency and consistency of its decision making and has moved to reduce the scope of officer discretion. Immigration lawyers and consultants are quick to jump on any apparent misstep in an officer's review procedures, or even poorly chosen words, to launch an appeal of a refusal decision. The growth in technology has arguably increased the sophistication of immigration-related fraud. Convincing-looking bank statements, birth certificates, employment letters, and university degrees and transcripts can all be made to order, and passports, visas, and residence permits can be outfitted with new identities and digitally massaged photographs. Citizenship and Immigration must work hard to stay abreast, applying ever more sophisticated technologies and investigative techniques to distinguish the genuine from the non-genuine (Salter 2011). New health risks appear, as a single international flight can enable disease to leap borders and continents. And, globalization has also brought attendant changes to the ways that people move around, to their identification with real and imagined ancestral homelands, and to the nature and strength of their transnational ties and connections. Some forms of transnationalism are benign and healthy: individuals send money to support relatives and friends back home, they fund the building of libraries and community centres, and they raise money for orphanages and shelters. But some types of transnationalism are not so healthy. Crime, whether in the form of human trafficking, drug smuggling, or money laundering, is taking on increasingly sophisticated international, and transnational, dimensions (Satzewich and Wong 2006). Though perhaps somewhat exaggerated, the apprehension regarding the export of terror to prosperous countries such as Canada is not simply manufactured by scare-mongering governments or sensationalist media.

The sociological literature on street-level bureaucrats was pioneered by ethnographers during the 1960s and 1970s, and masterfully pulled together by Michael Lipsky in 1980 (republished in 2010). As discussed above, it emphasizes that face-to-face interaction significantly influences the decisions of authorities, regardless of whether they are police officials, judges, social workers, or visa officers, as they work up cases as credible or not credible, pigeonhole certain kinds of people, and exercise their discretion. Does the general absence of face-to-face contact with visa applicants mean that the literature on discretion and street-level bureaucrats is no longer relevant (Alpes and Spire 2013)? It should be obvious by now that my answer to this question is "no." Though personal interactions are one component in the decision-making process, a myriad of factors enter into it and remain salient even today. As street-level bureaucrats, visa officers still ration the time they spend on certain kinds of files, still use typifications of normality to simplify complexity and categorize their caseload, and still apply broad understandings of how applicants conform or do not conform to the legal requirements of application procedure. They are still pressured by bosses and managers to be productive, still juggle competing goals, and still work in an environment that frames the extent of their discretionary power and shapes how they do their job. All of this enables discretionary decisions to be made in the absence of face-to-face interaction.

This is not to say that the lack of direct contact has no consequences for the decision-making process. At the practical level, officers no longer counsel successful permanent resident applicants. This task is now subcontracted to a third party, the International Organization for Migration (IOM 2014), but counselling is generally available only to people who are selected overseas as refugees. Though it is not clear whether the absence of counselling affects how immigrants settle into the country, Citizenship and Immigration does seem concerned that it may be one of the reasons why some groups face difficulties as they adjust to Canadian society.

Another consequence of the current decision-making process has to do with visa officers' attitudes regarding applicants and their level of job satisfaction. Since they tend to interact with applicants only when the paperwork has prompted concerns, or in problematic or ambiguous cases, they never really come face-to-face with "good" ones. Though interviews often conclude positively, and applicants do establish that they are eligible for a visa, they can also confirm an officer's suspicions that an individual is a cheat, using fraud and misrepresentation to finesse the system. Constantly operating in an atmosphere of distrust, where even someone who is a little too friendly can seem suspect, might be enough to sour anyone's point of view.

Though they understand that the department is under pressure to work through its caseload and produce decisions, and some still regard themselves as nation-builders whose mandate is to select good immigrants for Canada, many officers lament the fact that so little of their job involves personal contact with applicants. Some longer-serving officers often fondly recall the days before the Immigration and Refugee Protection Act, when interviews were the norm. They routinely saw good cases that led to an approval and hard cases that led to a refusal, and arguably got a more rounded picture of the applicant pool.

The limited contact with applicants, particularly with "good" ones, may mean that some officers eventually become somewhat jaded about their occupation. They can move on to a new posting every couple of years, which helps to change things up and keeps things fresh, but regardless of where they work, they will see only those cases that generate misgivings, or whose files are "ugly" or "hard." Thus, the sense of nation building that may once have been part of the job is now under threat.

Though it is fair to say that most of the officers whom I interviewed were happy to be employed in the Canadian foreign service and involved with overseas visa issuance, some did not see it as a long-term profession or calling. One new officer who worked in a busy, high-volume Temporary Resident Unit spoke about the long days spent reviewing a seemingly endless stream of paper in her small office and having little to no interaction with either applicants or friends, and said simply, "This is not what I thought I was getting into."[1] Other officers also admitted privately that they would probably be looking for another line of work because the job was not as interesting, fulfilling, or glamorous as it had seemed from the outside. In the public's mind, foreign service officers attend high-level meetings with other international players, grace glittering diplomatic functions, sip champagne at cocktail parties, and hobnob with the political and bureaucratic elites of the world (Carroll and Siegel 1999). The reality is, of course, quite different. Many take the bus or drive to the office, get stuck in traffic, start work early in the morning, and continue late into the afternoon. If they are parents, they worry about who collects the kids from school, who does the grocery shopping, who cooks dinner, and who helps with the homework. They also worry about whether their partner can find a job in the country. Some cities in which officers work might be interesting to visit as a tourist for a few days, but they are not particularly glamorous. And though Western brands of restaurants, coffee shops, and entertainment may span the globe, they are limited and hard to find in some postings.

This may contribute to the retention problems in the foreign service. Employee retention did not take up a huge amount of time in my interviews with senior managers, but several did comment on the fact that it is an issue in the foreign service generally and Citizenship and Immigration in particular. According to a Treasury Board of Canada report, half of Canada's foreign service officers leave the service within fourteen years of joining it, a figure that former ambassador Derek Burney and co-author Fen Hampson (2013) describe as a "terrible retention rate." Though the dispute between foreign service officers and the federal government during the summer of 2013 was mainly about pay, it was also arguably a reflection of visa officer dissatisfaction with broader working conditions.

Despite these changes in context, and in the receipt and processing of applications, the overall purpose of a visa officer's job has not changed much since the 1970s and 1980s. In the 1989 National Film Board video *Who Gets In?* a young officer named Mike Molloy explained that his job, simply put, was to select good immigrants for Canada and to "keep the rascals out." To phrase it in the more technocratic language of today, the job is to assess, and balance, credibility and risk. The world of immigration was, and is, big, messy, and ambiguous. Immigrants and visitors come to Canada from every corner of the globe. Depending on where they come from and for what purpose, they must apply for a visa to visit, live, work, or study in Canada. The backgrounds and biographies of individuals, their reasons for travelling to Canada, the documents they bring to support their applications, and the countries and contexts from which they come are all different. So, too, are the social contexts in which they live and work, the ways in which they gain their experience, and the mechanisms that their states employ to produce and document their identities.

In a context where no two visa applications are likely to be identical, attempting to apply an entirely mechanical system to assess eligibility, credibility, and risk, one devoid of subjective, discretionary judgments, would be a nightmare. The immigration system is already highly bureaucratized and rule and procedure heavy, and adding more rules and procedures to cover every possible contingency would no doubt produce more problems than it solved. And, as some legal scholars have pointed out, flexibility in the application of rules is necessary to recognize that some individual cases are special and unique, and cannot be slotted into a clearly defined box or processing category (Pratt 2005).

This is why it would be wrong to interpret visa officers, and their decision-making procedures and techniques, as capricious. Capriciousness is not synonymous with discretion. When it comes to border control decisions such as visa issuance, most states recognize that it is impossible to create a set of processing rules for every variable and consideration that goes into assessing credibility and risk. Nor it is possible to create a strict formula or balance sheet in which individual characteristics are measured, quantified, and weighed against each other to mechanically arrive at a decision. States can use immigration laws and regulations to specify various indicators, criteria, and procedures in assessing credibility and risk, but they ultimately delegate discretion to their border control officials. Though the scope for discretion has been progressively narrowed, it remains the case that Canadian visa officers are expected to exercise their discretion as they carry out their duties and make their decisions. They must choose whether to approve or refuse a visa, and they must make various other choices as they progress toward that decision. Legislation and processing manuals can outline the options that are available to them and can instruct them on procedure, but they cannot tell them what choice to make.

The question of how those choices are made ultimately leads to the issue of bias. Are the choices and final decisions of visa officers fair and reasonable, and are they free of bias? Various adjudication appeal bodies do sometimes find that the decisions of visa officers are faulty on the grounds that they are not reasonable or that proper procedures were not followed, so it would be foolish to think that officers are infallible. Many commentators argue that despite efforts to rid the system of partiality, bias nonetheless creeps into the process whereby officers approve or refuse visas. Of course, certain kinds of biases are built into the criteria that officers employ when they determine whether someone is deserving of a visa. The federal skilled worker selection system contains unabashed class biases that favour applicants with the financial resources to get a higher education, gain professional and skilled work experience, and speak English or French. The "adaptability" points on the selection grid for federal skilled workers are explicitly skewed in favour of people who already have certain family members in Canada.

There is also little question that biases stem from the way in which immigration policies and rules are carried out. Visa officers do not have the time to dig deeper into every case, so they must triage applications and use various shortcuts to assess credibility and risk. For example, as Chapter 6 shows, applicants from wealthier, developed countries are perceived as having little incentive to enter into a sham marriage with a Canadian, and thus officers tend not to dig as deeply into their files. People from countries that face relatively favourable global visa regimes also benefit from discretion because they are defined as having many opportunities to work and travel abroad, so have little need to enter Canada on an undocumented basis. And, as Chapter 8 reveals, applicants whose class resources have permitted previous travel to other Western countries may benefit because some officers will conclude that they are unlikely to jump in Canada. These biases, however, are more about socio-economic standing than about race per se. Profiles, based on past experience and past patterns in detected fraud, mean that some applicants are subject to greater scrutiny than others. Criminologists and police officers often say that "the more you look for crime, the more you find crime," and this may also apply to visa officers and fraud: "The more one looks for fraud, the more one finds fraud." If this is true, and it is by no means proven, fraud detection strategies and profiles may select for certain types of applicants. Conversely, some applicants may be getting what amounts to a free pass because officers are not attuned to the kinds of fraud that they practise.

As this book also demonstrates, individual-level characteristics may lead officers to take particular kinds of approaches to files. They vary in how much weight they place on certain kinds of documents and what types of factors they emphasize or de-emphasize as they assess credibility. For instance, as Chapter 6 notes, officers have various ways of determining whether a marriage is genuine: some concentrate on conformity to certain rituals, some look for compatibility, and some check whether the relatives showed up for the wedding. But even such individual differences in approach might be the product of social circumstances and are not necessarily purely individual in nature. For example, some officers are more facilitative than others. But where a particular officer stands on this continuum may depend, in part, on the stage of his or her career. Newer, less-experienced officers tend to stick to the book and loosen up as they gain confidence in their abilities. It may also depend on how they arrived at their present occupation. Canada-based officers who previously performed enforcement-related work in the immigration department or Border Services may be more enforcement-minded than facilitative.

It is, of course, entirely possible that individual officers do entertain ethnic or racial prejudices that cause them to look more thoroughly at some applications and lead them to refuse more visible minority applicants than white applicants. After all, in speaking with an academic researcher, they were not likely to display overtly negative attitudes about their client population and could have kept their personal prejudices to themselves as I interviewed them and observed them doing their work. However, the possibility that decisions are grounded in racism should not be overemphasized, because they are driven by structurally imposed checks and balances. As I have shown, because refusing an application entails more work than approving one, and because officers must meet processing targets and cope with time constraints, they arguably have an incentive to approve applications rather than refuse them. Racist officers whose decisions sprang from prejudice would probably have a higher refusal rate than their colleagues in the same office. They would also have trouble contributing to the office target, which would no doubt attract the attention of management. Moreover, as Chapter 5 documents, there is no evidence that approval rates are systematically lower in offices that presumably deal with mainly racialized applicants than in those that deal with presumably white ones.

In *Canada and Immigration: Public Policy and Public Concern,* political scientist Freda Hawkins (1988, 267) explains that a mix of "curiosity and frustration" led her to explore what went on in overseas visa offices during the 1960s. Though she had spent much of her academic career studying and teaching about immigration policy and management in Canada, she could find few academics, leaders of NGOs, or even immigration department employees who "appeared to know or care where the visa offices were or how they were run" (ibid.). During her visits, Hawkins spent a few days in each office, interviewing staff and observing routines and procedures. Her "personal impressions" of her tours were published as a short chapter in her book. One of the most notable focused on the merits of immigration officers. Whereas the public commonly regarded them as "rigid, narrow-minded, rather petty [and] ... restrictionist," she found them to be of "high quality" and noted that they displayed "a keen interest in the job and dedication to it" (ibid., 271). Some fifty years later, having conducted my own "tour" of overseas visa offices, I cannot fault her conclusion.

Appendix

Goals of the Immigration and Refugee Program

OBJECTIVES AND APPLICATION

Objectives – immigration

3.(1) The objectives of this Act with respect to immigration are

- (a) to permit Canada to pursue the maximum social, cultural and economic benefits of immigration;
- (b) to enrich and strengthen the social and cultural fabric of Canadian society, while respecting the federal, bilingual and multicultural character of Canada;
- (b.1) to support and assist the development of minority official languages communities in Canada;
- (c) to support the development of a strong and prosperous Canadian economy, in which the benefits of immigration are shared across all regions of Canada;
- (d) to see that families are reunited in Canada;
- (e) to promote the successful integration of permanent residents into Canada, while recognizing that integration involves mutual obligations for new immigrants and Canadian society;
- (f) to support, by means of consistent standards and prompt processing, the attainment of immigration goals established by the Government of Canada in consultation with the provinces;

(g) to facilitate the entry of visitors, students and temporary workers for purposes such as trade, commerce, tourism, international understanding and cultural, educational and scientific activities;
(h) to protect public health and safety and to maintain the security of Canadian society;
(i) to promote international justice and security by fostering respect for human rights and by denying access to Canadian territory to persons who are criminals or security risks; and
(j) to work in cooperation with the provinces to secure better recognition of the foreign credentials of permanent residents and their more rapid integration into society.

Objectives – refugees

(2) The objectives of this Act with respect to refugees are
(a) to recognize that the refugee program is in the first instance about saving lives and offering protection to the displaced and persecuted;
(b) to fulfill Canada's international legal obligations with respect to refugees and affirm Canada's commitment to international efforts to provide assistance to those in need of resettlement;
(c) to grant, as a fundamental expression of Canada's humanitarian ideals, fair consideration to those who come to Canada claiming persecution;
(d) to offer safe haven to persons with a well-founded fear of persecution based on race, religion, nationality, political opinion or membership in a particular social group, as well as those at risk of torture or cruel and unusual treatment or punishment;
(e) to establish fair and efficient procedures that will maintain the integrity of the Canadian refugee protection system, while upholding Canada's respect for the human rights and fundamental freedoms of all human beings;
(f) to support the self-sufficiency and the social and economic well-being of refugees by facilitating reunification with their family members in Canada;
(g) to protect the health and safety of Canadians and to maintain the security of Canadian society; and
(h) to promote international justice and security by denying access to Canadian territory to persons, including refugee claimants, who are security risks or serious criminals.

Source: Immigration and Refugee Protection Act (2001).

Notes

Introduction

1 The following account of a visa officer's interview with an applicant for spousal sponsorship is drawn from my field notes. Several details of the case have been altered to protect the anonymity of both.

2 Over the years, researchers in the social sciences and humanities have examined a variety of issues related to the immigration policy-making process (Goutor 2007; Simmons and Keohane 1992; Veugelers and Klassen 1994; Kelly and Trebilcock 1998; Fleras 2015; Anderson 2012), the experiences and consequences of particular immigration policies (Triadafilopoulos 2012; Satzewich 1991), immigrant settlement patterns and integration (Biles, Burstein, and Frideres 2008), and what makes a "welcoming community" for immigrants (Pathways to Prosperity 2014). At the same time, the immigration bureaucracy, the public servants who work in the bureaucracy, and the structures and processes that guide their decision making are under-researched in Canada and constitute something of a missing link to a more complete understanding of the migration process (see Paquet 2014; Tomkinson 2015).

3 Aside from public commentary, there is some limited social science research on the inside workings of the federal immigration department and how its officials carry out their jobs. Political scientist Freda Hawkins was one of the first scholars to systematically examine the intersection of immigration policy, law, and management in Canada. In her comprehensive study *Canada and Immigration: Public Policy and Public Concern,* first published in 1972, Hawkins (1988) examined the policy-making process, the workings of the post-war immigration bureaucracy, and the internal and external pressures placed on immigration managers and other decision-makers. An innovative aspect of her research involved three "tours" of overseas visa offices,

in 1964, 1966, and 1969. During the tours, Hawkins visited offices in London, The Hague, Paris, Copenhagen, Cologne, Rome, Vienna, Berne, Munich, Stuttgart, Berlin, Brussels, and Geneva.

Since then, only a few Canadian academics have been permitted to see the inside of a Canadian overseas visa office, let alone talk to officers about how they make their decisions. Geneviève Bouchard's (2000) PhD dissertation research on officer discretion was partially based on nineteen interviews with Citizenship and Immigration staff in Ottawa and in Toronto and Niagara Falls field offices. (She also conducted a few interviews with Canadian officers posted in Washington and Buffalo, nine with officials who worked for the Quebec immigration department, the Ministère des Relations avec les citoyens et de l'Immigration, and ten with officials in the US Department of State.) Margaret Walton-Roberts (2003) interviewed a few Immigration office staff in Delhi while researching Indian immigration to Canada in 1999 and 2000.

A few other academics have been allowed to study how Citizenship and Immigration works on the Canadian side of the border. Lorne Foster (1998), a former immigration officer and now a social scientist at York University, provides a detailed and highly critical "insider's" account of immigration officers in *Turnstile Immigration: Multiculturalism, Social Order and Social Justice in Canada*. Though his book is intended as a critique of Canadian immigration policy, much of his analysis focuses on his own experiences as a Toronto immigration officer during the 1980s and 1990s. He suggests that front-line immigration officers in Canada work in a black-and-white world of "good guys" and "bad guys." They often become fixated on keeping the "bad guys" out of Canada (mainly criminals and those who violate immigration rules), but they pay little attention to helping "good" immigrants settle, improve their lives, and contribute to Canadian society. In presenting the officers as bureaucratic agents of social control, Foster tends to characterize them as obsessed with the mundane details of applications, procedures, and rules, and as having lost sight of the bigger picture – immigration as a positive, nation-building process. His book is mainly about officers who work in Canada and whose jobs do involve enforcement and deportation; thus, it is perhaps not surprising that they become overly focused on unmasking undesirables. What we do not learn from Foster is how Canada's overseas officers perform, and make sense of, their jobs.

The line of argument in *Securing Borders: Detention and Deportation in Canada* (Pratt 2005) is much like that of Foster. Although author Anna Pratt concentrates on analyzing primary and secondary source documents related to deportation and removal policies and practices, she also conducted a microstudy of the Celebrity Inn (located just outside of Pearson International Airport), which at the time was one of three main immigrant detention facilities in Canada. Authorized to visit the facility, Pratt describes its physical layout and its rules and operating procedures. She does not seem to have spoken with its employees (or at least did not use interview material to describe its workings).

Thus, though she provides a fairly vivid, and harsh, picture of what the facility looks like and how it functions, we ultimately understand little about the roles and responsibilities of its officials, how they carry out their duties on a daily basis, how they make decisions, and how they feel about their jobs.

4 This topic fell by the wayside because of time and resource constraints, but it remains an interesting and important issue for exploration.

5 Interview, October 23, 2009.

6 Field notes, July 22, 2010, 18.

7 For reasons explained later, my visits focused on more than the selection process for federal skilled workers. I also interviewed locally engaged staff, who play support roles in the decision-making process. I conducted semi-structured interviews with ten immigration program managers (one was away during my visit), six deputy program managers, fifteen unit managers, thirty-eight visa officers (who were a mix of foreign service officers and those on secondment to International Region), thirty locally engaged staff who had varying levels of decision-making authority (designated immigration officers make decisions on most types of permanent resident applications, whereas non-immigrant officers make decisions on most types of temporary resident applications), eighteen locally engaged staff who provided support services but had no authority to make decisions, six migration integrity officers, one medical officer, and four other staff members who were not employed directly by the Canadian government (such as a UN High Commission for Refugees representative or an employee of a Visa Application Centre). According to the 2011 *Report of the Auditor General of Canada,* there were eighty-six Canadian missions abroad (though only about forty-four had immigration-related functions), where "about 270 Canada-based officers, 12 medical officers, and 1,305 locally engaged staff – including about 160 locally engaged visa officers – worked" in visa processing (Auditor General of Canada 2011, 6). This figure means that I conducted interviews at nearly 20 percent of all overseas offices, interviewed about 20 percent of all Canada-based officers (which includes immigration program managers, deputy program managers, foreign service visa officers, and those on secondment) and locally engaged decision makers, and 1.4 percent of locally engaged support staff.

8 Nine were with family class applicants, all involving spousal or partner sponsorship. Ten were in the economic class: one was an investor and one a provincial nominee, one was in the Canadian experience class, four were live-in caregivers, and three were federal skilled workers. Nine were refugees. In the Temporary Resident Units, thirteen interviews were for visitors to Canada, and one was for a temporary foreign worker visa applicant. I also observed two anti-fraud field investigations.

Chapter 1: Stated and Hidden Agendas

1 See, for example, Sassen (1998 and 2000), Milanovic (2011), Bauder (2006), Orozco (2013), and Preibisch and Binford (2008).

2 For a small selection of what amounts to a considerable literature, see Satzewich and Wong (2006), Salaff and Greve (2004), Frideres and Biles (2012), Boyd (2006), and Simon (2013).

Chapter 2: Delegated Discretion

1 Field notes, April 24, 2011, 15.
2 Field notes, January 16, 2011, 9.
3 For more information on this topic, see the Immigration Consultants of Canada Regulatory Council website at http://www.iccrc-crcic.ca/home.cfm?setLanCookie=En.
4 Field notes, December 13, 2011, 13.
5 As discussed in the next chapter, certain types of temporary resident visas are exempt from this general rule.
6 Field notes, December 13, 2011, 16.
7 Field notes, April 27, 2011, 39.

Chapter 3: Immigration Policy

1 Field notes, April 26, 2011, 21.
2 "Convention" here refers to the 1951 Geneva Convention Relating to the Status of Refugees.

Chapter 4: Visa Offices and Officers

1 Over the summer of 2013, foreign service officers who worked overseas for both Foreign Affairs and the immigration department engaged in job action to protest the discrepancy between their salaries and those of their counterparts in Canada.
2 Field notes, July 29, 2010, 33.
3 Field notes, December 15, 2011, 46.
4 Field notes, April 26, 2011, 17.
5 Field notes, December 15, 2011, 41.
6 Field notes, July 26, 2010, 7.
7 Field notes, May 4, 2011, 30.
8 Field notes, December 13, 2011, 15.
9 Field notes, July 25, 2010, 4.
10 Field notes, December 13, 2011, 15.
11 Field notes, July 28, 2010, 21.
12 Field notes, August 11, 2010, 34.
13 Ibid.
14 Ibid.
15 Field notes, January 10, 2012, 29.
16 Field notes, January 11, 2011, 29.
17 Field notes, May 5, 2011, 35.
18 Ibid.
19 Field notes, January 11, 2012, 29.
20 Field notes, May 5, 2011, 35.
21 Field notes, April 28, 2011, 45.
22 Field notes, May 5, 2011, 35.
23 Ibid.
24 Ibid.
25 Field notes, December 13, 2011, 15–16.

26 Field notes, April 28, 2011, 49.
27 Ibid.
28 Field notes, December 13, 2011, 16.
29 Field notes, December 13, 2010, 5.
30 Field notes, July 26, 2010, 11.
31 Ibid., 11; see also Canada Border Services Agency (2009).
32 Field notes, July 26, 2010, 10.
33 Ibid., 11.
34 Ibid.
35 Field notes, December 13, 2011, 16.
36 Ibid., 17.
37 Ibid.
38 Ibid., 16.
39 Field notes, July 20, 2010, 8.
40 Field notes, July 25, 2010, 9–10.

Chapter 5: Approval and Refusal Rates

1 Field notes, August 9, 2010, 6.
2 Field notes, December 13, 2011, 10.
3 Field notes, May 5, 2011, 35.
4 Field notes, December 13, 2011, 15.
5 Interview, May 11, 2010.
6 Field notes, July 11, 2010, 8.
7 Field notes, December 14, 2010, 10.
8 Field notes, February 21, 2011, 12.
9 Field notes, August 9, 2010, 6.
10 Field notes, December 15, 2010, 31.
11 Field notes, April 25, 2011, 15.
12 Ibid.
13 Field notes, April 26, 2011, 32.
14 Ibid.
15 Field notes, December 13, 2010, 9.

Chapter 6: Spousal and Partner Sponsorships

1 Field notes, January 9, 2012, 12.
2 Field notes, January 10, 2012, 16.
3 Field notes, December 14, 2010, 17.
4 Field notes, May 3, 2011, 14.
5 Field notes, April 26, 2011, 29.
6 Field notes, August 10, 2010, 18.
7 Field notes, February 21, 2011, 12.
8 Field notes, January 16, 2012, 6.
9 Field notes, December 15, 2010, 29.
10 Field notes, April 25, 2011, 12.
11 Field notes, December 13, 2011, 18.

12 Ibid.
13 Field notes, April 25, 2011, 13.
14 Field notes, April 27, 2011, 26–27.
15 Field notes, December 14, 2011, 25.
16 Field notes, January 10, 2012, 26.
17 Field notes, January 17, 2012, 6.
18 Field notes, July 26, 2010, 10.
19 Field notes, April 26, 2011, 20.
20 Field notes, May 3, 2011, 10.
21 Field notes, February 21, 2011, 8.
22 Ibid.
23 Ibid.
24 Field notes, January 11, 2012, 45.
25 Field notes, January 9, 2012, 14.
26 Field notes, January 10, 2012, 16.
27 Field notes, January 11, 2012, 45.
28 Ibid.
29 Field notes, January 9, 2012, 9.
30 Field notes, July 29, 2010, 34.
31 Field notes, January 10, 2012, 11.
32 Ibid., 18.
33 Field notes, December 14, 2010, 17.
34 Field notes, December 8, 2010, 15.
35 Field notes, January 10, 2012, 9.
36 Field notes, January 9, 2012, 9.
37 Field notes, December 14, 2010, 13.
38 Field notes, December 9, 2010, 29.
39 Field notes, December 14, 2010, 17.
40 Field notes, January 9, 2012, 10.
41 Field notes, December 14, 2010, 17.
42 Ibid., 14.
43 Field notes, January 10, 2012, 16.
44 Ibid.
45 Field notes, May 3, 2011, 6.
46 Field notes, December 8, 2010, 15.
47 Field notes, January 9, 2012, 12.
48 Field notes, January 10, 2012, 15.
49 Field notes, December 8, 2010, 15. Money transfer documents are also easily dismissed. After examining the documents regarding the money that a Canadian sponsor had sent to his spouse, the officer said, "These don't tell me much. She could be sending the money right back to him." Field notes, December 14, 2010, 16.
50 Field notes, February 21, 2011, 10.

Chapter 7: Federal Skilled Workers

1 Interview, October 23, 2009.
2 Interview, September 19, 2009.

3 Field notes, May 4, 2011, 26.
4 Field notes, December 9, 2010, 24.
5 Field notes, December 15, 2010, 20.
6 Field notes, December 9, 2010, 24.
7 Field notes, April 27, 2011, 33.
8 Field notes, December 13, 2011, 13.
9 Field notes, May 4, 2011, 29.
10 Ibid.
11 Ibid., 30.
12 Ibid.
13 Ibid., 31.
14 Ibid., 28.
15 Ibid.
16 Ibid.
17 Ibid.
18 Field notes, April 27, 2011, 34.
19 Field notes, December 14, 2010, 19.
20 Field notes, May 4, 2011, 31.
21 Ibid.
22 Field notes, December 14, 2010, 19.
23 Ibid., 20.
24 Field notes, August 9, 2010, 10.
25 Field notes, April 27, 2011, 34.
26 Field notes, May 4, 2011, 29.
27 Field notes, December 14, 2010, 20.
28 Field notes, April 27, 2011, 38.
29 Field notes, April 26, 2011, 23.
30 Field notes, May 4, 2011, 31–32.
31 Ibid., 32.
32 Field notes, December 9, 2010, 24.
33 Field notes, December 14, 2010, 20.
34 Field notes, May 4, 2011, 29.
35 Field notes, December 14, 2010, 20.
36 Ibid.

Chapter 8: Visitor Visas

1 Field notes, April 28, 2011, 41.
2 The department's new database, the Global Case Management System, permits individuals in some countries to electronically submit their applications for certain types of temporary resident visas. In part, their eligibility for this service depends on whether they must provide biometric information (be fingerprinted and photographed) as well. People who live in a country where biometric information is required cannot submit an application online and must drop it off at a Visa Application Centre.
3 Field notes, May 4, 2011, 19.
4 Field notes, December 13, 2011, 10.

5 Field notes, May 4, 2011, 19.
6 Field notes, January 11, 2012, 30.
7 Field notes, May 5, 2011, 19.
8 Field notes, May 4, 2011, 30.
9 Field notes, January 11, 2012, 33.
10 Ibid., 32.
11 Field notes, January 16, 2012, 8.
12 Field notes, January 16, 2011, 8.
13 Field notes, May 5, 2011, 25.
14 Ibid.
15 Field notes, December 15, 2011, 38.
16 Field notes, July 26, 2010, 7.
17 Field notes, May 4, 2011, 6.
18 Field notes, April 25, 2011, 4.
19 Field notes, December 15, 2011, 39.
20 Field notes, December 9, 2010, 23–24.
21 Field notes, July 25, 2010, 6.
22 Field notes, December 15, 2011, 39.
23 Field notes, December 9, 2011, 11.
24 Field notes, December 9, 2010, 23–24.
25 Field notes, December 15, 2011, 39.
26 Field notes, May 5, 2011, 26.
27 Field notes, July 25, 2010, 8.
28 Field notes, May 4, 2011, 19.
29 Field notes, December 13, 2011, 11.
30 Field notes, December 15, 2011, 39.
31 Field notes, December 9, 2010, 24.
32 Ibid., 23–24.
33 Field notes, December 15, 2011, 39.
34 Field notes, May 5, 2011, 25.
35 Field notes, December 9, 2010, 23.
36 Field notes, April 25, 2011, 5.
37 Field notes, December 8, 2010, 10.
38 Field notes, July 25, 2010, 7.
39 Field notes, May 5, 2011, 23.
40 Field notes, April 25, 2011, 6.
41 Ibid., 9.
42 Field notes, May 5, 2011, 25.
43 Ibid., 24–25.
44 Field notes, April 25, 2011, 6–7.
45 Field notes, May 5, 2011, 23.
46 Field notes, January 16, 2012, 6.
47 Field notes, July 26, 2010, 8.
48 Field notes, December 13, 2010, 6.
49 Field notes, April 25, 2011, 4.
50 Ibid., 8–9.

51 Field notes, May 5, 2011, 21.
52 Ibid.
53 Ibid., 25.
54 Field notes, July 26, 2010, 6.
55 Field notes, December 13, 2010, 7.
56 Field notes, May 5, 2011, 24.
57 Field notes, July 26, 2010, 25.
58 Field notes, April 25, 2011, 7.
59 Ibid., 10.
60 Field notes, December 13, 2010, 6.
61 Field notes, December 15, 2011, 40.

Chapter 9: The Interview

1 Field notes, August 11, 2010, 30.
2 Field notes, December 14, 2010, 1.
3 Field notes, July 29, 2010, 36.
4 Ibid.
5 Ibid., 35.
6 Ibid., 34.
7 Ibid., 24.
8 Field notes, August 10, 2010, 15–17.
9 Field notes, July 28, 2010, 26.
10 Field notes, August 10, 2010, 19–20.
11 Ibid., 20.
12 Ibid.
13 Field notes, May 3, 2011, 6.
14 Field notes, December 13, 2010, 4.
15 Field notes, April 25, 2011, 16.
16 Field notes, January 9, 2012, 4.
17 Field notes, February 22, 2011, 19–23.
18 Field notes, August 10, 2010, 20.
19 Field notes, February 21, 2011, 9.
20 Field notes, July 21, 2010, 10.
21 Field notes, April 26, 2011, 23.
22 Ibid., 24.
23 Field notes, December 9, 2010, 3.
24 Ibid., 30.
25 Field notes, December 8, 2010, 16.
26 Field notes, December 15, 2010, 29.
27 Field notes, December 9, 2010, 30.

Conclusion

1 Field notes, January 11, 2012, 33.

References

Abrams, Kerry. 2007. "Immigration Law and the Regulation of Marriage." *Minnesota Law Review* 91 (6): 1624–709.

Abu-Laban, Yasmeen. 1998. "Welcome/STAY OUT: The Contradiction of Canadian Immigration Policies at the Millennium." *Canadian Ethnic Studies* 30 (3): 190–211.

Abu-Laban, Yasmeen, and Christina Gabriel. 2002. *Selling Diversity: Immigration, Multiculturalism, Employment Equity and Globalization.* Peterborough: Broadview Press.

Aiken, Sharryn. 2007. "From Slavery to Expulsion: Racism, Canadian Immigration Law, and the Unfilled Promise of Modern Constitutionalism." In *Interrogating Race and Racism,* ed. Vijay Agnew, 55–111. Toronto: University of Toronto Press.

Alave, Kristine. 2008. "OSG Alarmed by Rising Marriage Annulment Cases." *Philippine Daily Inquirer,* February 10. http://newsinfo.inquirer.net/breakingnews/nation/view/20080210-117984/OSG-alarmed-by-rising-marriage-annulment-cases.

Alboim, Naomi. 2009. "Adjusting the Balance: Fixing Canada's Economic Immigration Policies." *Maytree: Policy in Focus* 10 (December): 1–64.

Alpes, Maybritt Jill, and Alexis Spire. 2013. "Dealing with Law in Migration Control: The Powers of Street-Level Bureaucrats at French Consulates." *Social and Legal Studies.* http://sls.sagepub.com/lookup/doi/10.1177/0964663913510927.

Anderson, Alan, and James Frideres. 1980. *Ethnicity in Canada: Theoretical Perspectives.* Toronto: Butterworths.

Anderson, Christopher. 2012. *Canadian Liberalism and the Politics of Border Control, 1867–1967.* Vancouver: UBC Press.

Auditor General of Canada. 2003. *Report of the Auditor General of Canada*. Ottawa: Minister of Supply and Services.

–. 2009. *Report of the Auditor General of Canada to the House of Commons*. Ottawa: Minister of Supply and Services.

–. 2011. *Report of the Auditor General of Canada to the House of Commons*. Ottawa: Minister of Supply and Services.

Aulakh, Raveena. 2010. "Fastest Way to Get to Canada – Marriage." *Toronto Star*, July 16. http://www.thestar.com/news/canada/2010/07/16/fastest_way_to_get_to_canada_marriage.html.

Avery, Donald. 1995. *Reluctant Host: Canada's Response to Immigrant Workers*. Toronto: McClelland and Stewart.

Bakan, Abigail, and Daiva Stasiulis. 1995. "Making the Match: Domestic Placement Agencies and the Racialization of Women's Household Work." *Signs* 20 (2): 303–35. http://dx.doi.org/10.1086/494976.

Baldwin, Robert, and Keith Hawkins. 1984. "Discretionary Justice: Davis Reconsidered." *Public Law* (Winter): 570–99.

Barber, Pauline, and Winnie Lem. 2012. "Migration, Political Economy and Ethnography." In *Migration in the 21st Century: Political Economy and Ethnography*, ed. Pauline Barber and Winnie Lem, 1–16. London: Routledge.

Bauder, Harald. 2006. *Labor Movement: How Migration Regulates Labor Markets*. Toronto: Oxford University Press.

Bauman, Zygmunt. 1989. *Modernity and the Holocaust*. Cambridge: Polity.

Beck, Ulrich. 1992. *Risk Society: Towards a New Modernity*. New Delhi: Sage.

Becker, Howard. 1970. *Sociological Work: Method and Substance*. New Brunswick, NJ: Transaction.

Bhabha, Jacqueline, and Sue Shutter. 1994. *Women's Movement: Women under Immigration, Nationality and Refugee Law*. Stoke-on-Trent, UK: Trentham Books.

Biles, John, Meyer Burstein, and James Frideres, eds. 2008. *Immigration and Integration in Canada in the Twenty-First Century*. Montreal and Kingston: McGill-Queen's University Press.

Boehmer, Charles, and Sergio Peña. 2012. "The Determinants of Open and Closed Borders." *Journal of Borderland Studies* 27 (3): 273–85. http://dx.doi.org/10.1080/08865655.2012.750950.

Bonjour, Saskia, and Betty de Hart. 2013. "A Proper Wife, and Proper Marriage: Constructions of 'Us' and 'Them' in Dutch Family Migration Policy." *European Journal of Women's Studies* 20 (1): 61–76.

Borjas, George. 1999. *Heaven's Door: Immigration Policy and the American Economy*. Princeton: Princeton University Press.

Bouchard, Geneviève. 2000. "Field Officer Discretion in the Implementation Process: Immigration Policy in Canada, Quebec and the United States." PhD thesis, McMaster University, Department of Political Science.

Bouchard, Geneviève, and Barbara Wake Carroll. 2002. "Policy-Making and Administrative Discretion: The Case of Immigration in Canada." *Canadian Public Administration* 45 (2): 239–57. http://dx.doi.org/10.1111/j.1754-7121.2002.tb01082.x.

Boyd, Monica. 2006. "Women in International Migration: The Context of Exit and Entry for Empowerment and Exploitation." Paper presented in the high-level panel "The Gender Dimension of International Migration," United Nations Commission on the Status of Women, New York City, March 2.

Brouwer, Andrew. 2003. "Attack of the Migration Integrity Specialists: Interdiction and the Threat to Asylum." Canadian Council for Refugees. http://ccrweb.ca/sites/ccrweb.ca/files/static-files/interdictionab.htm.

Burney, Derek, and Fen Hampson. 2013. "For PAFSO, a Question of Equity and Respect." *iPolitics,* July 15. http://www.ipolitics.ca/2013/07/15/for-pafso-a-question-of-equity-and-respect/.

Calavita, Kitty. 1991. *Inside the State: The Bracero Program, Immigration and the INS.* New York: Routledge.

Canada Border Services Agency. 2009. "Admissibility Screening and Supporting Intelligence Activities – Evaluation Study." http://www.cbsa-asfc.gc.ca/agency-agence/reports-rapports/ae-ve/2009/assia-aeasr-eng.html.

–. 2010. "CBSA Detentions and Removals Programs: Evaluation Study." http://www.cbsa-asfc.gc.ca/agency-agence/reports-rapports/ae-ve/2010/dr-rd-eng.html#s03.

Canada Immigration Forum. 2005. "Discussion Group." http://www.canada-city.ca/canada-immigration/posting.php?messageid=8852.

CanadaVisa.com. 2010. "How Many People Want to Give Up?" http://www.canadavisa.com/canada-immigration-discussion-board/how-many-people-want-to-give-up-t52441.120.html.

Canadian Bar Association. 2014. "National Immigration Law Section." http://www.cba.org/CBA/sections_Cship/main/.

Canadian Council for Refugees. 2008. "Bill C-50 – Proposed Amendments to IRPA: 10 Reasons to Be Concerned." https://ccrweb.ca/en/bill-c-50-proposed-amendments-irpa-10-reasons-be-concerned.

–. 2010. "Proposed Refugee Reform Undermines Fairness to Refugees." https://ccrweb.ca/en/bulletin/10/03/30.

Canadian Doctors for Refugee Care. 2014. "The Issue." http://www.doctorsforrefugeecare.ca/the-issue.html.

Canadian Race Relations Foundation. 2001. "Canada's Immigration Policies: Contradictions and Shortcomings." *CRFF Perspectives: Focus on Immigration and Refugee Issues* (Autumn-Winter). Online document, no longer available.

Canadian Tourism Commission. 2012. "Tourism Snapshot: 2012 Year-in-Review." 7th ed. http://en-corporate.canada.travel/?sc_url=corpdomain13.

Carroll, Barbara Wake, and David Siegel. 1999. *Service in the Field: The World of Front-Line Public Servants.* Montreal and Kingston: McGill-Queen's University Press.

Carter, Tom. 2012. "Provincial Nominee Programs and Temporary Worker Programs: A Comparative Assessment of Advantages and Disadvantages in Addressing Labour Shortages." In *Legislated Inequality: Temporary Labour Migration in Canada,* ed. Patti Lenard and Christine Straehle, 178–201. Montreal and Kingston: McGill-Queen's University Press.

Cartier, Geneviève. 2009. "Administrative Discretion and the Spirit of Legality: From Theory to Practice." *Canadian Journal of Law and Society* 24 (3): 313–35. http://dx.doi.org/10.1017/S0829320100010061.

Castles, Stephen, and Mark Miller. 2003. *The Age of Migration: International Population Movements in the International World.* 3rd ed. London: Macmillan.

CBC News. 2009. "Mexicans, Czechs Will Need Visas to Visit Canada." http://www.cbc.ca/news/canada/mexicans-czechs-will-need-visas-to-visit-canada-1.817998.

–. 2010. "New Immigration Rules Aim to Weed Out Marriage Fraud." http://www.cbc.ca/news/canada/new-immigration-rules-aim-to-weed-out-marriage-fraud-1.891888.

–. 2014a. "Canada Wants to Double Its International Student Body." http://www.cbc.ca/news/canada/british-columbia/canada-wants-to-double-its-international-student-body-1.2497819.

–. 2014b. "CBSA Immigration Arrests during Spot Checks Stir Controversy." http://www.cbc.ca/news/canada/toronto/cbsa-immigration-arrests-during-spot-checks-stir-controversy-1.2738337.

Chase, Steven. 2012. "Jason Kenney Faces Legal Uprising over Conrad Black Visa." *Toronto Globe and Mail,* August 2. http://www.theglobeandmail.com/news/politics/jason-kenney-faces-legal-uprising-over-conrad-black-visa/article4457055/).

Citizenship and Immigration Canada. 1998. "Towards a New Model of Selection: Current Selection Criteria: Indicators of Successful Establishment?" Ottawa, Economic Policy and Programs Division, Selection Branch.

–. 2001. "Regulatory Impact Analysis Statement, Immigration and Refugee Protection Regulations." *Canada Gazette,* December 15, 4477–99.

–. 2008. "Audit of the Immigration Program at the Canadian Mission in Beijing." October. http://www.cic.gc.ca/english/resources/audit/beijing.asp.

–. 2009a. "Audit of the Immigration Program at the Canadian Mission in Hong Kong." October. http://www.cic.gc.ca/english/resources/audit/hong_kong.asp.

–. 2009b. "Audit of the Immigration Program in the Canadian Mission in Tokyo." June. http://www.cic.gc.ca/english/resources/audit/beijing.asp.

–. 2010a. "Archived – Balanced Reforms Planned for Canada's Asylum System." http://news.gc.ca/web/index-en.do.

–. 2010b. "Audit of Immigration Program at the Canadian Mission in Kingston." June. http://www.cic.gc.ca/english/resources/audit/kingston.asp.

–. 2010c. "Audit of the Immigration Program at the Canadian High Commission in Singapore." October. http://www.cic.gc.ca/english/resources/audit/singapore.asp.

–. 2010d. *Evaluation of the Federal Skilled Worker Program.* Ottawa: Evaluation Division.

–. 2010e. *OP 23/IP 11 Anti-Fraud.* http://www.cic.gc.ca/ENGLISH/RESOURCES/manuals/op/op23-eng.pdf.

–. 2011a. "Audit of the Immigration Program at the Canadian Mission in Ankara." April. http://www.cic.gc.ca/english/resources/audit/ankara.asp.

–. 2011b. "Case Management Branch." PowerPoint presentation by Sharon Chomyn to Canadian Bar Association, Gatineau, May 3.

–. 2011c. *OP 2: Processing Members of the Family Class.* Ottawa: Citizenship and Immigration Canada.

–. 2012a. "Archived Citizenship and Immigration Canada Visa Application Centre Network to Reach Global Proportions." http://news.gc.ca/web/index-en.do.

–. 2012b. "Backgrounder – Overview of Canada's New Refugee System." http://www.cic.gc.ca/english/department/media/backgrounders/2012/2012-06-29c.asp.

–. 2012c. "Canada Facts and Figures: Immigrant Overview, Permanent and Temporary Residents." Ottawa: Minister of Public Works and Government Services.

–. 2012d. "IMM5490, Sponsored Spouse/Partner Questionnaire." Ottawa: Citizenship and Immigration Canada. http://www.cic.gc.ca/english/pdf/kits/forms/IMM5490E.pdf.

–. 2012e. "'The Jig Is Up on Marriage Fraud,' Says Minister Kenney." News release, October 26. http://news.gc.ca/web/article-en.do?nid=703499.

–. 2012f. "Permanent Resident Summary by Mission." http://open.canada.ca/data/en/dataset/fd6f93ed-6249-42a4-ac30-5a1a7aa48389.

–. 2012–13. *2012–2013 Report on Plans and Priorities.* Ottawa: Citizenship and Immigration Canada.

–. 2013a. *Annual Report to Parliament on Immigration.* Ottawa: Citizenship and Immigration Canada. http://www.cic.gc.ca/english/resources/publications/annual-report-2013/index.asp.

–. 2013b. "Audit of the Immigration Program at the Canadian Mission in Nairobi." June. http://www.cic.gc.ca/english/resources/audit/nairobi.asp.

–. 2013c. "Notice – Update on Fee Returns for Federal Skilled Worker Applicants Affected by the Backlog Elimination." http://www.cic.gc.ca/english/department/media/notices/notice-returns.asp.

–. 2013d. "Visiting Canada." Site now discontinued.

–. 2014a. "Amendments to the Immigration and Refugee Protection Regulations to Support Operational Modernization." http://www.cic.gc.ca/english/department/acts-regulations/forward-regulatory-plan/irpr-opmod.asp.

–. 2014b. "Application for Visitor Visa (Temporary Resident Visa – TRV)." http://www.cic.gc.ca/english/information/applications/visa.asp.

–. 2014c. "Applying for Visitor Visa (Temporary Resident Visa – IMM 5256)." http://www.cic.gc.ca/english/information/applications/guides/5256ETOC.asp.

–. 2014d. "Building a Fast and Flexible Immigration System." http://news.gc.ca/web/article-en.do?nid=814939.

–. 2014e. "Citizenship and Immigration Canada Offices." http://www.cic.gc.ca/english/information/offices/index.asp.

–. 2014f. "Countries and Territories Where Visas Are Required." http://www.cic.gc.ca/english/visit/visas-all.asp.

–. 2014g. "Determine Your Eligibility – Canadian Experience Class." http://www.cic.gc.ca/english/immigrate/cec/apply-who.asp.

–. 2014h. "Determine Your Eligibility – Sponsor Your Spouse, Partner or Children." http://www.cic.gc.ca/english/immigrate/sponsor/spouse-apply-who.asp.

–. 2014i. "Find Your Closest Visa Application Centre." http://www.cic.gc.ca/english/information/offices/vac.asp.

–. 2014j. “Government of Canada’s Immigration Planning Story: Operational Targets.” http://www.cic.gc.ca/english/department/ips/operational.asp.

–. 2014k. “Government of Canada’s Immigration Planning Story: Operational Targets by Office: (Economic).” http://www.cic.gc.ca/english/department/ips/operational.asp.

–. 2014l. “Government of Canada’s Immigration Planning Story: Operational Targets by Office: (Non-Economic).” http://www.cic.gc.ca/english/department/ips/non-economic.asp.

–. 2014m. “Instruments of Designation and Delegation: Immigration and Refugee Protection Act and Regulations.” Ottawa, Minister of Citizenship and Immigration. http://www.cic.gc.ca/english/resources/manuals/il/il3-eng.pdf.

–. 2014n. “Ministerial Instructions.” http://www.cic.gc.ca/english/department/mi/.

–. 2014o. “Processing Time for Temporary Resident Visa Applications Processed by Visa Offices outside of Canada.” http://www.cic.gc.ca/english/information/times/temp/visitors.asp.

–. 2014p. “Processing Times for Sponsorship of Spouses, Common-Law or Conjugal Partners and Dependent Children.” http://www.cic.gc.ca/english/information/times/perm/fc-spouses.asp.

–. 2014q. “Six Selection Factors — Federal Skilled Workers.” http://www.cic.gc.ca/english/immigrate/skilled/apply-factors.asp.

–. 2014r. “Sponsor Your Spouse, Partner or Children.” http://www.cic.gc.ca/english/immigrate/sponsor/spouse.asp.

–. 2014s. “Temporary Resident Permits.” http://www.cic.gc.ca/english/information/inadmissibility/permits.asp.

–. 2015. “Guide to the Private Sponsorship of Refugees Program.” http://www.cic.gc.ca/english/resources/publications/ref-sponsor/section-2.asp#a2.6.

Clark, Campbell. 2012. “Ottawa Ends UAE Feud with Nuclear Deal.” *Toronto Globe and Mail,* September 19, A4.

Clement, Tony. 2013. “Tony Clement: How – and Why – We’re Modernizing Canada’s Public Service.” *National Post* (Toronto), June 18. http://news.nationalpost.com/2013/06/18/tony-clement-how-and-why-were-modernizing-canadas-public-service/.

Collins, Jock. 1988. *Migrant Hands in a Distant Land: Australia’s Post-War Immigration.* Sydney: Pluto Press.

Comisión de Ayuda al Refugiado en Euskadi. 2013. “The Externalization of Borders: Migration Control and the Right to Asylum – A Framework for Advocacy.” Bizkaiko Foru Aldundia Diputación Foral de Bizkaia. https://docs.google.com/a/kisa.org.cy/file/d/0B0bim47ArAYzT1g0TXhYUk5BQzA/edit?pli=1.

Cyrus, Norbert, and Dita Vogel. 2003. “Work-Permit Decisions in the German Labour Administration: An Exploration of the Implementation Process.” *Journal of Ethnic and Migration Studies* 29 (2): 225–55. http://dx.doi.org/10.1080/1369183032000079602.

Daenzer, Patricia. 1993. *Regulating Class Privilege: Immigrant Servants in Canada, 1940s to 1990s.* Toronto: Canadian Scholars’ Press.

Daily Mail. 2011. "'Racist' Australia Compared to Apartheid South Africa by UN Human Rights Commissioner." May 25. http://www.dailymail.co.uk/news/article-1390748/Racist-Australia-compared-Apartheid-South-Africa-UN-Human-Rights-commissioner.html.

DeVoretz, Don. 2003. *Asian Skilled-Immigration Flows to Canada: A Supply Side Analysis.* Vancouver: Asia Pacific Foundation.

Digruber, Daniela, and Irene Messinger. 2006. "Marriage of Residence in Austria." *European Journal of Migration and Law* 8 (3): 281–302. http://dx.doi.org/10.1163/157181606778882618.

Ditchburn, Jennifer. 2013. "Immigration Department Unsure Whether MP-Backed Visa Visitors Ever Ultimately Left Canada." *National Post* (Toronto), April 4. http://news.nationalpost.com/2013/04/04/immigration-department-unsure-whether-mp-backed-visa-visitors-ever-ultimately-left-canada/.

Düvell, Franck, and Bill Jordan. 2003. "Immigration Control and Management of Economic Migration in the United Kingdom: Organizational Culture, Implementation, Enforcement and Identity Processes in Public Services." *Journal of Ethnic and Migration Studies* 29 (2): 299–336. http://dx.doi.org/10.1080/1369183032000079620.

Dworkin, Ronald. 1977. *Taking Rights Seriously.* Cambridge, MA: Harvard University Press.

Economic Community of West African States. 2014. "ECOWAS in Brief." http://www.comm.ecowas.int/sec/index.php?id=about_a&lang=en.

Economist. 2014. "America's Deportation Machine: The Great Expulsion." *Economist,* February 8.

Eggebø, Helga. 2013a. "A Real Marriage? Applying for Marriage Migration to Norway." *Journal of Ethnic and Migration Studies* 39 (5): 773–89. http://dx.doi.org/10.1080/1369183X.2013.756678.

–. 2013b. "'With a Heavy Heart': Ethics, Emotions and Rationality in Norwegian Immigration Administration." *Sociology* 47 (2): 301–17. http://soc.sagepub.com/cgi/doi/10.1177/0038038512437895.

Ekberg, Merryn. 2007. "The Parameters of the Risk Society: A Review and Exploration." *Current Sociology* 55 (3): 343–66. http://dx.doi.org/10.1177/0011392107076080.

Emerson, Robert. 1994. "Constructing Serious Violence and Its Victims: Processing a Domestic Violence Restraining Order." *Perspectives on Social Problems* 6: 3–28.

Emerson, Robert, and Blair Paley. 2001. "Organizational Horizons and Complaint-Filing." In *The Uses of Discretion,* ed. Keith Hawkins, 231–48. Oxford: Oxford University Press.

Europa. 2013. "Family Reunification." http://europa.eu/legislation_summaries/justice_freedom_security/free_movement_of_persons_asylum_immigration/l33118_en.htm.

Fassin, Didier. 2011. "Policing Borders, Producing Boundaries: The Governmentality of Immigration in Dark Times." *Annual Review of Anthropology* 40 (1): 213–26. http://dx.doi.org/10.1146/annurev-anthro-081309-145847.

Federal Accountability Initiative for Reform. 2014. "Corruption and Cover Up (W5)." http://fairwhistleblower.ca/content/corruption-and-cover-w5.

Fleras, Augie. 2015. *Immigration Canada: Evolving Realities and Emerging Challenges in a Postnational World.* Vancouver: UBC Press.

Foblets, Marie-Claire, and Dirk Vanheule. 2006. "Marriages of Convenience in Belgium: The Punitive Approach Gains Ground in Migration Law." *European Journal of Migration and Law* 8 (3): 263–80. http://dx.doi.org/10.1163/157181606778882564.

Ford, Michele, Lenore Lyons, and Willem van Schendel. 2012. "Labour Migration and Human Trafficking: An Introduction." In *Labour Migration and Human Trafficking in Southeast Asia: Critical Perspectives,* ed. Michele Ford, Lenore Lyons, and Willem van Schendel, 1–23. London: Routledge.

Foreign Affairs and International Trade Canada. 2009. "Summative Evaluation of the Governance Model for Support to Missions Abroad." http://www.international.gc.ca/about-a_propos/oig-big/2009/evaluation/csa_sce09.aspx?lang=eng#a1_1.

Forsyth, Lacey. 2010. "Gender, Race, and Marriage in Immigration: The Spousal Sponsorship Appeal Process in Canada." Master's thesis, Simon Fraser University, Department of Sociology.

Foster, Lorne. 1998. *Turnstile Immigration: Multiculturalism, Social Order and Social Justice in Canada.* Toronto: Thompson Educational.

Frideres, James, and John Biles, eds. 2012. *International Perspectives: Integration and Inclusion.* Kingston: Queen's Policy Studies.

Frohmann, Lisa. 1991. "Discrediting Victims' Allegations of Sexual Assault: Prosecutorial Accounts of Case Rejections." *Social Problems* 38 (2): 213–26. http://dx.doi.org/10.2307/800530.

Galabuzi, Grace-Edward. 2006. *Canada's Economic Apartheid: The Social Exclusion of Racialized Groups in the New Century.* Toronto: Canadian Scholars' Press.

Ganor, Boaz. 2002. "Defining Terrorism: Is One Man's Terrorist Another Man's Freedom Fighter?" *Police Practice and Research* 3 (4): 287–304. http://dx.doi.org/10.1080/1561426022000032060.

Garner, Steve. 2010. *Racisms: An Introduction.* Los Angeles: Sage.

Gauntlett, David. 2002. *Media, Gender and Identity: An Introduction.* London: Routledge. http://dx.doi.org/10.4324/9780203360798.

Ghana Immigration Service. 2011. "AENEAS 'Countering Document Fraud' Programme, 2007–2010." Paper presented to "Experts Meeting on Improving Civil Status Registration Systems and Combating Document Fraud," International Centre for Migration Policy Development, Warsaw, May 9–11.

Giddens, Anthony. 1992. *The Transformation of Intimacy: Sexuality, Love and Eroticism.* Oxford: Polity Press.

–. 1999. "Risk and Responsibility." *Modern Law Review* 62 (1): 1–10. http://dx.doi.org/10.1111/1468-2230.00188.

Gilboy, Janet. 1991. "Deciding Who Gets In: Decision Making by Immigration Inspectors." *Law and Society Review* 25 (3): 571–600. http://dx.doi.org/10.2307/3053727.

–. 1992. "Penetrability of Administrative Systems: Political 'Casework' and Immigration Inspections." *Law and Society Review* 26 (2): 273–314. http://dx.doi.org/10.2307/3053899.

GMA News. 2007. "Canada's Famous Donut Chain Hiring Pinoys – Brion." *GMA News Online*, March 7. http://www.gmanetwork.com/news/story/33384/ulatfilipino/balitangpinoy/canada-s-famous-donut-chain-hiring-pinoys-brion.

Goffman, Erving. 1952. "On Cooling the Mark Out: Some Aspects of Adaptation to Failure." *Psychiatry: Journal of Interpersonal Relations* 15 (November): 451–63.

Golash-Boza, Tanya. 2012. *Immigration Nation: Raids, Detentions and Deportations in Post 9/11 America*. Boulder: Paradigm.

Goutor, David. 2007. *Guarding the Gates: The Canadian Labour Movement and Immigration, 1872–1934*. Vancouver: UBC Press.

Government Accountability Office. 2007. *Border Security: Fraud Risks Complicate State's Ability to Manage Diversity Visa Program*. Washington, DC: Government Accountability Office.

Government of Canada. 2014a. "Canada's Economic Action Plan: The Road to Balance." http://actionplan.gc.ca/blog/road-balance.

–. 2014b. "CIC Program Assistant: Position Information." http://www.canadainternational.gc.ca/italy-italie/offices-bureaux/COMP01-2014.aspx?lang=en.

Hall, Alexandra. 2010. "'These People Could be Anyone': Fear, Contempt (and Empathy) in a British Immigration Removal Centre." *Journal of Ethnic and Migration Studies* 36 (6): 881–98.

Hall, Rachel. 2002. "When Is a Wife Not a Wife? Some Observations on the Immigration Experiences of South Asian Women in West Yorkshire." *Contemporary Politics* 8 (1): 55–68. http://dx.doi.org/10.1080/13569770220130121.

Hallock, Erin. 2009. "Gender Stereotypes in Canadian Immigration." Paper presented at the "John and Mary Yaremko Forum on Multiculturalism and Human Rights: Student Symposium on Women's Human Rights," University of Toronto, Faculty of Law, March 6.

Hammar, Tomas. 1990. *Democracy and the Nation State: Aliens, Denizens, and Citizens in a World of International Migration*. London: Avebury.

Hanley, Jill, Eric Shragge, Andre Rivard, and Jahhon Koo. 2012. "'Good Enough to Work? Good Enough to Stay!' Organizing among Temporary Foreign Workers." In *Legislated Inequality in Canada: Temporary Labour Migration in Canada*, ed. Patti Tamara Lenard and Christine Straehle, 245–71. Montreal and Kingston: McGill-Queen's University Press.

Hannah-Moffat, Kelly, Paula Maurutto, and Sarah Turnbull. 2009. "Negotiated Risk: Actuarial Illusions and Discretion in Probation." *Canadian Journal of Law and Society* 24 (3): 391–409. http://dx.doi.org/10.1017/S0829320100010097.

Hardcastle, Leonie, Andrew Parkin, Alan Simmons and Nobuaki Suyama. 1994. "The Making of Immigration and Refugee Policy: Politicians, Bureaucrats and Citizens." In *Immigration and Refugee Policy: Australia and Canada Compared*. Vol. 1, ed. Howard Adelman, Allan Borowski, Meyer Burstein and Lois Foster, 95–124. Toronto: University of Toronto Press.

Harris, Nigel. 2007. "The Economics and Politics of the Free Movement of People." In *Migration without Borders: Essays on the Free Movement of People,* ed. Antoine Pécoud and Paul de Guchteneire, 33–50. New York: Berghahn Books.

Hawkins, Freda. 1988. *Canada and Immigration: Public Policy and Public Concern.* Montreal and Kingston: McGill-Queen's University Press.

–. 1989. *Critical Years in Immigration: Canada and Australia Compared.* Montreal and Kingston: McGill-Queen's University Press.

Hawkins Keith. 2002. *Law as a Last Resort: Prosecution Decision Making in a Regulatory Agency.* Oxford: Oxford University Press.

Helleiner, Jane. 2012. "Whiteness and Narratives of a Racialized Canada/US Border at Niagara." *Canadian Journal of Sociology* 37 (2): 109–35.

Henry, Frances, and Carol Tator. 2010. *The Colour of Democracy: Racism in Canada.* 4th ed. Toronto: Nelson.

Heyman, Josiah Mc. 1998. "State Effects on Labour Exploitation: The INS and Undocumented Immigrants and the Mexican-United States Border." *Critique of Anthropology* 18 (2): 157–79. http://dx.doi.org/10.1177/0308275X9801800203.

–. 2001a. "Class and Classification at the U.S.-Mexico Border." *Human Organization* 60 (2): 128–40.

–. 2001b. "U.S. Ports of Entry on the Mexican Border." *Journal of the Southwest* 43 (4): 681–700.

–. 2009. "Trust, Privilege, and Discretion in the Governance of the US Borderlands with Mexico." *Canadian Journal of Law and Society* 24 (3): 367–90. http://dx.doi.org/10.1017/S0829320100010085.

Higuchi, Naoto. 2006. "Brazilian Migration to Japan: Trends, Modalities and Impact." Paper presented to the "Expert Group Meeting on International Migration and Development in Latin America and the Caribbean," Population Division, Department of Economic and Social Affairs, United Nations Secretariat, Mexico City, 30 November–2 December.

Hollifield, James. 2008. "The Politics of International Migration." In *Migration Theory: Talking across Disciplines,* 2nd ed., ed. Caroline Brettell and James Hollifield, 183–238. London: Routledge.

Howard-Hassmann, Rhoda. 1999. "'Canadian' as an Ethnic Category: Implications for Multiculturalism and National Unity." *Canadian Public Policy* 25 (4): 523–37. http://dx.doi.org/10.2307/3552426.

Hughes, Everett C. 1958. *Men and Their Work.* New York: Free Press.

Human Rights Watch. 2008. "The Netherlands: Discrimination in the Name of Integration: Migrants' Rights under the Integration Abroad Act." May 13. http://www.hrw.org/reports/2009/04/13/netherlands-discrimination-name-integration.

Iacovetta, Franca. 2007. *Gatekeepers: Reshaping Immigrant Lives in Cold War Canada.* Toronto: Between the Lines Press.

–. 2014. "Refugee Appeal Division Changes Resulting from New Legislation." http://www.irb-cisr.gc.ca/Eng/RefApp/Pages/RadSarC31Impact.aspx.

Immigration and Refugee Protection Act. 2001. SC 2001, c. 27. http://laws-lois.justice.gc.ca.

IOM (International Organization for Migration). 2014. "Canadian Orientation Abroad: Helping Future Immigrants Adapt to Life in Canada." http://www.iom.

int/cms/render/live/en/sites/iom/home/what-we-do/resettlement-assistance/canadian-orientation-abroad-helping-fut.html.

Jakubowski, Lisa Marie. 1997. *Immigration and the Legalization of Racism.* Toronto: Fernwood Press.

Jamaican High Commission in the United Kingdom. 2014. "Do I Need a Visa to Enter Jamaica?" http://www.jhcuk.org/visitors/visa-requirements/do-i-need-a-visa-to-enter-jamaica.

Joppke, Christian. 2005. *Selecting by Origin: Ethnic Migration in the Liberal State.* Cambridge, MA: Harvard University Press.

Jordan, Bill, Bo Stråth, and Anna Triandafyllidou. 2003a. "Comparing Cultures of Discretion." *Journal of Ethnic and Migration Studies* 29 (2): 373–95. http://dx.doi.org/10.1080/1369183032000079648.

–. 2003b. "Contextualizing Immigration Policy Implementation in Europe." *Journal of Ethnic and Migration Studies* 29 (2): 195–224. http://dx.doi.org/10.1080/1369183032000079594.

Juss, Satvinder. 1997. *Discretion and Deviation in the Administration of Immigration Control.* London: Sweet and Maxwell.

Kallen, Evelyn. 2003. *Ethnicity and Human Rights in Canada.* 3rd ed. Toronto: Oxford University Press.

Kelly, Ninette, and Michael Trebilcock. 1998. *The Making of the Mosaic: A History of Canadian Immigration Policy.* Toronto: University of Toronto Press.

Kenney, Jason. 2013a. "Action Plan for Faster Immigration Producing Real Results." Presentation in Mississauga, March 26.

–. 2013b. "A Message from Minister Jason Kenney to All CIC Employees." http://www.jasonkenney.ca/news/a-message-from-minister-jason-kenney-to-all-cic-employees-message-du-ministre-jason-kenney-a-lintention-de-tous-les-employes-de-cic/.

Keung, Nicholas. 2008. "'Rent-a-Guest' Schemes Tipped Off Immigration." *Toronto Star,* May 23. http://www.thestar.com/news/gta/2008/05/23/rentaguest_schemes_tipped_off_immigration.html.

Khoo, Siew-Ean. 2001. "The Context of Spouse Migration to Australia." *International Migration* (Geneva) 39 (1): 111–32. http://dx.doi.org/10.1111/1468-2435.00137.

Kingwell, Daniel. 2008. "Appeals of Refused Spousal Sponsorship Applications." *Canadian Newcomer Magazine: Settlement Guide to Southwestern Ontario* (July-August): n.p.

Kirkham, Della. 1998. "The Reform Party of Canada: A Discourse on Race, Ethnicity and Equality." In *Racism and Social Inequality in Canada,* ed. Vic Satzewich, 243–68. Toronto: Thompson Educational.

Knowles, Valerie. 1992. *Strangers at Our Gates: Canadian Immigration and Immigration Policy, 1540–1990.* Toronto: Dundurn Press.

Koopmans, Ruud, Paul Statham, Marco Giugni, and Florence Passy. 2005. *Contested Citizenship: Immigration and Cultural Diversity in Europe.* Minneapolis: University of Minnesota Press.

Kukushkin, Vadim. 2009. "Immigrant Friendly Communities: Making Immigration Work for Employers and Other Stakeholders." Ottawa, Conference Board of Canada, October.

Lahav, Gallya. 2000. "The Rise of Nonstate Actors in Migration Regulation in the United States and Europe: Changing the Gatekeepers or Bringing Back the State?" In *Immigration Research for a New Century,* ed. Nancy Foner, Ruben Rumbaut, and Steven Gold, 215–41. New York: Russell Sage Foundation.

LaViolette, Nicole. 2004. "Coming Out to Canada: The Immigration of Same-Sex Couples under the Immigration and Refugee Protection Act." *McGill Law Journal* 49: 970–1003.

Lenard, Patti. 2012. "How Does Canada Fare? Canadian Temporary Labour Migration in Comparative Context." In *Legislated Inequality: Temporary Labour Migration in Canada,* ed. Patti Lenard and Christine Straehle, 272–96. Montreal and Kingston: McGill-Queen's University Press.

Lenard, Patti, and Christine Straehle, eds. 2012. *Legislated Inequality: Temporary Labour Migration in Canada.* Montreal and Kingston: McGill-Queen's University Press.

Li, Peter. 2003. *Destination Canada: Immigration Debates and Issues.* Toronto: Oxford University Press.

Lipsky, Michael. 2010. *Street-Level Bureaucracy: Dilemmas of the Individual in Public Services.* New York: Russell Sage.

Macaluso, Grace. 2012. "Michigan Muslims Sue FBI and U.S. Border Agents over 'Discriminatory' Treatment." *Windsor Star,* April 13. http://blogs.windsorstar.com/news/26229.

MacLeod, Peter. 2006. "How to Organize an Effective Constituency Office." *Canadian Parliamentary Review* 29 (6): 9–12.

Mahrouse, Gada. 2010. "'Reasonable Accommodation' in Quebec: The Limits of Participation and Dialogue." *Race and Class* 52 (1): 85–96. http://dx.doi.org/10.1177/0306396810371768.

Makaremi, Chowra. 2009. "Governing Borders in France: From Extraterritorial to Humanitarian Confinement." *Canadian Journal of Law and Society* 24 (3): 411–32. http://dx.doi.org/10.1017/S0829320100010103.

Marginson, Simon. 2014. "Internationalisation under Threat from Anti-Immigration Populism." *University World News* 00318, May 4. http://www.universityworldnews.com/article.php?story=20140501102653421.

Marshall, Ray. 2011. *Value Added Immigration: Lessons for the United States from Canada, Australia and the United Kingdom.* Washington, DC: Economic Policy Unit.

Martin, Peter. 2003. *Bordering on Control: Combating Irregular Migration in North America and Europe*. Migration Research Series 13. Geneva: International Organization for Migration.

Mas, Susana. 2013. "More Foreign Caregivers to Be Offered Residency in 2014." CBC News, October 29. http://www.cbc.ca/news/politics/more-foreign-caregivers-to-be-offered-residency-in-2014-1.2287138.

Massey, Douglas. 1999. "Why Does Immigration Occur? A Theoretical Synthesis." In *The Handbook of International Migration,* ed. Charles Hirschman, Philip Kasinitz, and Josh DeWind, 34–52. New York: Russell Sage Foundation.

Matthews, Kim, and Vic Satzewich. 2006. "The Invisible Transnationals? Americans in Canada." In *Transnational Identities and Practices in Canada,* ed. Vic Satzewich and Lloyd Wong, 164–79. Vancouver: UBC Press.

Meehan, Albert. 1986. "Record Keeping Practices in the Policing of Juveniles." *Urban Life* 15 (1): 70–102.

Meurrens, Steven. 2013. "The CBSA Databases – ICES, FOSS, CPIC, and NCIC." Meurrens on Immigration. http://www.stevenmeurrens.com/2013/07/the-cbsa-databases-ices-foss-cpic-and-ncic/.

Migration Observatory. 2011. "Deportations, Removals and Voluntary Departures from the UK." http://www.migrationobservatory.ox.ac.uk/briefings/deportations-removals-and-voluntary-departures-uk.

Milanovic, Branko. 2011. *Global Inequality: From Class to Location, from Proletarians to Migrants.* Policy Research Working Paper 5820. New York: World Bank.

Miles, R., and M. Brown. 2003. *Racism.* 2nd ed. London: Routledge.

Mosey, Ann-Marie. 2004. *The Canadian Foreign Service in the 21st Century: An Analysis of Research on the Compensation System and Retention Rates at the Department of Foreign Affairs and International Trade.* Occasional Paper 45. Ottawa: Norman Patterson School of International Affairs.

Muller Myrdahl, Eileen. 2010. "Legislating Love: Norwegian Family Reunification as a Racial Project." *Social and Cultural Geography* 11 (2): 103–16.

Nakache, Delphine, and Sarah D'Aoust. 2012. "Provincial/Territorial Nominee Programs: An Avenue to Permanent Residency for Low-Skilled Temporary Foreign Workers." In *Legislated Inequality: Temporary Labour Migration in Canada,* ed. Patti Lenard and Christine Straehle, 158–77. Montreal and Kingston: McGill-Queen's University Press.

National Conference of State Legislatures. 2012. "Arizona's Immigration Enforcement Laws." http://www.ncsl.org/research/immigration/analysis-of-arizonas-immigration-law.aspx.

National Joint Council. 2012a. "Appendix A – Post Differential Allowance." http://www.njc-cnm.gc.ca/directive/index.php?sid=495&lang=eng.

–. 2012b. "Appendix B – Post Ratings." http://www.njc-cnm.gc.ca/directive/index.php?sid=496&lang=eng.

Newman, David. 2003. "On Borders and Power: A Theoretical Framework." *Journal of Borderland Studies* 18 (1): 13–25. http://dx.doi.org/10.1080/08865655.2003.9695598.

OECD. 2013. *International Migration Outlook, 2013.* N.p.: OECD Publishing. http://dx.doi.org/10.1787/migr_outlook-2013-en.

Orozco, Manuel. 2013. *Migrant Remittances and Development in the Global Economy.* Boulder: Lynne Rienner.

O'Shea, Edwina. 2009. *Missing the Point(s): The Declining Fortunes of Canada's Economic Immigration Program.* Washington, DC: Transatlantic Academy.

Pacific Immigration Canada. 2011. "Parents and Grandparents Extended Stay Temporary Resident Visa (Super Visa) and Authorized Period of Extended Stay." http://www.pacificimmigration.ca/en/news/parents-and-grandparents-extended-stay-temporary-resident-visa-super-visa-and-authorized-period-of-extended-stay.

Palmer, Wayne. 2012. "Discretion and the Trafficking-Like Practices of the Indonesian State." In *Labour Migration and Human Trafficking in Southeast Asia: Critical Perspectives,* ed. Michele Ford, Lenore Lyons, and Willem van Schendel, 149–66. London: Routledge.

Papademetriou, Demetrios. 2005. "The 'Regularization' Option in Managing Illegal Migration More Effectively: A Comparative Perspective." *Policy Brief* (Migration Policy Institute) 4 (September).

Papademetriou, Demetrios, and Stephen Yale-Loeher. 1996. *Balancing Interests: Rethinking U.S. Selection of Skilled Immigrants.* Washington, DC: Carnegie Endowment for International Peace.

Paquet, Mireille. 2014. "Public Servants as Heroes: Process-Tracing and Elite Interviews in a Politically Sensitive Field." Paper presented at the annual meeting of the Canadian Political Science Association, Brock University, St. Catharines, May 27.

Pathways to Prosperity. 2014. "Pan-Canadian Research Themes." http://p2pcanada.ca/current-research/p2p-pan-canadian-research/.

Pécoud, Antoine, and Paul de Guchteneire. 2007. "Introduction: The Migration without Borders Scenario." In *Migration without Borders: Essays on the Free Movement of People,* ed. Antoine Pécoud and Paul de Guchteneire, 1–32. Paris: UNESCO.

Portes, Alejandro. 1999. "Immigration Theory for a New Century: Some Problems and Opportunities." In *The Handbook of International Migration,* ed. Charles Hirschman, Philip Kasinitz, and Josh DeWind, 21–33. New York: Russell Sage Foundation.

Pratt, Anna. 2005. *Securing Borders: Detention and Deportation in Canada.* Vancouver: UBC Press.

Pratt, Anna, and Lorne Sossin. 2009. "A Brief Introduction of the Puzzle of Discretion." *Canadian Journal of Law and Society* 24 (3): 301–12. http://dx.doi.org/10.1017/S082932010001005X.

Preibisch, Kerry, and Leigh Binford. 2007. "Interrogating Racialized Global Labour Supply: An Exploration of the Racial/National Replacement of Foreign Agricultural Workers in Canada." *Canadian Review of Sociology* 44 (1): 5–36. http://dx.doi.org/10.1111/j.1755-618X.2007.tb01146.x.

Preibisch, Kerry, and Jenna Hennebry. 2012. "Buy Local, Hire Global: Temporary Migration in Canadian Agriculture." In *Legislated Inequality: Temporary Labour Migration in Canada,* ed. Patti Lenard and Christine Straehle, 48–72. Montreal and Kingston: McGill-Queen's University Press.

Protecting Canada's Immigration System Act. 2012. SC 2012, c. 17. http://laws-lois.justice.gc.ca/eng/annualstatutes/2012_17/page-1.html.

Prus, Robert. 1997. *Subcultural Mosaics and Intersubjective Realities: An Ethnographic Research Agenda for Pragmatizing the Social Sciences.* Albany: State University of New York Press.

Psimmenos, Iordanis, and Koula Kassimati. 2003. "Immigration Control Pathways: Organizational Culture and Work Values of Greek Welfare Officers." *Journal of Ethnic and Migration Studies* 29 (2): 337–71. http://dx.doi.org/10.1080/1369183032000079639.

Razack, Sherene. 1999. "Making Canada White: Law and the Policing of Bodies of Colour in the 1990s." *Canadian Journal of Law and Society* 14 (1): 159–84. http://dx.doi.org/10.1017/S0829320100005974.

Rowe, Roger. 2008. "*Baker* Revisited 2007." *Journal of Black Studies* 38 (3): 338–45. http://dx.doi.org/10.1177/0021934707306569.

Roy, Patricia. 1989. *A White Man's Province: British Columbia Politicians and Chinese and Japanese Immigrants, 1858–1914.* Vancouver: UBC Press.

Royal Canadian Mounted Police. 2014. "Immigration and Passport." http://www.rcmp-grc.gc.ca/imm-passp/index-eng.htm.

Rygiel, Kim. 2010. *Globalizing Citizenship.* Vancouver: UBC Press.

Salaff, Janet, and Arent Greve. 2004. "Can Women's Social Networks Migrate?" *Women's Studies International Forum* 27 (2): 149–62. http://dx.doi.org/10.1016/j.wsif.2004.06.005.

Salter, Mark. 2006. "The Global Visa Regime and the Political Technologies of the International Self: Borders, Bodies, Biopolitics." *Alternatives: Global, Local, Political* 31 (2): 167–89. http://dx.doi.org/10.1177/030437540603100203.

–. 2011. "International Cooperation on Travel Document Security in the Developed World." In *Global Mobility Regimes,* ed. Rey Koslowski, 115–30. New York: Palgrave Macmillan. http://dx.doi.org/10.1057/9781137001948.0013.

Sassen, Saskia. 1988. *The Mobility of Capital and Labor: A Study in International Investment and Labor Flow.* Cambridge: Cambridge University Press. http://dx.doi.org/10.1017/CBO9780511598296.

–. 2000. *Guests and Aliens.* New York: New Press.

–. 2006. *A Sociology of Globalization.* New York: W.W. Norton.

Satzewich, Vic. 1991. *Racism and the Incorporation of Foreign Labour: Farm Labour Migration to Canada since 1945.* London: Routledge.

–. 2002. *The Ukrainian Diaspora.* London: Routledge.

–. 2007. "Business or Bureaucratic Dominance in Immigration Policymaking in Canada: Why Was Mexico Added to the Caribbean Agricultural Workers Program in 1974?" *Journal of International Migration and Integration* 8 (3): 255–75.

–. 2007–08. "Multiculturalism, Transnationalism and the Hijacking of Canadian Foreign Policy: A Pseudo-Problem?" *International Journal* 63 (1): 43–67.

Satzewich, Vic, and Nik Liodakis. 2013. *"Race" and Ethnicity in Canada: A Critical Introduction.* Toronto: Oxford University Press.

Satzewich, Vic, and William Shaffir. 2009. "Racism versus Professionalism: Claims and Counter Claims about Racial Profiling." *Canadian Journal of Criminology and Criminal Justice* 51 (2): 199–226. http://dx.doi.org/10.3138/cjccj.51.2.199.

Satzewich, Vic, and Lloyd Wong, eds. 2006. *Transnational Identities and Practices in Canada.* Vancouver: UBC Press.

Schneider, Carl. 1992. "Discretion and Rules: A Lawyer's View." In *The Uses of Discretion,* ed. Keith Hawkins, 47–88. London: Oxford University Press.

Schrover, Marlou, and Willem Schinkel. 2013. "Introduction: The Language of Inclusion and Exclusion in the Context of Immigration and Integration." *Ethnic and Racial Studies* 36 (7): 1123–41. http://dx.doi.org/10.1080/01419870.2013.783711.

Schuck, Peter. 2008. "Law and the Study of Migration." In *Migration Theory: Talking across Disciplines,* ed. Caroline Brettell and James Hollifield, 239–58. London: Routledge.

Sharma, Nandita. 2006. *Home Economics: Nationalism and the Making of "Migrant Workers" in Canada.* Toronto: University of Toronto Press.

–. 2012. "The 'Difference' That Borders Make: 'Temporary Foreign Workers' and the Social Organization of Unfreedom in Canada." In *Legislated Inequality: Temporary Labour Migration in Canada,* ed. Patti Lenard and Christine Straehle, 26–47. Montreal and Kingston: McGill-Queen's University Press.

Simmons, Alan. 1998. "Racism and Immigration Policy." In *Racism and Social Inequality in Canada: Concepts, Controversies and Strategies of Resistance,* ed. Vic Satzewich, 87–114. Toronto: Thompson Educational.

–. 2010. *Immigration and Canada.* Toronto: Canadian Scholars' Press.

Simmons, Alan, and Kieran Keohane. 1992. "Shifts in Canadian Immigration Policy: State Strategies and the Quest for Legitimacy." *Canadian Review of Sociology and Anthropology* 29 (4): 421–52. http://dx.doi.org/10.1111/j.1755-618X.1992.tb02446.x.

Simon, Patrick. 2013. "Discrimination against Immigrants – Measurement, Incidence and Policy Instruments." In *OECD, International Migration Outlook, 2013.* Paris: OECD Publishing. http://dx.doi.org/10.1787/migr_outlook-2013-7-en.

Smith, Donna. 2007. "Senate Kills Bush Immigration Reform Bill." Reuters, June 29. http://www.reuters.com/article/2007/06/29/us-usa-immigration-idUSN2742643820070629.

Stanford, Jim. 2014. "TFWs Threatened the Conservative Coalition." *Toronto Globe and Mail,* April 30, A13.

Stasiulis, Daiva, and Abigail Bakan. 2005. *Negotiating Citizenship: Migrant Women in Canada and the Global System.* Toronto: University of Toronto Press.

Steinecke, Julia. 2009. "Border Skirmishes." *Toronto Star,* August 15. http://www.thestar.com/news/2009/08/15/border_skirmishes.html.

Tomkinson, Sule. 2015. "Doing Research on State Organizations in Democratic Settings: Ethical Issues of Research in Refugee Decision Making." *Forum Qualitative Sozial Forschung* 16 (1): Art. 6.

Treasury Board of Canada Secretariat. 2012. "Appendix A: FS-Foreign Service Group Annual Rates of Pay." http://www.njc-cnm.gc.ca/directive/index.php?sid=495&lang=eng.

Triadafilopoulos, Phil. 2012. *Becoming Multicultural: Immigration and the Politics of Membership in Canada and Germany.* Vancouver: UBC Press.

Triandafyllidou, Anna. 2003. "Immigration Policy Implementation in Italy: Organizational Culture, Identity Processes and Labour Market Control." *Journal of Ethnic and Migration Studies* 29 (2): 257–97. http://dx.doi.org/10.1080/1369183032000079611.

United Nations High Commissioner for Refugees. 2014. "World Refugee Day: Global Forced Displacement Tops 50 Million for First Time in Post-World War II Era." http://www.unhcr.org/53a155bc6.html.

Veugelers, John. 2000. "State-Society Relations in the Making of Canadian Immigration Policy during the Mulroney Era." *Canadian Review of Sociology and Anthropology* 37 (1): 95–110. http://dx.doi.org/10.1111/j.1755-618X.2000.tb00588.x.

Veugelers, John, and Thomas Klassen. 1994. "Continuity and Change in Canada's Unemployment-Immigration Linkage." *Canadian Journal of Sociology* 19 (3): 351–69. http://dx.doi.org/10.2307/3340722.

VFS Global Group. 2014. "About Us." http://www.vfsglobal.com/about_us/company_profile.asp.

Visa Services Canada. 2013. "Democratic People's Republic of Korea." http://visaservicescanada.ca/countries/north_korea.php.

Waegel, William. 1981. "Case Routinization in Investigative Police Work." *Social Problems* 28 (3): 263–75. http://dx.doi.org/10.2307/800302.

Waldman, Lorne. 2009. "Compassion in Canada's Immigration Programme: Discretionary Relief in Immigration Processing and a Review of the Refugee Determination Process." Paper presented at the Canadian Bar Association annual meeting, Dublin, August 19.

Walton-Roberts, Margaret. 2003. "Transnational Geographies: Indian Immigration to Canada." *Canadian Geographer* 47 (3): 235–50. http://dx.doi.org/10.1111/1541-0064.00020.

–. 2004. "Rescaling Citizenship: Gendering Canadian Immigration Policy." *Political Geography* 23 (3): 265–81. http://dx.doi.org/10.1016/j.polgeo.2003.12.016.

Webber, Frances. 2012. *Borderline Justice: The Fight for Refugee and Migrant Rights.* London: Pluto Press.

Weber, Leanne. 2013. *Policing Non-Citizens.* Abingdon, UK: Routledge.

Weber, Max. 1964. *The Theory of Social and Economic Organization.* New York: Free Press.

Whitaker, Reg. 1987. *Double Standard: The Secret History of Canadian Immigration.* Toronto: Lester and Orpen Dennys.

Willis, Paul. 1981. "Cultural Production Is Different from Cultural Reproduction Is Different from Social Reproduction Is Different from Reproduction." *Interchange* 12 (2–3): 48–67. http://dx.doi.org/10.1007/BF01192107.

Wong, Lloyd, and Nancy Netting. 1992. "Business Immigration to Canada: Social Impact and Racism." In *Deconstructing a Nation: Immigration, Multiculturalism and Racism in '90s Canada,* ed. Vic Satzewich, 93–122. Halifax: Fernwood Press.

World Bank. 2014. "International Tourism, Number of Arrivals." http://data.worldbank.org/indicator/ST.INT.ARVL.

Wray, H. 2006. "An Ideal Husband? Marriages of Convenience, Moral Gate-Keeping and Immigration to the UK." *European Journal of Migration and Law* 8 (3): 303–20. http://dx.doi.org/10.1163/157181606778882582.

York, Geoffrey. 2012. "Ottawa Set to Lift Entry Ban on ANC Members." *Toronto Globe and Mail,* September 6. http://m.theglobeandmail.com/news/politics/ottawa-set-to-lift-entry-ban-on-anc-members/article2356094/?service=mobile.

Zolberg, Aristide. 1999. "Matters of State: Theorizing Immigration Policy." In *The Handbook of International Migration,* ed. Charles Hirschman, Philip Kasinitz, and Josh DeWind, 71–93. New York: Russell Sage Foundation.

Index

Note: "(f)" after a page number indicates a figure; "(t)" after a page number indicates a table. "CIC," in parenthetical glosses and subentries, stands for Citizenship and Immigration Canada; "skilled worker(s)," in subentries, refers to federal skilled workers.

advocacy groups, 42; on race-based bias, 168–69; on refugee claims, 191

African National Congress, 77

agendas, hidden: in border control process, 28–32; in Canada's immigration system, 32–36, 37, 245–47. *See also* bias; border control; discretion, as exercised by visa officers

agendas, stated/official: in border control process, 26–28. *See also* border control

airport interdiction: and airline sanctions, 23, 98; migration integrity officers handling, 97–100

Alexander, Chris, 8

anti-fraud migration integrity officers, 98, 100–1, 156

approval and refusal rates, 105–38; as affected by competing goals, 120–21, 138; as affected by organizational culture, 120–37, 138; for family class and skilled workers, 106–20; perceived bias of, 16, 118–20, 137–38, 247. *See also entry below*; refusals of visas

approvals of visas: by category (2012), 106, 107–8(t), 109; as "easy," 204–5; by office (2012), 109, 110–11(t), 112; by region/category (2012), 112, 113(t); by region/office – C-50 skilled worker, 115, 116–17(t), 117–18, 119–20; by region/office – spousal/partner, 112, 113–15(t), 115, 119, 120; as reversible, 205, 221–22

asylum, refugees seeking, 72, 73

Australia, 25, 31, 62, 73, 119; points system of, 164; as visa exempt, 189; white-only immigration policy of, 29

backlog, of visa applications, 2, 17, 87, 121, 123; Bill C-50/Ministerial

Instructions and, 65–66, 68, 71, 171–73, 191
backlog reduction offices: approval rates for (2012), 110(t), 112
Baker v. Canada (Minister of Citizenship and Immigration) (Supreme Court case), 45
bias: in border control process, 28–32, 37; in Canada's immigration system, 32–36, 37, 245–47; and exercise of discretion, 15–18, 19, 37–38; need for serious consideration of, 35–36; and path-dependent nature of immigration, 35, 47–48, 137–38; public's perception of, 7–8, 96, 234. *See also* class-based bias; gender-based bias; race-based bias
bigamy and polygamy, 149–50
Bill C-50 (2008 federal budget): and skilled worker cases, 10, 40, 63, 65–66, 106–20, 171–73, 191. *See also* Conservative government, changes made by; Immigration and Refugee Protection Act; Kenney, Jason; Ministerial Instructions
Black, Conrad, 7
border control, 19–36; airline sanctions as, 23, 98; cost of, 26; inclusion-exclusion process of, 21–26; macro-micro-meso analysis of, 20; at physical border, 23–25; in post-9/11 era, 24; profiling and, 148–49; reasons for (stated/official), 26–28; reasons for (unstated/hidden), 28–32, 37; by regulated access to citizenship, 25–26; by removal/deportation, 25; state sovereignty and, 21; at visa issuance stage, 22–23, 244–45; and visa officers' discretion, 37, 47–48, 49, 50, 56, 244–45; visitor visa requirements and, 198
Bouchard, Geneviève, 250*n*3
Buffalo visa office, 11–12; approval rates at, 114(t), 117(t); closure of, 83, 112
bureaucrats, senior, at CIC, 42, 169–70. *See also* street-level bureaucrats, visa officers as
Bush, George W., 27
business delegations/groups, as visitors, 210
business immigrants, 67, 68–69, 124; approval rates for (2012), 107(t), 109; as entrepreneurs, 68–69, 118; as investors, 64, 68–69, 82, 109, 177–78; as self-employed, 68, 69, 82, 109

Canada Border Services Agency, 3–4, 24, 77, 87, 93, 94; enforcement role of, 25, 43, 75, 80, 222, 246; and migration integrity officers, 97–100
Canadian Bar Association, 44
Canadian Council for Refugees, 42, 191
Canadian Experience Class, 69–70, 77, 82; approval rate for (2012), 107(t); finalized application targets for (2014), 124, 125(t), 126–27(t), 128–29(t)
Canadian Food Inspection Agency, 43
Canadian Immigration Historical Society, 10, 11
Canadian Marriage Fraud Victims Society, 42
Canadian Race Relations Foundation, 34
Canadian Security Intelligence Service (CSIS), 43, 87
Caribbean: live-in caregivers from, 33–34, 69; removal cases from, 158; seasonal agricultural workers from, 33, 42, 76–77; visa exempt countries of, 189
case analysts, 102, 103; and marriage fraud, 155–56, 158–60, 161
Case Processing Centres, 82, 83, 112; Mississauga, 83, 142, 156; Sydney, 83, 85
caseload: of visa officers, 49, 56, 57, 105, 121, 170, 188, 192–93, 209; of visa offices, 89, 91–92, 112, 192, 194, 242
C.D. Howe Institute, 42

Centralized Intake office (Sydney), 82–83
citizenship: access to, 21–22, 25–26, 31; Black's renunciation of, 7; and right to vote, 39
Citizenship and Immigration Canada (CIC): author's interactions with, 8–14; budgetary pressures of, 79, 240; employee retention at, 243–44; as high-caseload department, 57, 121; inter-organizational work of, 42–43; modernization agenda of, 79, 80–85, 112, 122, 124, 193, 240; senior bureaucrats at, 42, 169–70; sensitivity to public criticism of, 206–8, 233; visa officers' employment for, 86; website of, 8–9, 122, 194, 216–17
class-based bias, 16–17, 19, 34, 35, 245–46; neo-liberalism and, 32, 61; social reproduction and, 60–61
Committee on Representation Abroad, 87
Computer Assisted Immigration Processing System (CAIPS) database, 80–81, 174
Conservative government, changes made by: family class and, 40–41, 71, 139; refugees and, 72–74, 191–92, 199; skilled workers and, 10, 40, 63, 65–66, 106–20, 171–73, 191. *See also* Immigration and Refugee Protection Act; Kenney, Jason; Ministerial Instructions
consultants, 6, 17, 44, 57, 81, 122, 200, 216–17, 233; and appeals, 45, 58, 185, 241; as critics of process, 151, 181; as crooked, 147, 149; as former visa officers/staff, 11–12, 92–93; rise of, 45; and substituted evaluations, 11–12, 181, 185
convention refugees, 72, 73
Council on American-Islamic Relations, 24
courts, 45–46, 58; and substituted evaluations, 185–86. *See also specific courts and judicial bodies*
credibility, assessment of, 50–52; and "balance of probabilities," 15–16, 51–52, 143; databases used in, 80–81; at interviews, 17–18, 55–56, 135, 143, 196–97, 216, 225–32, 241–43; locally engaged staff and, 102; profiling and, 99, 148–49, 175–76; as re-evaluated based on new information, 221–22; in spousal/partner sponsorship cases, 2–6, 140–45, 151–63; time pressures on, 196–97; in visitor visa cases, 196–97, 209–14. *See also entry below*
credibility and risk, assessment of, 15–16, 17, 34, 50–54, 244–47; decision-making variables involved in, 54–58; by "digging deeper," 140–42; embassy staff members and, 88; at interviews, 55–56, 135, 216, 222, 241–43; locally engaged staff and, 17, 57; perceived racialization of, 35, 137–38; in refugee cases, 51, 53–54, 100; Visa Application Centres as factor in, 84, 222; in visitor visa cases, 187–214
crime: drug trafficking, 26, 241; fraud, 7; human trafficking, 20, 26, 43, 212, 241; smuggling, 99
crimes, of visa applicants/visitors, 27, 80–81, 101, 106, 109, 137, 142, 198, 201, 235, 246, 249; drunk driving, 24, 233; fraud/misrepresentation, 16–17, 43, 91, 97–101, 102, 103, 176–78, 197, 206, 210, 220, 241, 242, 246; high-ranking visitors and, 77; investor category and, 177–78; terrorism, 6–7, 26, 52–53, 59, 62, 80, 184, 241; war crimes/human rights violations, 25, 52–53, 62, 237. *See also* marriages of convenience
Czech Republic, 84; visa requirement imposed on, 189, 191–92

Daily Wrap (electronic newsletter), 233
Damascus visa office, 86, 112
databases, CIC, 3, 80–81, 136, 156, 170, 174, 196, 210–11, 219, 222, 223;

replacement system for, 80–81, 133, 256*n*2
decision making. *See* discretionary decisions, factors in
deportation, 22, 25; *Baker* case and, 45; Border Services and, 43; CIC database tracking of, 80; circumvention of, 26; of failed refugee claimants, 74; perceived racism of, 29, 35; and potential marriage fraud, 3, 158; of temporary foreign workers, 76–77
designated immigration officers, 101, 103; and *Daily Wrap*, 233; and "jumpers," 203–4; and marriage fraud, 143, 146, 151–52, 155, 161, 226; online attacks on, 234–35; Ottawa-based training of, 102; and skilled worker cases, 175–76; target pressures on, 134
"digging deeper," 16–17, 54, 55, 80, 140–42, 214; organizational factors affecting, 121, 183, 188, 245; in skilled worker cases, 167, 175–78, 183; social constitution of, 16–17, 141–42, 175–78; in spousal/partner sponsorship cases, 3–6, 140–42, 145–50, 154–56, 162–63, 175, 227–32; in visitor visa cases, 188, 210–11
discretion, as exercised by visa officers, 6, 7, 15–18, 37–58, 241–42, 244–45; and credibility/risk, 15–16, 17, 34, 50–54, 244–47; criticism of, 34–35; and decision-making process, 54–58; delegation of, 48–50; fettering of, 40–41, 50, 54, 77, 87, 90–91, 184, 203; and immigration policy creation/implementation, 38–47; and importance of being "satisfied," 2–3, 5–6, 49–50, 143, 178, 221; and increasing rarity of interviews, 17–18, 55, 135–36, 215–16, 242–43; and need to "dig deeper," 16–17, 140–42, 145–50, 175–78; vs organizational culture/structure, 38, 39, 56–57, 120–37, 138; racialization of, 16, 34–35, 118, 120, 137–38, 240; reduction of, 169–75, 241; and rule of law, 37–38; in skilled worker cases/points system, 9–12, 34, 164–86; social constitution of, 16–17, 57, 138, 141–42, 175–78; in spousal/partner sponsorship cases, 139–63, 227–32; and stated/hidden agendas, 19, 32, 34; in street-level bureaucratic role, 47–58, 121, 138, 141–42, 216–17, 241–42; in substituted evaluations, 11–12, 34, 166, 171, 173–75, 178–86; in visitor visa cases, 186, 188, 204–14, 216. *See also entry below*; credibility, assessment of, *and entry following*; fettering of discretion; immigration policy, *and entry following*
discretionary decisions, factors in, 54–58; "balance of probabilities," 15–16, 51–52, 143; caseload, 56, 57, 105, 121, 170, 188, 193, 242; decision horizons/appeal process, 58; enforcement vs facilitative approach, 15–16, 56, 57, 163, 196–204, 246; experience, 16, 17, 55, 56, 57, 90, 94–95, 147–48, 186, 246; face-to-face interaction, 1–6, 17–18, 55–56, 196–97, 215–38, 241–43; immigration policy, 38–47, 57, 59–78, 121; national identity/nation-building, 17, 44, 56, 74, 121, 135, 240, 242–43; organizational culture/structure, 38, 39, 56–57, 120–37, 138; political pressure, 39–41, 57, 77, 122–23, 204; professional identity/sense of responsibility, 56, 121; target pressures, 133–37, 183–84; time pressures, 134–37, 140, 163, 196–98, 240–42, 246–47
drug trafficking, 26, 241

"easy" cases, 55, 204–6
economic class immigrants, 40, 46, 64–70, 71, 163; approval rate for

(2012), 112, 113(t); Centralized Intake Office and, 82–83; finalized application targets for (2014), 124, 126–28(t); as outnumbered by temporary foreign workers, 76; reduced discretion in selection of, 169–75; weighting of entry rules for, 35, 138. *See also entry below*
economic class immigrants (specific): business immigrants, 68–69; Canadian experience class, 69–70; live-in caregivers, 69; provincial nominees, 66–68; skilled workers, 64–66. *See also specific types of economic immigrants*; Federal Skilled Worker Program; Quebec skilled workers
Economic Class Units, of visa offices, 89, 174–79; managers of, 172, 174–75, 177, 178–79, 181–83
embassies and consulates, as visa office locations, 84, 85–88, 194, 211, 225; business activity/fraud conducted near, 92, 177; and business delegations, 210; and embassy staff, 87–88, 95, 210; and locally engaged staff, 102–3, 218; security precautions at, 14, 218, 237–38
employers, 28, 44, 63; and access to offshore labour, 41–42, 43, 44, 60, 76–77, 150; and employee credentials, 164, 214; mistreatment/abuse by, 54, 230; and provincial nominees, 41, 67–68, 109
enforcement, as Border Services/police responsibility, 22–26, 43; database for, 80; and goal of immigration system integrity, 27–28; racialization of, 29–31. *See also entry below*; selection, as CIC/Human Resources responsibility
enforcement approach, as taken by visa officers, 15–16, 56, 57, 135, 163, 186, 195, 246; and goal of immigration system integrity, 144–45, 198; in provincial nominee cases, 67–68; and screening out of "jumpers," 198–204; and substituted evaluations, 178–79, 183. *See also* facilitative approach, as taken by visa officers
English-/French-language skills, 35, 64, 66, 138; in points system, 65, 65(t), 166–68, 169, 170, 245; refugee training in, 72; of visa office staff, 102
Europe/European Union: applicants' previous travel to, 212, 213; border control/racism in, 21, 22, 24, 29–32; immigration to Canada from, 32–33, 34, 118–19, 165; live-in caregivers from, 33, 69; refugees to Canada from, 73, 112; visa exempt countries in, 189; visa offices in, 83, 112, 115, 235, 236

facilitative approach, as taken by visa officers, 15–16, 56, 57, 163, 246; and applicants from Philippines, 150, 195; and new "super visa," 40–41; and permitting of applicant interviews, 197; and screening out of "jumpers," 198–204; and substituted evaluations, 183. *See also* enforcement approach, as taken by visa officers
family class immigrants, 40, 46, 64, 70–71, 118; approval rate for (2012), 106, 107–8(t), 109; approval rates for (by office, 2012), 112, 113–15(t), 115; finalized application targets for (2014), 124, 125(t), 129–32(t), 133; humanitarian/compassionate cases of, 74; interviews of, 135–36, 225–32; perceived bias in selection of, 34–35; recent modifications to process for, 71. *See also* marriages of convenience; spousal and partner sponsorships
Family Class Units, of visa offices, 89; interviews at, 225–32; officers' safety at, 234

Federal Court of Canada: appeals to, 46, 81, 121, 136, 170–71, 185, 233
federal political parties/politicians, 39–41, 57, 77, 122–23, 204. *See also* Kenney, Jason
Federal Skilled Trades Program, 66
Federal Skilled Worker Program, 9, 10, 64–66, 164–86; application backlog in, 65–66, 171–73, 191; approval rate for (2012), 106, 107(t), 109; approval rates for (C-50 class, by office, 2012), 115, 116–17(t), 118, 119–20; Bill C-50 changes to, 10, 40, 63, 65–66, 106–20, 171–73, 191; "digging deeper" in applications to, 167, 175–78, 183; finalized application targets for (2014), 124, 125(t), 126–27(t), 128–29(t); Ministerial Instructions for, 40, 63, 65–66, 71, 82–83, 106, 109, 115, 171–73; perceived selection bias of, 34, 35, 165–70, 178–79; personal suitability criteria of, 166, 167–75, 186; points system of, 64–65, 69, 164–75, 178–86; substituted evaluations and, 11–12, 34, 166, 171, 173–75, 178–86; targets for, 171–73, 182, 183–84, 185, 186, 246–47. *See also* points system
fettering of discretion: "justified reasons" for, 77; as legally prohibited, 50, 54, 87; managers' balancing act in avoiding, 90–91, 203; in "super visa" cases, 40–41; target/time pressures and, 184
Field Operations Support System (FOSS) database, 3, 80–81, 156, 210–11, 222
Foreign Affairs and International Trade, Department of, 43; Global Citizens Strategy of, 12–13; and visa offices/staff, 78, 85–87, 93, 95, 103
Foreign Service Development Program (FSDP), 86, 93, 102, 182–83
Foster, Lorne, 250*n*3
fraud, 16–17, 43, 91, 102, 103, 176–78, 197, 206, 210, 220, 241, 242, 246; migration integrity officers handling, 97–101, 156
front-line bureaucrats. *See* street-level bureaucrats, visa officers as

gender-based bias, 19, 32–34, 37; transgender persons and, 24–25
Germany, 26, 63, 84, 119
Ghana: British mission in, 149; visa requirements of, 189–90
Global Case Management System (GCMS), 80–81, 133, 256*n*2
Go, Avvy, 34–35
Great Britain, 68, 90, 118, 119, 151, 212; deportations from, 25; domestics recruited from, 33, 69; perceived racism of immigration control process in, 29–30; and refusal rate of Ghana visa office, 149; as visa exempt, 189, 190

"hard" cases, 55, 206–8
Hawkins, Freda, 11, 42, 247, 250*n*3
health: in era of global disease, 241; and inadmissibility, 6, 41, 43, 46, 61, 62, 106, 109, 166, 249; at visa offices, 86; in visitor visa cases, 189, 190, 195, 198, 201, 205
health care system: potential abuse of/demands on, 7, 26–27, 52, 62; refugees and, 74, 98, 191; visitors and, 75
Homeland Security, U.S. Department of, 29
Hong Kong, 67, 68, 189; visa office in, 86, 93, 112, 118, 119, 120, 122, 133
Human Resources and Skills Development Canada, 43, 109
human rights violations: refugees fleeing, 72, 73; by visa applicants, 25, 52–53
human trafficking/smuggling, 20, 26, 43, 212, 241

humanitarian and compassionate grounds: approval rates on (2012), 108(t), 109; backlog reduction offices and, 112; in *Baker* case, 45; finalized application targets on (2014), 125(t); office definitions/use of, 90–91, 178, 207–8; for refugee admission, 61, 74, 109

immigrants, categories of, 64–77; economic class, 64–70; family class, 70–71; refugees, 71–74; temporary residents, 74–77. *See also specific categories*
immigration, to Canada: history/scope of (since 2001), 62–64; and nation-building , 17, 44, 56, 74, 121, 135, 240, 242–43; path-dependent nature of, 35, 47–48, 137–38
Immigration and Refugee Board: about, 46; access to case notes by, 81; database tracking of decisions by, 80; immigration hearings/appeals at, 46, 121, 136, 143; refugee hearings/ appeals at, 4, 46, 73–74, 227–28
Immigration and Refugee Program: goals of, 61, 121, 248–49
Immigration and Refugee Protection Act: amendments to, 40, 63, 171–73; and concept of being "satisfied," 5–6, 49–50, 143, 178, 221; era preceding, 135, 170, 174–75, 239–40, 242–43; and family class, 40–41, 71, 74; and humanitarian/compassionate cases, 74; on inadmissibility, 61–62, 64, 74; and increasing rarity of interviews, 55, 215–16, 239–40, 242–43; introduction of, 169; objectives of, 6, 27, 61, 105, 121, 188, 248–49; and skilled workers, 10, 40, 63, 65–66, 71, 106–20, 165, 167, 170–73, 181, 183–84; visa officer training in, 93; and visitors, 188, 204. *See also* Ministerial Instructions
Immigration Appeal Board, 46
immigration policy, 59–78; and border control, 19–36; and categories of immigrants, 64–77; and class-gender-race bias, 32–36; and immigration trends/overview (since 2001), 62–64; under Kenney, 28, 40, 63, 72–74, 191; and objectives of economic development/social reproduction, 60–62; parties involved in, 38–47; target groups of, 39, 44–47; and undesirability/inadmissibility, 61–62; and visa office administration, 77–78. *See also entry below*; immigrants, categories of; Kenney, Jason
immigration policy, parties involved in creating/implementing, 38–47; advocacy groups, 42; courts/judicial bodies, 45–46; employers, 44; federal and provincial governments/ police forces, 42–43; federal and provincial parties/politicians, 39–41, 57; lawyers/consultants, 44–45, 57; lobby/interest groups, 41–42; provincial nominee programs, 44; senior bureaucrats, 42; trade unions, 42. *See also entries for specific parties*
immigration program managers, 59, 88, 90–93, 95; author's interactions with, 9, 12, 13–14; conflict of interest concerns for, 92–93; and discretionary decisions, 50, 51, 57, 174, 175, 184; and International Region, 90, 91, 96; and "jumpers," 198–99, 201–4; on organizational chart, 88, 89(f); and potential malfeasance, 103; salaries of, 86; and substituted evaluations, 174, 182–83; target pressures on, 2, 133–35, 137, 184; time pressures on, 195–96; and visa officer staffing decisions, 95–97
Immigration Regulations, 6, 10, 49–50, 63, 186
In Person offices, 82
International Organization for Migration, 91–92, 242

International Region branch (CIC): author's interactions with, 10–14; and *Daily Wrap* newsletter, 233; functions of, 82, 83; and interviews, 216, 219; and "jumpers," 199, 200–1; and office productivity/targets, 122, 133–35, 193; poor website presence of, 8; and program managers, 90, 91, 96; and visa officers, 93–96, 199, 216
interpreters, 102, 161, 219
interview, face-to-face, 215–38; booth for, 1, 55, 219, 220, 224, 227–29, 232, 235; examples of, 1–6, 227–32; increasing rarity of, 17–18, 55, 135–36, 215–16, 239–40, 242–43; micro-level interaction of, 55–56, 216, 219–22, 227–32, 241–43; as permitted or not, 196–97; as reinforcing applicants' client/subordinate status, 216–22, 227–32; and safety of visa officers/staff, 1, 14, 218–19, 225, 232–38; in spousal/partner sponsorship cases, 225–32; time needed for, 2, 18, 136, 170; and triaging of applications, 222–25; in visitor visa cases, 196, 197, 201, 212, 214, 216, 221–22, 223–24, 235, 240
investors, 64, 82, 109; pause on applications by, 68–69; "source of funds" issues for, 177–78

"jumpers," 198–208; costs of, 98, 100, 191, 200; database research on, 81, 210–12; definitions of, 198–99; vs genuine visitors, 204–8, 209; as group visitors, 210; inter-office comparisons of, 201–2; protection of system/taxpayer from, 191–92, 198–204; refugee claimants as, 53, 80–81, 98, 188, 198–201, 211, 214, 225; in sickness/death cases, 206–8; and timing of jump, 200; unpredictability of, 188, 201, 204, 214; on visa officers' records, 200–4

Kenney, Jason: and increasing rarity of interviews, 239–40; on marriages of convenience, 139; Ministerial Instructions introduced by, 40, 63, 172; and refugee determination system, 72–74, 191–92; and safety-security-prosperity mantra, 28; and skilled workers, 63, 65–66, 171–73, 191. *See also* Ministerial Instructions
Kingston (Jamaica) visa office, 118, 120, 122, 133; organization of, 88, 89(f)

language proficiency, as component of points system, 65, 65(t), 166–68, 169, 170, 245
lawyers, 6, 17, 20, 44–45, 57, 81, 92, 122, 147, 212, 216–17, 233; and appeals, 44, 58, 185, 241; and substituted evaluations, 181, 185
LGBT community, 24–25, 225, 227; same-sex couples, 71, 151
Lipsky, Michael, 47, 121, 163, 216, 241–42
Live-in Caregiver Program, 69, 77; approval rate for (2012), 107(t), 109; finalized application targets for (2014), 124, 125(t), 126–27(t), 128–29(t); perceived sexism/racism of, 33–34
lobby/interest groups, 41–42
locally engaged staff, 9, 17, 88–89, 101–4, 252*n*7; factors affecting decision-making by, 101–3; as Foreign Affairs employees, 85, 86; as interpreters, 102, 161, 219; on organizational chart, 88, 89(f); promotion of, 102–3; safety concerns of, 237–38; target pressures on, 134; tensions among, 103–4; time pressures on, 196; triaging of applications by, 57, 222–25; as visa applicants, 221–22; visa officers and, 96, 155–56; and visa refusals, 153, 196–97. *See also entry below*

locally engaged staff (specific): case analysts, 102, 103; designated immigration officers, 101, 102, 103; non-immigrant officers, 101, 102, 103, 192; program assistants, 2, 89, 102, 103; receptionists, 102, 211, 218, 219; security guards, 14, 218, 219, 225. *See also entries for specific positions*
London visa office, 115, 118, 119, 120, 122, 124, 133

macro-level factors, in immigration process, 19, 20, 55, 57, 138, 141–42, 162, 163, 182, 186, 192, 214; fraud by client, 147–49; migration opportunities/socio-economic development, 145–47; overseas legal contexts, 149–50; weak ties to country of residence, 205–6
marriages of convenience, 2–6; age differences as sign of, 161; case analysts/program assistants' handling of, 155–56, 158–60, 161; designated immigration officers' handling of, 143, 146, 151–52, 155, 161, 226; government crackdown on, 139–40; involving deportees, 3, 158; photographs as exposing, 4, 159–60; "poison pen letters" sent to expose, 156–57. *See also* spousal and partner sponsorships, *and entries following*
Maytree Foundation, 42
Members of Parliament (MPs), 39–40, 57, 77, 122–23, 204
meso-level factors, in immigration process, 20, 55, 182, 186; visa offices/officers and, 19, 20, 35, 56–57, 186
Mexico, 73, 190; seasonal agricultural workers from, 33, 42, 76–77; U.S. border control issues with, 26; visa requirement imposed on, 191–92
micro-level factors, in immigration process, 19, 20, 34, 55, 141–42, 182, 186, 192; interviews, 55–56, 216, 219–22, 227–32
migration integrity officers, 97–101; and airport interdiction, 97–100; anti-fraud, 98, 100–1, 156; international contacts cultivated by, 99, 100–1
Ministerial Instructions, 63; for business immigrants, 68; for parent/grandparent sponsorships, 40–41, 71; for skilled workers, 40, 63, 65–66, 71, 82–83, 106, 109, 115, 171–73
modernization initiatives, at CIC, 79, 80–85, 112, 122, 124, 193, 240; Canada-based visa processing, 81–84; new database system, 80–81; Visa Application Centres, 84–85
Molloy, Mike, 9–10, 244
"Mr. X" (bureaucrat/former visa officer), 10–11
Muslims, as targeted by border control/immigration authorities, 24, 29–30, 31

neo-liberalism, 32, 61
Netherlands, 31–32, 84, 119
non-governmental organizations (NGOs), 34, 39, 42, 102, 168–69, 247
Non-Immigrant Employment Authorization Program, 33
non-immigrant officers, 101, 103, 192; and difficult cases, 206, 223; and "jumpers," 204, 205; Ottawa-based training of, 102; and "self-serving" letters of employment, 196–97; time pressures on, 196; and visiting groups, 210
North American Free Trade Agreement, 190
North Korea, 22
Norway, 31, 151, 206

parent and grandparent sponsorships, 70–71; approval rates for (2012), 108(t), 109; finalized application targets for (2014), 124, 125(t), 129–32(t); and "super visa," 40–41, 71

pass mark, of points system, 65, 83, 166, 170, 171–72, 183; as not difficult to attain, 182; as resulting in refusal, 185; for self-employed applicants, 69; and substituted evaluations, 166, 171, 174, 184, 186
Permanent Resident Units, of visa offices, 89, 192
personal suitability, as component of points system, 166, 167–71, 186; perceived bias of, 168–69; removal of, 169, 173–75
Philippines, 63, 195; live-in caregivers from, 34, 69; spousal/partner sponsorship issues of, 145–46, 149–50
points system, 64–65, 65(t), 164–65; history of, 165–73; international praise for, 164, 166; language proficiency and, 65, 166–68, 169, 170, 245; as not required for provincial nominees, 67; pass marks of, 65, 69, 83, 166, 170, 171–72, 174, 182, 183–85, 186; personal suitability and, 166, 167–71, 173–75, 186; reduced officer discretion in, 169–71, 173–75; for self-employed, 69; substituted evaluations and, 166, 171, 178–86. *See also* pass mark, of points system; personal suitability, as component of points system
police: and border control, 24, 25, 43; on "looking for crime," 246; as street-level bureaucrats, 47, 48, 140, 241
Pratt, Anna, 35, 250*n*3; and Lorne Sossin, 37–38, 48
processing times: applicant inquiries about, 82, 84; CIC publication of, 122–23; for difficult applications, 217–18; and parents/grandparents' backlog, 71; and skilled workers' backlog, 65–66; Visa Application Centres and, 193–96
Professional Association of Foreign Service Officers, 86
profiling, 99, 175–76, 246; of "jumpers," 81, 214; in spousal/partner sponsorship cases, 148–49, 154
program assistants, 2, 89, 102, 103; and checking/screening of applications, 57, 102, 192, 209, 210, 222; and fraud, 147; and marriage fraud, 155–56; triaging of applications by, 57, 222–25; and visitor visas, 209, 210–12
provincial governments, 41. *See also entry below*; Quebec, *and entry following*
Provincial Nominee Program, 41, 66–68, 82; approval rate for (2012), 107(t), 109; finalized application targets for (2014), 124, 125(t), 126–27(t), 128–29(t); Manitoba origins of, 41, 67
Public Safety, Department of, 43
Punjabi marriages, 153–55, 160, 161

Quebec: provincial immigration program of, 41, 64, 67; refugees to, 129–30(t), 132(t); regional offices/personnel in, 82, 111(t), 112
Quebec skilled workers, 64, 82, 118; approval rate for (2012), 106, 107(t), 109; finalized application targets for (2014), 124, 125(t), 126–27(t), 128–29(t)
queue jumpers. *See* "jumpers"

race-based bias, 20, 29–30, 31, 32–35, 245–47; and approval/refusal rates, 16, 118–20, 137–38, 247; and personal suitability points, 168–69; and visa office locations, 34, 87; and visa officers' discretion, 16, 34–35, 118, 120, 137–38, 240
receptionists, 102, 211, 218, 219; triaging of applications by, 222–25
refugee claims, 3–4; in Britain, 29, 30; costs of, 98, 100, 191, 200; refusals of, 25, 46; by visitors, 53, 80–81, 98,

188, 198–201, 211, 214, 225. *See also entries below*; "jumpers"
refugee determination system, 3–4; and costs of claims/deportations, 98, 100, 191, 200; perceived bias of, 32–33; recent controversial modifications to, 72–74, 191–92
Refugee Program: goals of, 61, 121, 249
refugees, 33, 42, 43, 64, 71–74, 93–94; admission process for, 3–4; approval rates for (2012), 108(t), 109, 112, 113(t); in Britain, 29, 30; credibility/risk issues of, 51, 53–54, 100; finalized application targets for (2014), 124, 125(t), 129–32(t), 133; as "jumpers," 53, 80–81, 98, 188, 198–201, 211, 214, 225; offices handling, 89, 133; in *Singh* case, 46. *See also* "jumpers"
refugees (specific categories): government-assisted, 72, 109, 214; humanitarian/compassionate cases, 61, 74, 109; in-Canada (protected), 72, 73–74, 82, 109; outside Canada (convention), 72, 73; outside Canada (country of asylum), 72; privately-sponsored, 72, 109, 214
refusals of visas: appeals of, 44, 45–46, 121, 136, 143, 153, 170–71, 178, 179–80, 184–85, 186, 188, 233, 241; in *Baker* and *Singh* cases, 45–46; bias and, 245–47; as "easy," 153, 204, 205–6; and inadmissibility, 47–48, 106, 109; interviews in cases of, 135–36, 143, 170, 196–97, 216, 217–18, 225, 227–38, 243; "jumpers" and, 201, 203–4, 210; letters for, 49–50, 178, 236; as more work than approvals, 16, 136, 170–71, 184, 246–47; negative publicity about, 7, 91, 207–8, 233–35; rates of, 105–38; as reversible, 208; and safety of visa officers, 217, 233–38; in sickness/death cases, 206–8; in skilled worker cases, 165–66, 170; in spousal/partner sponsorship cases, 140, 141, 143, 149, 153–54, 163; target/time pressures and, 136–37, 163, 184–85, 196, 246–47; for visitors, 186, 188, 196–98, 201, 203–13
Research and Evaluation Branch (CIC), 10–11, 12
risk, management of, 52–54; at backlog reduction offices, 112; in checks of applicant/family, 81, 205–6; and criteria for exclusion, 59–60; and handling of "jumpers," 203–4; at interviews, 55; in promotion of locally engaged staff, 102–3; in spousal/partner sponsorship cases, 143–44; target pressures and, 136; as varying among visa officers, 134–35, 183, 186, 197; and visa office safety, 1, 232–38; in visitor visa cases, 190, 192, 195, 197–98, 205–6, 209. *See also* credibility, assessment of, *and entry following*
Royal Canadian Mounted Police (RCMP), 43, 87

safety, public: and inadmissibility, 6, 26–28, 41, 43, 46, 52, 53, 61–62, 106, 109, 218, 249; in visitor visa cases, 197–98, 200, 201. *See also* crime, *and entry following*
safety at visa offices, 86, 218–19; bulletproof glass and, 1, 219, 235; concealment of identity/job information and, 236–38; security guards and, 14, 218, 219, 225
safety threats, to visa officers/staff, 217, 218–19, 232–38; intimidation/threats, 235–36; online attacks, 234–35; publicity/controversy, 233
"satisfied," as key term in approvals, 2–3, 5–6, 49–50, 143, 178, 221
Seasonal Agricultural Worker Program, 33, 42, 76–77
security: and inadmissibility, 6, 41, 43, 46, 61, 62, 106, 109, 166, 201; in

visitor visa cases, 189, 190, 197–98, 201, 218–19. *See also* safety, public, *and entries following*
security guards, 14, 218, 219, 225
selection, as CIC/Human Resources responsibility, 43; database for, 80; and provincial nominee cases, 67–68; racialization of, 16, 32–35, 119–20, 137–38. *See also* enforcement, as Border Services/police responsibility
self-employed business immigrants, 68, 69, 82, 109
Shaffir, Billy, 11
Singh v. Minister of Employment and Immigration (Supreme Court case), 45, 46
skilled workers. *See* Federal Skilled Worker Program; Quebec skilled workers
South Korea, 31, 63, 145, 189
spousal and partner sponsorships, 70–71, 139–63; application process for, 142–45; approval rates for (2012), 106, 107(t), 112, 113–15(t), 115, 119, 120; and bigamy/polygamy, 149–50; credibility of, 2–6, 140–45, 151–63; and culture/normality, 151–55; "digging deeper" into, 3–6, 140–42, 145–50, 154–56, 162–63, 175, 227–32; and factors indicating real relationships, 155–62; finalized application targets for (2014), 124, 125(t), 129–32(t), 133; interviews for, 225–32; macro-level contexts of, 145–50; non-linear process of assessing, 162–63; photographs provided to support, 4, 143, 144, 154, 159–60; "poison pen letters" sent to scuttle, 156–57. *See also entries below*; marriages of convenience
spousal and partner sponsorships, and factors indicating real relationships, 155–62; communication, 161–62; compatibility, 160–61; logical progression of relationship, 158–60; migration/marriage history, 156–58
spousal and partner sponsorships, macro-level contexts of, 145–50; fraud by client, 147–49; migration opportunities/socio-economic development in country of origin, 145–47; overseas legal contexts/marriage irregularities, 149–50
Start-Up Visa Program, 69
street-level bureaucrats, visa officers as, 39, 47–58, 241–42; and credibility/risk, 50–54; decision-making process of, 54–58; and delegation of discretion, 48–50; and face-to-face interaction with clients, 17–18, 170, 216–17; vs organizational culture/structure, 120–21, 138; and reduction of discretion, 169–70, 241; and social constitution of discretion, 141–42
students, international, 21, 75–76, 84, 94, 188, 192; as allowed to apply for permanent residency within Canada, 22; as hindered by long visa processing times, 123; as "jumpers," 191, 199, 200, 220; in PhD programs, 66, 76; potential fraud/abuse involving, 176, 177; university recruitment of, 27, 75–76
substituted evaluations, 11–12, 34, 173–75, 178–86; and points system, 166, 171, 174, 184, 186
"super visa" (multiple-entry visitor visa), 40–41, 71
Supreme Court of Canada: *Baker* and *Singh* rulings by, 45–46
Supreme Court (U.S.): and Arizona immigration law, 25

target groups, of immigration policy, 39, 44–47. *See also* immigration policy, parties involved in creating/implementing
targets, 2, 16, 17, 83, 90–91, 123–37, 138; change in definition of, 123–24,

137; for finalized applications (2014), 124, 125(t); for finalized applications (economic visas, 2014), 124, 126–28(t); for finalized applications (non-economic visas, 2014), 124, 129–32(t), 133; International Region and, 133–35; and pressures on staff, 133–37, 183–84; and processing times, 122–23; and reduction of interviews, 135–36; for skilled worker applications, 171–73, 182, 183–84, 185, 186, 246–47

Temporary Foreign Worker Program, 76–77; perceived racism/sexism of, 33–34; and permanent residency applications within Canada, 22, 77; recent controversy over, 28, 41–42. *See also* Live-in Caregiver Program; Seasonal Agricultural Worker Program

Temporary Resident Units, of visa offices, 89, 192, 197–214; and "jumpers," 198–208; managers of, 193–94, 196, 198, 199–203, 208; as real front line, 213–14; stress/workload at, 197–98, 243; triaging/applicant assessment at, 222–25; and Visa Application Centres, 193–94

temporary residents, 74–77, 188; as issued permits for "justified reasons," 77; and peak time for applications, 14, 94, 123, 192; students, 75–76; temporary foreign workers, 76–77; visitors/tourists, 75, 187–214. *See also entry above*; students, international; tourists; visitor visas, *and entry following*

terrorism, 6–7, 26, 52–53, 59, 62, 80, 184, 241

Tim Hortons, 41

time: for "digging deeper," 175–78; for "hard" cases, 206; for interviews, 2, 18, 135–36, 170; pressures of, 134–37, 140, 163, 196–98, 240–42, 246–47; for processing applications, 65–66, 71, 82, 84, 122–23, 140, 193–96, 217–18; rationing of, 105, 121, 138, 140, 175–76, 242; strategies for managing, 17, 55, 57, 138, 245; for substituted evaluations, 183–86; for visitor visas, 188, 196–98, 201, 206, 214

tourists, 21, 192; economic benefits of, 27, 61, 75, 187–88. *See also* visitor visas

trade unions, 42, 73

triage process, at visa offices, 17, 55, 140, 148, 245; by locally engaged staff, 57, 222–25

Ukraine, 187, 189, 190

United Arab Emirates, 190

United Food and Commercial Workers Union, 42

United Nations: employees of, as "jumpers," 201; High Commission for Refugees, 72, 93; Human Rights Commissioner, 29

United States, 31, 62, 63, 164, 165, 199; border control/citizenship issues of, 24–26, 149; Canada's safe third country agreement with, 73; Canadians' travel to, 187; deportations from, 3, 25, 29; and spousal/partner sponsorship cases, 1–6, 146, 149, 156, 158; as visa exempt, 23, 24, 189, 190; visa offices in, 14, 34, 83, 128(t), 132(t), 223; and visitor visa cases, 197, 212, 221–22

units, visa office, 89, 192; case analysts in, 102; managers of, 133, 134. *See also specific units below*

units, visa office (specific): Economic Class, 89, 172, 174–79, 181–83; Family Class, 89, 225–32, 234; Permanent Resident, 89, 192; Refugee, 89; Temporary Resident, 89, 192, 193–94, 196, 197–214, 222–25, 243

VFS Global Group, 84, 193

Visa Application Centres, 84–85, 123, 192–96, 215, 222

visa exempt countries, 23, 24, 75, 188, 189–90
visa officers, 1–18, 93–97, 239–47; decision-making process of, 54–58; discretion exercised by, 6, 7, 15–18, 37–58, 241–42, 244–45; "easy" and "hard" cases for, 55, 204–8; enforcement vs facilitative approach of, 15–16, 56, 57, 163, 196–204, 246; interviews conducted by, 1–6, 17–18, 55–56, 196–97, 215–38, 241–43; and "jumpers," 200–4; managers' role in postings of, 95–97; mandated silence of, 7–8; posting rotations/preferences of, 94–95; retention rate of, 243–44; safety of, 217, 218–19, 232–38; salaries of, 86; and spousal employment, 95; as street-level bureaucrats, 47–58, 121, 138, 141–42, 216–17, 241–42; training/probation of, 93–94. *See also* discretion, as exercised by visa officers, *and entry following*; enforcement approach, as taken by visa officers; facilitative approach, as taken by visa officers; fettering of discretion; interviews, face-to-face; street-level bureaucrats, visa officers as
visa offices. *See entries below;* selection, as CIC/Human Resources responsibility
visa offices, Canadian, 22, 81–83; backlog reduction offices, 112; Case Processing Centres, 82, 83, 85, 112, 142, 156; Centralized Intake office, 82–83; In Person offices, 82
visa offices, overseas, 22, 79–104; about, 83–85; applications processed by, 6, 106–20; approval/refusal rates at, 105–38; closure of, 83, 86, 88, 112; dearth of scholarship on, 11, 15, 247, 250*n*3; and departmental budgetary pressures, 79; and departmental modernization agenda, 79, 80–85; embassy/consulate locations of, 85–88; employees of, 88–101; "hardship scale" of difficulty in staffing, 86; and immigration policy, 77–78; and "jumpers," 198–208; locally engaged staff at, 101–4; malfeasance at, 102–3; perceived bias in location choices of, 34, 87; regional divisions of, 112; safety concerns at, 1, 14, 86, 217, 218–19, 232–38; targets assigned to, 2, 16, 17, 83, 90–91, 123–37, 138; types of, 84; unit divisions within, 89, 192. *See also entries below*; embassies and consulates, as visa office locations
visa offices, overseas, employees of, 88–101; and embassy/consulate staff, 87–88; organizational chart of, 88, 89(f); tensions among, 103–4
visa offices, overseas, employees of (specific): immigration program manager, 90–93; locally engaged staff working with, 101–4; migration integrity officers, 97–101; visa officers, 93–97. *See also entries for specific positions*
visitor visas, 187–214; about, 192–96; and applicants' credibility, 196–97, 209–14; and applicants' travel history, 211–13; Application Centres for, 84–85, 123, 192–96, 215, 222; as border control mechanism, 198; "digging deeper" into, 188, 210–11; discretionary decisions on, 186, 188, 204–14, 216; exemption of countries from, 23, 24, 75, 188, 189–90; exemption of high-ranking visitors from, 77; and genuine vs non-genuine visitors, 204–8; for groups, 210; interviews for, 196, 197, 201, 212, 214, 216, 221–22, 223–24, 235, 240; and "jumpers," 53, 80–81, 98, 188, 198–201, 211, 214; politics of,

189–92; real front line process for, 213–14; refusals of, 186, 188, 196–98, 201, 203–13; risk management and, 190, 192, 195, 197–98, 205–6, 209; spring/summer peak time for, 14, 94, 123, 192; and "super visa," 40–41, 71; time pressures and, 188, 196–98, 201, 206, 214

visitors, 21–22; to Canada, 75, 187–88; refugee claims by, 53, 80–81, 98, 188, 198–201, 211, 214, 225. *See also entry above*; refugees; tourists

Walton-Roberts, Margaret, 153, 250*n*3

war crimes, 25, 52–53, 62, 237. *See also* human rights violations

Weber, Max, 36, 217

Who Gets In? (documentary), 9, 244

Zuma, Jacob, 77

Printed and bound in Canada by Friesens

Set in Segoe and Warnock by Apex CoVantage, LLC

Copy editor: Deborah Kerr

Proofreader: Sophie Pouyanne

Indexer: Cheryl Lemmens